New Directions in the Study of Work and Employment

New Directions in the Study of Work and Employment

Revitalizing Industrial Relations as an Academic Enterprise

Edited by

Charles J. Whalen

Utica College and Cornell University, USA

Edward Elgar
Cheltenham, UK • Northampton, MA, USA

HD
6960.5
.U5
N49
2008

Published by
Edward Elgar Publishing Limited
The Lypiatts
15 Lansdown Road
Cheltenham
Glos GL50 2JA
UK

Edward Elgar Publishing, Inc.
William Pratt House
9 Dewey Court
Northampton
Massachusetts 01060
USA

A catalogue record for this book
is available from the British Library

Library of Congress Cataloging in Publication Data
New directions in the study of work and employment : revitalizing industrial relations as an academic enterprise / edited by Charles J. Whalen.
    p.   cm.
  Includes bibliographical references and index.
  1. Industrial relations—Study and teaching (Higher)—United States. I. Whalen, Charles J., 1960–
   HD6960.5.U5N49 2008
   331.071'173–dc22

                           2008001733

ISBN 978 1 84720 452 3

Printed and bound in Great Britain by MPG Books Ltd, Bodmin, Cornwall

Contents

List of figures and tables		vii
List of contributors		ix
Preface		xi

Introduction: new directions in the study of work and employment   1
Charles J. Whalen

PART 1   RETHINKING INDUSTRIAL RELATIONS

1. Reconceptualizing industrial relations in a global, knowledge-driven economy   15
   Joel Cutcher-Gershenfeld
2. The original industrial relations paradigm: foundation for revitalizing the field   31
   Bruce E. Kaufman
3. A meta-paradigm for revitalizing industrial relations   48
   John W. Budd
4. An institutional environments approach to industrial relations   68
   John Godard

PART 2   RECONSTRUCTING INSTITUTIONS

5. Social capital and the labor movement   89
   David B. Lipsky and Ronald L. Seeber
6. Industrial relations and the law   110
   William B. Gould IV
7. How industrial relations is marginalized in business schools: using institutional theory to examine our home base   123
   Daphne Taras
8. Let a thousand journals bloom: the precarious landscape of labor and employment publishing   142
   Immanuel Ness, Bruce Nissen and Charles J. Whalen

PART 3   REENERGIZING PRACTICE

 9.   Revitalizing industrial relations   163
        Michael J. Piore
10.   Varieties of capitalism and employment relations under
        globalization: evidence from the auto industry   173
        Nick Wailes, Russell D. Lansbury and Jim Kitay
11.   Evolving labor relations in the women's apparel industry   194
        Katie Quan
12.   Immigrant workers and the new American labor movement   211
        Kent Wong and Janna Shadduck-Hernández

Conclusion: the future of industrial relations, a.k.a. work and
employment relations   225
Thomas A. Kochan

Index   237

Figures and tables

FIGURES

2.1 Wage/employment determination in a competitive labor
market   38
3.1 Analyzing comparative industrial relations systems   58
5.1 Federal mediation and conciliation service total
revenue in nominal and real terms, 1949–2003   97
5.2 The American Arbitration Association: revenue
from labor relations activities as a proportion of
total revenue, 1971–2000   99
5.3 Labor relations degrees as a proportion of degrees
granted in labor relations, human resource management
and organizational behavior, 1970–2001   105
7A.1 Journal citation scores for selected journals ranked by
the *Financial Times*   138
7A.2 Journal citation scores for selected industrial
relations journals   140

TABLES

1.1 Year of establishment for US and Canadian schools,
institutes, centers and departments specializing in industrial
relations or human resources management   23
5.1 Types and names of organizations in the study   95
7.1 The *Financial Times* 40 top journals, 2007   130
10.1 The GERAB framework   182

Contributors

John W. Budd is Industrial Relations Landgrant Professor at Carlson School of Management, University of Minnesota.

Joel Cutcher-Gershenfeld is professor and dean of the Institute of Labor and Industrial Relations, University of Illinois, Urbana-Champaign.

John Godard is professor of business administration at I.H. Asper School of Business, University of Manitoba.

William B. Gould IV is Charles A. Beardsley Professor of Law, Emeritus at Stanford Law School. He was chairman of the National Labor Relations Board from 1994 to 1998.

Bruce E. Kaufman is professor of economics at Andrew Young School of Policy Studies and senior associate at W.T. Beebe Institute of Personnel and Employment Relations, Georgia State University.

Jim Kitay is honorary associate professor of work and organizational studies at University of Sydney.

Thomas A. Kochan is George Maverick Bunker Professor of Management and co-director of the Institute for Work and Employment Research, Massachusetts Institute of Technology.

Russell D. Lansbury is professor of work and organizational studies at University of Sydney.

David B. Lipsky is Anne Evans Estabrook Professor of Dispute Resolution and director of the Martin and Laura Scheinman Institute on Conflict Resolution, School of Industrial and Labor Relations, Cornell University.

Immanuel Ness is professor of political science at Brooklyn College and teaches in the Graduate Center for Worker Education, City University of New York.

Bruce Nissen is director of research at the Center for Labor Research and Studies, Florida International University.

Michael J. Piore is David W. Skinner Professor of Political Economy at Massachusetts Institute of Technology.

Katie Quan is associate chair of the Center for Labor Research and Education, University of California, Berkeley.

Ronald L. Seeber is vice provost for land grant affairs and professor of industrial and labor relations at Cornell University.

Janna Shadduck-Hernández is project director at the Downtown Labor Center of University of California, Los Angeles.

Daphne Taras is area chair and professor of industrial relations in the Department of Human Resources and Organizational Dynamics at Haskayne School of Business, University of Calgary.

Nick Wailes is associate professor of work and organizational studies at University of Sydney.

Charles J. Whalen is professor of economics and director of business and economics at Utica College and visiting fellow at the School of Industrial and Labor Relations, Cornell University.

Kent Wong is director of the Center for Labor Research and Education, University of California, Los Angeles.

y20

Preface

au: Whalen, Charles J.

This book stems from my involvement in the Labor and Employment Relations Association (LERA). Although my affiliation with the organization began in the early 1980s, I became editor of its journal, *Perspectives on Work*, in late 2001, a position that provides a superb vantage point from which to view work and employment relations. Established as the Industrial Relations Research Association in the United States during the 1940s, LERA is currently reexamining all aspects of its mission, activities and plans in the wake of decreasing academic and practitioner membership that is part of an overall decline affecting the intellectual community associated with 'industrial relations,' especially in the United States and Canada. That ongoing reexamination, and the erosion that sparked it, prompted me to organize and prepare this volume.

While I am one who believes strongly that the academic enterprise of industrial relations needs to survive (indeed, even flourish), I believe just as fervently in the need for the field to change. New directions in the study of work and employment are warranted, and charting and pursuing them requires – as this book shows – a rethinking of institutions, practices and concepts; it may even be necessary to rename the field ('employment relations' is currently the top contender). At the same time, this collection of essays demonstrates that moving forward does not mean turning our backs on the past. In fact, key insights from the early days of industrial relations may now be more important than ever.

This book focuses primarily on industrial relations as it is practiced in the United States, but not all of its contributors are based in that country. Indeed, the project is collectively informed by training, teaching and scholarship that are global in scope. Due to unanticipated developments, plans to cast an even wider net in the current volume did not work out, but this collection is not intended to be the final word on the subject. Moreover, the book that came together provides a solid foundation for wider collaboration in the future.

My job as the volume's editor has been made easier due to the talent and collegiality of the contributors, and I thank each of them for cheerfully participating in this project. I received much valuable assistance – especially in the project's early stages, when it was needed most – from Bruce Kaufman and John Budd, and I wish to acknowledge their help. Similarly, I want to recognize the help and guidance provided by Alan Sturmer and Bob Pickens at Edward Elgar Publishing. Finally, on behalf of the contributors, I wish to thank the members of LERA who shared their ideas on how to revitalize the field during a 2007 symposium that addressed this topic at the organization's annual meeting. This book is dedicated to all those in LERA now engaged in efforts to revitalize the association and the field. Let the dialogue continue.

Introduction: new directions in the study of work and employment

Charles J. Whalen

INDUSTRIAL RELATIONS IN CRISIS

Work and employment have been subjects of academic research and teaching for over a century. Their study emerged out of the examination of social problems and evolved into a field called industrial relations (IR), which was born in the United States around 1920. Since its inception, IR has generally been considered interdisciplinary terrain devoted to both science building and real-world problem solving (Kaufman, 2004).

In the current era, IR should be flourishing. Across the academy, one can find a growing recognition of the value of crossing traditional boundaries and engaging in interdisciplinary scientific research. Problems regarding jobs and employment relations, meanwhile, are a major concern for workers, managers and government representatives across the globe. As Bruce E. Kaufman writes at the conclusion of his sweeping history of the global evolution of IR, 'Who today would say that the subject of employment and contemporary developments in the world of work is less important today than two or three decades ago? Few, I wager, and most would probably say the opposite – that the world of work is more important than ever for peoples and nations across the globe' (Kaufman, 2004: 621).

Nevertheless, academic units devoted to IR are facing tough times – especially in the English-speaking world – and the number of scholars associated with the field is shrinking.[1] Many observers say the problem is that IR researchers became too focused on issues involving organized labor, especially collective bargaining, and thus the fortunes of the field faded over time with the erosion of union membership and power. Others tell a more complicated story that involves a number of decisions made by IR scholars (about the field's conceptual makeup, relationship to other fields, and research methods, for example) and the impact upon the field of a variety of social and institutional developments that have taken place outside IR academic units (see, for instance, Kaufman, 2004). There may be disagreements about the exact source of the problem, but what is clear

1

is that the word 'crisis' is increasingly being used, and there has even been recent talk about the possibility of the field's extinction.

Letting IR wither and fade away is not a sensible option. No other field of academic inquiry is devoted exclusively to studying the world of work. Other fields often examine elements found in the IR realm, but the practical results are largely disappointing. As Michael J. Piore writes in chapter 9 of this volume, scholars in mainstream disciplines break up IR's 'key methodological and empirical issues into a series of separate components and parcel them out to different social sciences – disciplines that speak to each other in very limited and stylized ways or not at all. . . . This leaves space in the intellectual landscape for a more integrated, interdisciplinary approach.' Indeed, the present era cries out for the insights of such an approach. It is for this reason that IR should be revitalized; society deserves a scholarly community devoted to the world of work.

To revitalize IR as an academic enterprise, new directions in the study of work and employment are needed. The scope and intellectual content of the field must be reconsidered; its institutions must be reinforced or reshaped; and cutting-edge conceptual and practical issues must receive attention in the course of revitalizing its practice. This volume, which developed out of a symposium held at the annual meeting of the Labor and Employment Relations Association (LERA) in 2007, identifies such new directions by assembling some of the field's most creative and insightful scholars.

Rethinking IR means reconnecting with its origin as a field grounded in an understanding of institutional and historical reality, concerned with all aspects of work, and populated by scholars committed to the resolution of pressing labor problems. IR can no longer be synonymous with the study of just unions and collective bargaining, which became the view of many in recent decades. It must be a broad expanse – conducive to theory development, open to a multiplicity of paradigms, and accommodative of the fact that employment relationships come in many varieties and can be structured to seek any of a diverse set of objectives. Chapters in Part 1 examine how this can be accomplished.

Rebuilding IR institutions must begin in the academy, as it exists today; IR scholars cannot sit tight and wait for social changes to occur first. Such rebuilding requires a hard look at the status of IR within centers of higher learning and construction of an aggressive plan for resurgence. In addition, there must be both introspection regarding the way the field judges its own scholarship and a reconsideration of the social impact of IR research. The rebuilding must also involve an effort to breathe new life into the legal framework and social institutions that structure employment relations for society at large. Chapters in Part 2 address these matters.

Reenergizing IR practice involves recognizing that the performance and management of work now occurs in a dynamic, global economy that is different in many ways from the economy that existed immediately following World War II. This environment demands refashioned IR curricula. It also requires close scholarly attention to the interplay between worldwide trends (especially those involving or influencing international job and labor mobility), national economic systems, business and labor strategies, and employment-relations practices. Not all researchers must turn their attention from investigations of union-management relations in manufacturing to scholarship on service employment or emerging industries, but even the study of longstanding industries such as apparel must recognize the transnational realities faced by today's workers and employers. Chapters in Part 3 flesh out the issues at stake and examine specific developments and sectoral examples capable of moving the field forward. A concluding chapter by Thomas A. Kochan offers further thoughts on the future of the field in light of all the chapters that precede it.

THE FIELD OF INDUSTRIAL RELATIONS

Although the field of IR may not have emerged until the twentieth century, it bears a name that reveals deep roots traceable to the Industrial Revolution. In Chapter 1, Joel Cutcher-Gershenfeld reflects on the separate and joint use of the terms 'industrial' and 'relations,' and explains how they take on new and broader meaning in today's knowledge-driven economy. Cutcher-Gershenfeld admits he is not sure whether the IR label can adapt well to the new era and acknowledges that 'employment relations' is an alternative that more fully reflects the spectrum of contemporary workplace relationships. Nevertheless, a field's guiding principles are even more important than its name, and Chapter 1 demonstrates the enduring applicability of the principles adopted by IR scholars and academic units decades ago – namely, the need for blending theory, practice and policy; valuing balance between labor and management (now expanded to include other stakeholders as well); and assembling cross-disciplinary faculties.

Bruce Kaufman also finds that the history of the IR field contains a set of ideas with enduring value. In Chapter 2, he introduces those ideas as the 'original' IR paradigm, which emerged in the United States in the 1920s, and offers it as an alternative to the paradigm that treats IR as involving only the study of unions and union-management relations, a view holding a prominent place in the field since at least the 1970s. Since Kaufman sees no major resurgence of unions on the horizon, he argues that restructuring and repositioning IR according to its original paradigm is the best way to prevent the field from suffering further decline, especially in the United States.

The original IR paradigm has what Kaufman calls 'three faces' – a commitment to science building; a focus on practical problem solving; and a belief in the values of economic efficiency, social fairness, and human self-actualization. The core principle uniting these faces is that 'labor is not a commodity,' which can be stated alternatively as 'rejection of the orthodox competitive demand/supply labor market model as the appropriate frame-work' for analyzing the real world. The result is an expansive field, cover-ing all aspects of the employment relationship and capable of including a wide range of scholars and practitioners, regardless of whether they specialize in labor-oriented, management-oriented, or policy-oriented solutions to employment problems.

While Kaufman's chapter calls for choosing between two paradigms, the present's narrow one and the past's more inclusive one, John W. Budd's recent scholarship has focused on finding a way to bridge IR's four 'schools of thought' (Budd, 2004). In Chapter 3, Budd presents those schools as each generating a distinctive model of the employment relationship. (He calls them the egoist, unitarist, pluralist, and critical employment-relations models; and they are associated with neoclassical economics, personnel or human resource management, institutional economics, and Marxism, respectively.) Budd's approach to the revitalization of IR involves not only spelling out and calling for widespread recognition of a meta-paradigm capable of encompassing the field's various models (paradigms), but also promoting dialogue among scholars with differing perspectives. The cen-terpiece of his approach is an emphasis on making IR objectives, assump-tions and predictions explicit.

The views of Budd and Kaufman overlap in a number of important respects. For example, both place the whole employment relationship – rather than just the study of unions – at the heart of IR. In addition, Budd's list of possible objectives of the employment relationship (which are what he deems the 'starting point' for IR scholarship) consists of efficiency, equity and voice, which closely parallel the elements Kaufman identifies as characteristic of the ethical/ideological face of the original IR paradigm. The authors also have a common aim: to recast IR as a broad field, open to diverse voices, and committed to science building and problem solving.

Chapter 4, by John Godard, extends the reconsideration of IR by emphasizing the need for a systematic study of the institutions of labor and employment. The central message of Godard's chapter is that an 'insti-tutional environments' approach to IR research can help the field 'regain its intellectual bearings.' His chapter explains the tenets of such an approach and illustrates its usefulness by exploring two research examples:

a comparative examination of the role of unions in Canada and England, and an inquiry into the exceptional decline of the US labor movement.

THE INSTITUTIONS OF INDUSTRIAL RELATIONS

Revitalizing IR requires reforming and reconstructing institutions as well as studying them. Chapter 5 sets the stage for a discussion of the latter by cataloging how the weakening of the US labor movement 'caused collateral damage to organizations and institutions that have a close relationship to unions.' In particular, co-authors David B. Lipsky and Ronald L. Seeber examine the 'social capital' implications of labor's decline upon federal agencies, neutral and professional associations (such as the LERA and the American Arbitration Association), university IR programs, and other organizations with a mission relating in some way to organized labor.

Now that the social network that helped to support the labor movement 'has substantially withered,' can a revitalization of unions occur? Lipsky and Seeber offer a nuanced answer. On the one hand, initiating and sustaining a union resurgence might be easier in the presence of institutions designed to support and foster labor's growth. On the other hand, US labor history indicates that successful union organizing and expansion do not require the existence of a large stock of social capital.

Of course, one institution that has played a major role in the growth of US unions is labor law. Private-sector union membership surged dramatically in the decade following passage of the National Labor Relations Act of 1935, and public-sector membership grew rapidly a few decades later in response to state and federal legislation that gave government workers the right to organize and bargain collectively. Similarly, subsequent legal changes (in the form of amendments and administrative rulings) have contributed to the erosion of the US labor movement. In light of the important connection between IR and the law, William B. Gould surveys key aspects of this topic, including the future of labor law reform, in Chapter 6.

Attention to the challenges associated with shoring up IR institutions within the academy is the focus of Chapters 7 and 8. In Chapter 7, Daphne Taras documents how IR is marginalized in business schools, which is the institutional home for a substantial number of IR scholars. The causes Taras identifies are the pursuit of rankings according to benchmarking systems that exclude IR journals; reliance on scoring systems that give virtually no recognition for books or book chapters; and use of reward systems that overlook the 'town–gown interactions' that have long been a tradition in IR. Her conclusion is that an extensive and coordinated effort is required to reform the academic and scholarly institutions of the field (an endeavor that would, for example, include collective action to establish IR professorships, obtain stable funding sources for research on work and employment matters, and better integrate IR into business-school offerings).

Chapter 8, by Immanuel Ness, Bruce Nissen and Charles Whalen, sketches a historical account of the evolution of labor and employment journals over the past century (with special attention to academically oriented publications produced in the United States). While many of the field's publications are currently reaching more readers and are resting on a more secure financial footing than in the past, the authors – all journal editors – find that the IR journal landscape is actually somewhat precarious due to trends that are fragmenting the study of work and employment and causing such scholarship to become increasingly the product of a subfield within traditional disciplines. They conclude that today's IR scholars must devote more attention to producing successful, interdisciplinary journals; and they recommend that members of the field explore recent, ongoing initiatives that use electronic technologies to create new forms of scholarly communication and enhance competition in scientific publishing.

THE PRACTICE OF INDUSTRIAL RELATIONS

There is no single path to reinvigorated IR teaching and research. Nevertheless, a number of IR scholars have found strategies and methods they find promising. Chapter 9, by Michael J. Piore, discusses the approach that he and his colleagues at the Massachusetts Institute of Technology (MIT) have adopted to keep their IR curriculum intellectually stimulating and professionally relevant in an economic, social and academic environment that is quite different from that of the period immediately following World War II, when IR flourished. At MIT, IR is conceived as an interdisciplinary field that includes all aspects of work and employment, but professors also stress that insights from IR can be applied more broadly and that work-related social relations do not need to be studied in isolation from other social movements, problems and institutions. In addition, MIT's IR graduate students are required to supplement IR course work by taking the core curriculum in one of the major social-science disciplines.

Chapter 10, by Nick Wailes, Russell D. Lansbury and Jim Kitay, complements Piore's chapter by illustrating a promising path to greater IR research vitality. Their approach is similar to that recommended by Godard; indeed, Chapters 4 and 10 both draw on and extend elements of scholarship falling under the 'new institutionalism' and 'varieties of capitalism' rubrics. In Chapter 10, however, the focus is on exploring the relationship between economic globalization and employment relations by drawing on a research project that examines the automobile industry in seven countries.

The relationship between globalization and IR also figures prominently in Chapter 11, by Katie Quan. Her chapter, which considers the need to redesign labor relations in the global garment industry, shows the continued relevance of research that returns to the problem-solving focus that was once a core characteristic of IR scholarship. Quan also identifies innovative ways that IR scholars can use their expertise and skills to simultaneously enhance their understanding of work and employment relations and further advance real-world problem solving.

Chapter 12, by Kent Wong and Janna Shadduck-Hernández, closes Part 3 with an examination of immigrant workers and 'the new American labor movement.' By discussing the UCLA Center for Labor Research and Education, the authors explain how 'university programs that focus on supporting and repositioning immigrant workers as central players in society and within contemporary social movements hold the potential of redefining labor and industrial relations programs nationally.' While Kaufman's chapter calls for restructuring IR according to the field's original paradigm largely because he sees no resurgence of unions on the horizon, Chapter 12 points toward the revitalization of IR and the labor movement at the same time. 'The linkages and prospects of coalition building among immigrant workers (both union and nonunion), their communities and labor organizations create important opportunities for labor educators, students and universities,' write Wong and Shadduck-Hernández.

THE FUTURE OF INDUSTRIAL RELATIONS

This book is designed to foster dialogue on the future of IR as an academic enterprise, not to be a comprehensive guide or to promote the 'one best way' forward.[2] Nevertheless, while the book's contributors were invited to present a personal view of the challenges and opportunities ahead for IR, a common thread emerges just the same: the vision of IR as a broad, interdisciplinary field that strives for both science building and practical problem solving. These chapters also reinforce a view of my own. Like Kaufman, I contend that part of what is necessary to advance the field is for IR scholars to reconnect with their roots.

As the editor of a journal published by the LERA, I recently reviewed some of the earliest documents of that organization – originally called the Industrial Relations Research Association (IRRA) – while preparing for its sixtieth anniversary. In the process, I was reminded that in 1948 the group's first president was Edwin E. Witte, an economics professor at the University of Wisconsin and a former student of John R. Commons, arguably the most influential scholar in the history of IR.[3] Since the careers of Commons and Witte span perhaps the most vibrant period of US IR scholarship – including a long stretch during which organized labor accounted for a tiny fraction of the nation's labor force – I decided to expand my historical investigations and become reacquainted with various writings of Witte, Commons, and other early IR contributors. I was looking at the past to find insights that would help IR to progress in the years ahead, and I quickly learned that the early pioneers of IR seemed almost eager to oblige. My research revealed three findings.

The first finding is that Commons and Witte both grounded their IR in institutional economics, which was conceived not as a narrow discipline but as an expansive, interdisciplinary study of social problems. Indeed, institutionalism was partly an attempt at the marriage of economics and an array of disciplines, including law, sociology, political science, history and psychology. In a 1954 journal article, for example, Witte describes his conception of institutional economics: 'It is not so much a connected body of economic thought as a method of approaching economic problems. This method is what might be called a practical problems approach.' Institutional economists, he adds, are interested in studying actual economic phenomena for the purpose of social improvement, while many other economists are concerned primarily with expressing the 'timeless and placeless' principles that govern the price system. Institutionalists believe in building and using theories in their work, but they insist on grounding those theories in history and institutional reality (Witte, 1954: 133–5).

The second finding is that Commons, Witte and their colleagues defined their field broadly. A Social Science Research Council report, written with the involvement of Commons, defines IR as including examinations of workers in relation to their work, their employers, their fellow workers and the public (Social Science Research Council, 1928: 22). Similarly, a 1931 report prepared by the National Industrial Conference Board states, 'The term "industrial relations" comprises *every incident that grows out of the fact of employment*' (quoted in Kaufman, 2004: 95, emphasis added). An early IR textbook edited by Commons devotes as much attention to 'labor management' (personnel management) as to labor unions, and also covers other issues, including both labor law and worker security (unemployment, accidents and workers' compensation, and employee health issues). Indeed, in that book (and elsewhere) Commons underscores the importance he assigns to the issue of economic security by identifying the business cycle as 'the greatest of all labor problems' (Commons, 1921: 4; see also Whalen, 1993).

The third finding is that Witte, Commons, and even Commons's professor, Richard T. Ely (a founder of the American Economic Association), were acutely aware of the creative role that government plays in economic life. In addition to serving as president of the IRRA, Witte ascended to the presidency of the American Economic Association (AEA). In his presidential address to the AEA, Witte focused on the relationship between economics and public policy. He stressed that 'there never was a time when *laissez faire* prevailed in the United States' and expressed support for the preeminent plank in the 1886 platform of the AEA, which declares that its founders regarded the state 'as an agency whose positive assistance is one of the indispensable conditions of human progress' (Witte, 1957: 1, 5). As Warren J. Samuels has written about Witte's university seminars and scholarly writings on public policy, 'Foremost of Witte's conclusions was that of the inseparability of government and economy' (Samuels, 1967: 134).

In the Commons–Witte view of the state, government is much more than a regulator of economic activity. To be sure, these scholars recognized government as a rule maker and umpire, 'inextricably involved in the promulgation of the basic economic institutions that make capitalism or free enterprise what it is' (Samuels, 1967: 136). But they also saw government as a social partner, and envisioned it working alongside individual initiative and private enterprise in an effort to promote overall economic wellbeing. For example, quoting Abraham Lincoln, Witte wrote, 'Government should do for a people what they cannot do for themselves or that which they cannot do so well for themselves in their individual capacities.' He could have just as easily quoted Commons, who stressed that collective action involves not just coercion or control, but also the liberation and expansion of individual action.[4]

The problems of today are not identical to those of Commons's day, and, of course, nobody wants to turn back the clock and disregard decades of subsequent theory-building and practice, but reconnecting with IR's roots can still provide guidance for the IR scholars of today and tomorrow. The Commons–Witte insights presented above remain promising as a basis for research, teaching, and dialogue on labor and employment relations. Moreover, there is guidance to be obtained not only at a foundational or conceptual level, but also at a more practical level.

Commons's attention to the business cycle, for example, is a reminder that IR scholars have long considered human resources from a national or macroeconomic perspective. In the 1960s and 1970s, federal policymakers' attention to employment and training policies helped sustain academic interest in the nation's human resources, though, understandably, most scholars became specialists and focused on a particular labor-market segment or policy area. Although high-quality research in this area continues (much of it sponsored by the W.E. Upjohn Institute for Employment Research), IR scholars' interest in managing the nation's human resources has dropped considerably in recent decades and the focus has instead moved to enterprise-level human resource management. With global forces exerting a greater influence on the US labor market each year, however, the macro realm is quickly becoming an area in great need of the involvement of IR scholars.[5]

Since only a small fraction of recent IR scholarship has centered on unemployment, workforce development and other aspects of macro-human resource management, it might appear convenient for IR to cede that area to economists. Doing so, however, would be a huge mistake. Although US economic policy has helped keep unemployment rates low for a number of years, much contemporary economic theory remains dismissive of the subject of unemployment (because joblessness is assumed to be a matter of individual choice). Moreover, almost the entire economics profession has ignored the fact that beyond the low rate of US unemployment are job 'offshoring' and other serious challenges – most tied to an ongoing transformation of the structure of the economy – that put financial security and a rising standard of living at risk for many working families.[6]

In the end, reconnecting with IR's history reveals that the field's evolution has always depended upon human decisions (this is a point Cutcher-Gershenfeld addresses in Chapter 1). There has never been much that is inevitable about work, the way it is studied, or the makeup and vitality of the academic enterprise associated with such studies. The field's past can be a springboard, not an albatross. The conceptual, institutional and practical insights contained in the present volume can help stimulate constructive dialogue and additional creativity. And the future of IR – under that name, 'employment relations,' or some label not yet invented – can be bright.[7]

NOTES

1. The erosion of IR as a field of study has been particularly severe in the United States. (For discussions of IR outside the United States, see, for example, Kaufman, 2004; and Ackers and Wilkinson, 2003. According to Kaufman, there are two reasons why the field of IR stabilized in the United Kingdom in the past decade or so: union membership stabilized when the Labor Party came to power in the late 1990s and British IR broadened its domain 'to give greater room to social policy' (Kaufman, 2004, 612).)
2. Actually, this book seeks to foster the continuation of a dialogue on the future of IR. Scholars and practitioners have addressed aspects of this subject in the past, both in the pages of the *Proceedings* of the annual meetings of the LERA (formerly the Industrial Relations Research Association) and elsewhere (see, for example, Adams and Meltz, 1993; and Whitfield and Strauss, 1998). Most recently, scholars have collaborated to examine the future of the study of labor and employment relations by means of a focus on the

United Kingdom (Ackers and Wilkinson, 2003) and Australia (Hearn and Michelson, 2006). This volume complements those efforts by focusing on North America, especially the United States, though many of its insights should be applicable to the study of IR in other countries.
3. Although Commons had a great impact as a professor, one must recall that the writings of Sidney and Beatrice Webb were an important influence on Commons's scholarship involving labor issues and that their works continue to be recognized as seminal to the IR literature.
4. For an extended discussion of my examination of early IR scholarship, see Whalen (2008a: 22–6). That article addresses the fact that Commons and Witte acknowledged there are dangers and challenges associated with public action, but emphasizes they ultimately concluded that government remains an inescapable fact of life. The article also gives some attention to how IR scholars can constructively contribute to shaping and promoting the public purpose.
5. In fact, there is an increasing need for greater attention to human resource development and utilization at the international level as well. Indeed, whereas early IR scholars devoted most of their energy to establishment of groups and working rules that were local and national, it will likely be necessary for twenty-first century IR scholars to fashion and improve organizations and institutions that are global.
6. For discussions of contemporary challenges facing working families in the United States, see, for example, Hacker (2006) and Whalen (2005; 2008b).
7. The author thanks Bruce Kaufman and Linda Whalen for reading this chapter in draft form and offering valuable suggestions.

REFERENCES

Ackers, Peter and Wilkinson, Adrian (2003), *Understanding Work and Employment: Industrial Relations in Transition*, Oxford, UK: Oxford University Press.

Adams, Roy J. and Meltz, Noah M. (1993), *Industrial Relations Theory: Its Nature, Scope, and Pedagogy*, Lanham, MD: The Scarecrow Press.

Budd, John W. (2004), *Employment with a Human Face: Balancing Efficiency, Equity and Voice*, Ithaca, NY: ILR Press.

Commons, John R. (ed.) (1921), *Trade Unionism and Labor Problems*, Second Series, Boston, MA: Ginn and Company.

Hacker, Jacob S. (2006), *The Great Risk Shift*. New York: Oxford University Press.

Hearn, Mark and Michelson, Grant (2006), *Rethinking Work: Time, Space and Discourse*, Melbourne, Australia: Cambridge University Press.

Kaufman, Bruce E. (2004), *The Global Evolution of Industrial Relations: Events, Ideas and the IIRA*, Geneva: International Labor Office.

Samuels, Warren J. (1967), 'Edwin E. Witte's concept of the role of government in the economy,' *Land Economics* **43** (2), 131–47.

Social Science Research Council (1928), *Survey of Research in the Field of Industrial Relations*, New York: Social Science Research Council.

Whalen, Charles J. (1993), 'Saving capitalism by making it good: the monetary economics of John R. Commons,' *Journal of Economic Issues* **27** (4), 1155–79.

Whalen, Charles J. (2005), 'Sending jobs offshore from the United States: what are the consequences?' *Intervention: Journal of Economics* **2** (2), 33–40.

Whalen, Charles J. (2008a), 'LERA's anniversary: an opportunity to reconnect with our roots,' *Perspectives on Work*, **11** (2): 22–6.

Whalen, Charles J. (2008b), 'Post-Keynesian institutionalism and the anxious society,' in Sandra S. Batie and Nicholas Mercuro (eds), *Alternative Institutional Structures: Evolution and Impact*, London: Routledge, pp. 273–99.

Whitfield, Keith and George Strauss (1998), *Researching the World of Work: Strategies and Methods in Studying Industrial Relations*, Ithaca, NY: ILR Press.

Witte, Edwin E. (1954), 'Institutional economics as seen by an institutional economist,' *Southern Economic Journal* **21** (2), 131–40.

Witte, Edwin E. (1957), 'Economics and public policy,' *American Economic Review* **47** (1), 1–21.

PART 1

Rethinking industrial relations

1. Reconceptualizing industrial relations in a global, knowledge-driven economy

Joel Cutcher-Gershenfeld

INTRODUCTION

The words 'industrial' and 'relations' came together about a century ago to describe what was then a new and important field of study – emerging in response to the rise of industrialization. The establishment of industrial relations schools, institutes, departments and other academic programs served to codify and advance this new field. Today, as the very nature of work, technology and markets are shifting again – toward what some have termed a global, knowledge-driven economy – it is not clear whether the concept of 'industrial relations' will adapt. Words do matter, and this chapter stands as a meditation on these key words in their changing context.

ORIGINS

The Industrial Revolution provided the crucible from which the field of industrial relations (IR) emerged. In most writings prior to the mid-1700s on farming, metalworking, woodworking, shipping, exchange and other occupations, the focus was on the object of the work, rather than the work itself. While there are notable exceptions – in the Bible and other places where issues such as fair compensation are discussed – prior to industrialization there was not an established literature on work and employment relations as such.

Industrialization provided new modes of production for agriculture and manufacturing, bringing with it ways of working that were different – typically more efficient, but also less safe, requiring different skill sets, drawing different workforces, and affecting many other aspects of life. As one observer commented, looking back on these changes in the United States,

'The Industrial Revolution . . . involved . . . the invention of power machinery and substitution of the factory system for individual crafts-manship and the domestic system. The term "revolution" merely indicates the sweeping changes involved in the complete reorganization of our eco-nomic life' (Patterson, 1929, p. 3). In this context, work stood out as a sep-arate domain of interest because it was now literally a variable. Instead of being a relatively fixed part of the background, work moved to the fore-ground as a separate subject of study. Writings on work and employment from the early 1800s forward were essentially comparative studies, docu-menting new patterns either explicitly or implicitly in comparison to earlier ways of doing things.

For some, the perspective was practical – focused on understanding and improving the way work was done in these various contexts. Technical encyclopedias were published in England and France, 'study tours' were organized in the 1800s to visit particular factories or regions (what today we call benchmarking trips), and industrial education programs were estab-lished. In the United States, the archetypical contributor from this perspective is Frederick Taylor, as is reflected in the following quote:

> This paper has been written: First. To point out, through a series of simple illus-trations, the great loss which the whole country is suffering through inefficiency in almost all of our daily acts. Second. To try to convince the reader that the remedy for this inefficiency lies in systematic management, rather than in search-ing for some unusual or extraordinary man. Third. To prove that the best man-agement is a true science, resting upon clearly defined laws, rules, and principles, as a foundation. And further to show that the fundamental principles of scientific management are applicable to all kinds of human activities, from our simplest individual acts to the work of our great corporations, which call for the most elaborate cooperation. And, briefly, through a series of illustrations, to convince the reader that whenever these principles are correctly applied, results must follow which are truly astounding. (Taylor, 1911)

For others, the perspective was more critical and analytical – focused on surfacing and understanding the dynamics and implications of these new patterns of work. This included various industrial commissions in Europe beginning in the 1800s and in the United States beginning in the early 1900s, as well as scholars who we now celebrate as the founders of IR as a field. For example, John R. Commons invoked a comparative perspective in introducing the principles of labor legislation:

> This spectacle of the free laborer, without property but with the ballot, bargain-ing for his livelihood but electing his rulers, is something new and unaccustomed, measured by the lives of nations. It has come about through what may be called industrial, legal and political changes. (Commons and Andrews, 1916: 2)

Similarly, Max Weber, in discussing the social aspects of the division of labor, contrasted appropriated labor (serfs, slaves, family members) with free labor, a concept that was taking on new meaning in an industrialized society (Weber, 1947: 238–46). Observers were drawn to this contrast after sufficient changes had taken place to make the phenomena visible. As Commons wrote in 1918:

> While the country was engrossed in Civil War and Reconstruction, the American labor movement developed for the first time, *almost unnoticed*, its characteristic national features. This period witnessed the distinctive American philosophies of greenbackism and the eight-hour day; the rise of the agitation for the exclusion of Oriental labor; the invention the trade union label; the first national trade agreement; the establishment of the first government bureau of labor; the organization of the first permanent labor lobby at Washington; the enactment of the first eight-hour legislation and the earliest laws against 'conspiracy' and 'intimidation.' The period also saw the organization of the first national employers' association, and the first national labor party. (Commons *et al.*, 1918. 3, italics added)

The institutional developments were, as Commons pointed out, 'almost unnoticed' initially, but came to be seen as parts of a larger set of shifts. While not all of the developments were necessarily to be celebrated, they were all part of changes that were visible in contrast to what preceded them.[1] It is helpful to know, as Bruce Kaufman documents, that the term 'industrial relations' dates back at least to the 1912 Presidential Commission on Industrial Relations (Kaufman, 1993). It is more important, however, to appreciate how work and employment became visible as distinct phenomena, separate from the associated activities. The roots of IR as a field are thus comparative in nature and based on practices and policy choices that were only made visible by a concurrent set of shifts in markets, technology and society.

Understanding the origins of IR is important because today we are again facing a set of fundamental shifts in markets, technology and society (Piore and Sabel, 1984). There are already many different terms that have been offered to characterize this era as a successor to the industrial, mass production era. These include labels that emphasize flexible specialization, information technology, global markets, and others. In my own writing, I have highlighted the central role of knowledge-driven work (Cutcher-Gershenfeld *et al.*, 1998). This includes the importance of knowledge as a source of competitive advantage in all jobs, not just a limited number of jobs involving so-called 'knowledge workers.' Regardless of the final label provided by future historians, what is most important is that social relations in the workplace and labor markets are shifting in ways that represent a fundamental set of choices for the field.

CHOICES AND PRINCIPLES

The emergence of a field of study and its guiding principles, like most social and institutional changes, does not happen as a single event. Nor, however, does this necessarily happen as a completely gradual, incremental process. In documenting a transformation in a particular labor-management relationship, it was helpful to identify a sequence of what were termed 'pivotal events' during which the transformation itself was at stake (Cutcher-Gershenfeld, 1988). The parties faced choices that, in retrospect, served to reinforce and extend the transformation (or to limit and constrain it). It was the sequence of events that served to make visible the nature and scope of the transformation. In a similar way, the emergence and establishment of key principles for the entire field of IR can be seen as the product of a series of pivotal moments and ideas.

The aim here is not to recount this full sequence of events that shaped the field of IR, but to highlight a few of those that may take on new meaning in the current context. I focus on key choices made at the conclusion of World War II when many states chose to establish schools, institutes and centers focused on labor and industrial relations in response to a wave of post-war strikes and in recognition of the growth of employer-based benefits (pensions, health care and others). These choices in establishing the post-war schools, institutes and centers – blending theory, practice and policy; valuing balance between labor and management; and assembling cross-disciplinary faculties – were all pivotal in that other choices were possible and whatever choice would have been made would have important consequences for the field. In each case, there is a follow-on story regarding the consequences of the choice for the present era.

In many cases, the labor movement supported the establishment of these new academic programs, often over initial opposition from some in the employers' community. As a result, most of these programs featured some faculty and staff focused on practical labor education in the field, modeled on the land-grant university agricultural extension model. This signaled a principle of valuing practical applications in addition to advances in theory and policy. Management education arms were also common, signaling a principle of balance between labor and management. These programs drew their faculties from a diverse mix of fields, including economics, history, industrial engineering, organizational studies, psychology, sociology, statistics and others. This marked the establishment of highly interdisciplinary academic units a full half century before the current interest in increased interdisciplinary scholarship in many colleges and universities. In addition to signaling a principle of cross-disciplinary investigation, it also reflected the problem-centered motivation in setting up these academic programs.

The first choice, blending theory, practice and policy, has persisted in part and been undermined in part in the subsequent years. There continues to be attention to all three domains (theory, practice and policy) reflected within the conference programs of what is now known as the Labor and Employment Relations Association (LERA), which was founded in 1947 as the Industrial Relations Research Association and now has over 3000 national members as well as at least a comparable number of local members in over fifty local chapters. On the other hand, the rise of two other professional associations, the Society for Human Resource Management (SHRM) and the Academy of Management (particularly the Human Resource Division), both reflect a splitting up of theory, practice and policy. SHRM was founded in 1948 and now has approximately 225000 members. It is focused primarily on practice, with occasional links to leading-edge scholarship. The Academy of Management was founded in 1936 and now has over 18000 members. It is focused primarily on theory, with modest (though increasing) attention to practice (Rynes, 2007) and still relatively little attention to public policy. Aligned with business schools, the Academy of Management has enjoyed substantial growth in the past few decades; aligned with the profession of human resource management (HRM), SHRM has also recently enjoyed substantial growth.

While SHRM and the Academy of Management have grown, LERA has experienced a gradual, but steady decline in membership. Moreover, the past half-century has seen the establishment, decline and dissolution of other organizations that also adhered to the principle of bridging theory, practice and policy. These include the Work in America Institute, the American Productivity Center, the National Policy Forum, and others. Thus, 60 years after the establishment of university schools, institutes and centers, we find that theory and practice are more divided and policy is under-emphasized. Today, as the nature of work, markets and society shifts again, it will be important to rebuild these three-way bridges.

A second principle articulated 60 years ago in IR academic units was the notion of balance between labor and management. This was reflected in labor and management extension (or outreach) and professional education, representation on advisory boards, and other aspects of operations. Over time, the same division of theory, practice and policy that can be found among professional associations is also reflected in a polarization of management and labor communities. The rise of the HRM profession, the decline of the labor movement, and the ideological divides between labor and management have all been well documented (Kochan *et al.*, 1984;

Kaufman, 1993). This is also reflected in the declining funding (now at zero) by Congress for the National Labor-Management Cooperation Act, the elimination of Labor-Management Cooperation programs in the US Department of Labor, and the elimination of support for federal sector initiatives under the Federal Labor-Management Partnership Act.

Even within the ranks of labor and management, there are increasing fissures. The departure of 6 million union members and their respective organizations to form the 'Change to Win Coalition' has left 10 million workers and their unions in the AFL-CIO. In 1935, the establishment of the CIO as a split from the then AFL was rooted in the shift from craft to industrial work, with two distinct representational forms. Today's split centers more on organizing tactics with respect to the growing service sector and debates over leadership than on the deeper shift from the industrial, hierarchal model of work to the networked, knowledge-driven model. Still, it does represent an important internal split within labor. Within management the splits are less visible, but no less important. In industries that have faced deregulation, such as airlines, banking, utilities and others, the traditional management organizations have lost what some have described as a congenial and even cozy culture as the various member organization now see each other as competitors and possible targets for acquisition. Moreover, management organizations that have historically taken a constructive approach to collective bargaining, such as the Industrial Relations Counselors (founded in 1926 to foster constructive engagement by management with unions), now have members with sharply different views on the role of unions as legitimate institutional actors.

Today, LERA, with support from the Sloan Foundation, is working to establish and sustain industry councils that can bring together labor, management and third parties in new, industry-level institutional arrangements. This is explicitly intended to fill an institutional gap in our society, but it is not something that has been deeply embraced by labor or management. There are, of course, many prominent labor–management partnerships in the public and private sectors. In addition, approximately 1500 practitioners attend the National Labor–Management Conference hosted by the Federal Mediation and Conciliation Service every other year. Still, the principle of labor-management balance that was articulated in that pivotal post-war period has been followed by a sequence of choices by parties and government officials that have largely resulted in a polarization between labor and management at a societal and institutional level.

The third principle – a multi-disciplinary approach to labor and employment relations – was contrary to a dominant trend in higher education. In many other domains of scholarship, it was specialization within disciplines and sub-disciplines that fueled success. For example, there was an international movement of polytechnics and trade colleges to reinvent themselves as modern, engineering research universities. The Massachusetts Institute of Technology (MIT) and a handful of other elite engineering programs were the exemplars, with success in most cases resting on embracing principles of scientific rigor within well-delineated disciplinary domains.[2] This same specialization within defined disciplinary domains has characterized many business schools. Classic social science disciplines, such as psychology, economics, sociology and history, have all seen an expansion of sub-disciplinary groupings as well. Against this backdrop, the field of IR has had a complex uneasy relationship with these various disciplinary domains.

On the one hand, many scholars have come into IR from various disciplinary homes and each has brought the associated rigor that has characterized the advance of applied social sciences in the second half of the twentieth century. On the other hand, the problem-centered, multi-disciplinary orientation of IR has led these scholars to be looked down upon as somehow less rigorous or less 'scientific' than those still operating within the disciplinary domain. In psychology, for example, the industrial and organizational psychologists maintain links with both the more practitioner-focused American Psychological Association and the more discipline-centered Association for Psychological Science, but do not fit neatly in either camp.

Interestingly, today many universities, foundations, and other institutional stakeholders (such as the National Science Foundation and the National Academies) are calling for more problem-centered, multi-disciplinary scholarship. Labor economics, which was once looked down up by mainstream economics as somehow less pure as a result of its consideration of institutions and practical problems, is now seen as one of the leading domains in the discipline precisely because of the demonstrated ability to blend rigorous theory and methods with attention to complex institutional and practical problems.

Of the three pivotal choices, reflected in the schools, institutes and programs established over 60 years ago, one – an interdisciplinary, problem-centered focus – has come full circle and is now highly valued by many key stakeholders in society. The principle of integrating theory, practice and policy is still posited as an ideal, but the reality is that there are few institutional homes outside of LERA where this is reflected in the organization's structure and operation. For the most part, the domains of theory, practice and policy are distinct, which will hamper the renewed appreciation of an interdisciplinary, problem-centered approach. Similarly, the principle of balance between labor and management has also not stood the test of time well – relations today are polarized and becoming more so.

FROM 'INDUSTRIAL' TO 'INDUSTRY'

The 'industrial' part of IR never limited the field to the study of industrial work – many early studies involved craft (Commons *et al.*, 1918) or service work (Whyte, 1959). Indeed, with the rise of public-sector collective bargaining in the 1970s, labor relations in the public sector dominated the literature for a while. Still, the term 'industrial relations' continued to be the overarching label for the field, presumably reflecting the focus on the new patterns of relations in the industrial sector that marked the founding of the field. However, as the 'industrial relations' function in organizations became increasingly centered in union relations, with 'human resources' replacing it as the overarching term (Kochan *et al.*, 1984), the word 'industrial' stood out as increasingly anachronistic.

Today, the rise of what some have termed the knowledge economy has even transformed old-line industrial jobs. As a result, the leading professional association in the field has changed its name from the Industrial Relations Research Association to the Labor and Employment Relations Association as noted above. Table 1.1 provides a representative listing of graduate degree-granting programs and other key programs in the field. As Rezler (1968) notes, a great wave of new programs were established in the decades following World War II. Today, seven of the 14 programs established during this period or earlier have changed their names, with all but one of the name changes involving the elimination of the word 'industrial.' Programs established more recently have use the term 'human resources' or terms other than IR. This is in contrast to many other parts of the world, where terms such as IR and its translations continue to be widely used.

Early on, 'industrialization' was treated as a natural correlate of IR (Harbison and Meyers, 1959). While the initial thesis of a global convergence of IR practice, driven by the logic of industrialization, proved overly deterministic, there are consequences of industrialization that are still very much in the literature. These center particularly in developing economies where the consequences of industrialization for labor markets and the environment are of particular concern. Thus, the continued use of 'industrial relations' in many parts of the world is paired with a continued interest in industrialization and its consequences.

An important further development has also happened in the field, which is the rise of what is termed 'industry studies' – scholarship that considers work, technology, trade, productivity, public policy, labor markets and institutions at the industry level of analysis or that is particularly relevant to a given industry. There are currently over 25 industry centers in the United States, established with Sloan Foundation support and based at a range of different universities. The annual industry studies conferences

*Table 1.1 Year of establishment for US and Canadian schools, institutes,
centers and departments specializing in industrial relations or
human resources management (with current name and founding
name indicated where different)*

1920s–1930s Total *N*=2	1940s–1950s Total *N*=13	1960s–1970s Total *N*=13	1980s–1990s Total *N*=9

Programs that grant or have granted graduate degrees (Masters or Ph.D.) in
industrial relations or human resource management

1920s–1930s	1940s–1950s	1960s–1970s	1980s–1990s
	Cornell University • New York State School of Industrial and Labor Relations University of Illinois at Urbana-Champaign • School of Labor and Employment Relations Loyola University of Chicago • Institute of Human Resources and Industrial Relations (was originally the Institute of Industrial Relations) Michigan State University • School of Labor and Industrial Relations University of Michigan • Institute for Research on Labour, Employment, and the Economy	University of Alabama-Tuscaloosa • Human Resources Institute George Washington University • Human Resource Development Programs Indiana University of Pennsylvania • Graduate Department of Industrial and Labor Relations University of Iowa • Center for Labor and Management (now restructured and partially disbanded) Université Laval (Canada) • Departement des relations industrielles University of Massachusetts – Amherst • Labor Relations and Research Center New School University	California State Polytechnic University, Pomona • Department of Management and Human Resources Claremont Graduate University • School of Behavioral and Organizational Sciences Cleveland State University • Department of Management and Labor Relations Georgia State University • WT Beebe Institute of Personnel and Employment Relations University of Louisville • Department of Leadership, Foundations and Human Resource Education

Table 1.1 (continued)

1920s–1930s Total $N=2$	1940s–1950s Total $N=13$	1960s–1970s Total $N=13$	1980s–1990s Total $N=9$
	University of Minnesota • Industrial Relations Center Université de Montréal • École de relations industrielles Pennsylvania State University • Department of Labor Studies and Employment Relations (was originally Department of Labor Studies and Industrial Relations) Rutgers University • School of Management and Labor Relations University of Wisconsin • Industrial Relations Research Institute (now restructured and partly disbanded)	• Department of Human Resources Management (undergoing reorganization) University of Oregon • Institute of Industrial and Labor Relations (now restructured and partially disbanded) Purdue University • Department of Organizational Behavior and Human Resource Management Queen's University (Canada) • Industrial Relations Centre Temple University • Department of Human Resource Administration (was originally the Department of Industrial Relations and Organizational Behavior) University of Toronto (Canada) • Centre for Industrial Relations and Human Resources Wayne State University • Institute of Labor	Rollins College • Human Resource Research Institute Ohio State University • Department of Management and Human Resources

Table 1.1　(continued)

1920s–1930s Total $N=2$	1940s–1950s Total $N=13$	1960s–1970s Total $N=13$	1980s–1990s Total $N=9$
		Relations (now restructured and partially disbanded)	

Additional Programs with Research Faculties and Graduate Course Offerings in Industrial Relations or Human Resource Management

Massachusetts Institute of Technology • Institute for Work and Employment Research (was originally the Industrial Relations Section) Princeton University • Industrial Relations Section	University of California-Berkeley • Institute for Research on Labor and Employment (was originally the Institute of Industrial Relations) University of California-Los Angeles • Institute for Research on Labor and Employment (was originally the Institute of Industrial Relations) University of Hawaii • Industrial Relations Center	Boston University • Human Resources Policy Institute West Virginia University • Department of Industrial Relations and Management	Empire State College, State University of New York • Harry Van Arsdale Jr. Center for Labor Studies University of Rhode Island • Schmidt Labor Research Center (was originally the Labor Research Center)

Note:　The list of programs prior to the 1960s is based on those identified by Rezler in a national survey conducted in 1968; subsequent programs were identified based on graduate degree programs listed in the directory provided by the Labor and Employment Relations Association and additional follow-up by phone and internet search (not including programs that are just MBA or Labor Studies without a link to a doctoral program or other relevant IR or HR programming). The focus on graduate programs was selected to ensure the presence of research faculties. Some programs are separate degree granting schools or institutes, some are departments in schools of business, social science and humanities units or other locations, and some are centers or other such academic units. The listing is relatively complete in the early years and broadly representative in the later years. Apologies are offered in advance for any programs that are misclassified, misrepresented, or missing.

draw an increasing number of leading scholars and many of their doctoral students.

What is the attraction of industry studies? There is certainly a long history of industry-focused scholarship in the field (Dunlop, 1958; Walton and McKersie, 1965). Although many politicians have resisted the notion of having an industrial policy, scholars have found that conducting research in an industry context yields useful insights. This reflects an important institutional development. While national policies and individual firm choices continue to be important, the work of the industry studies community documents innovations in trade, technology, labor markets and other industry-level developments that have more leverage than traditional sources of competitive advantage, such as more generic forms of geography, capital, or technology that are not in an industry context. For example, the rise of lean production, as documented by the book *The Machine that Changed the World* (Womack *et al.*, 1991), is an industry-specific, knowledge-driven development that has been transformational, first in the auto industry and then as a focus of attention in other sectors such as aerospace (Murman, *et al.*, 2002) and textiles (Abernathy *et al.*, 1999) where the primary research question centers on the transferability of the innovation from one industry to another. Today, the concept of 'industry' is fresh, even if 'industrial' is dated.

FROM 'LABOR-MANAGEMENT' TO 'STAKEHOLDER' RELATIONS

As noted earlier, the focus on 'relations' between labor and management has been a hallmark of the field. It was tensions in these relations in the 1940s that gave rise to many of the leading degree-granting schools, institutes and centers in the field. Relations among trade union representatives and human resource professionals are still at the core of professional practice in the field. At the same time, the direct relations between employers and their workforce in the absence of a union, the relations among co-workers on the job, and the relations among workers and their families and communities are all long-standing and growing areas of focus for many scholars in the field.

This focus on relations brings with it a number of key assumptions and implications. First, the concept of 'relations' implies actors who are at once independent and interdependent. That is, the parties are acting independently (at least to some degree), but their actions affect one another. Further, there is a related pluralistic assumption of both common and competing interests associated with these relationships – they are neither at the extremes of atomistic competition or completely unified in their existence. Tying the parties together is a social contract, which is an enduring theme in the field (Gershenfeld *et al.*, 2008). In addition, the concept of relations has a longitudinal connotation – relations take place over time, and the social contract may be stable, deteriorating or expanding. That is, there is a sense of trajectory associated with a focus on relations.

In today's world, the concept of relations takes on meaning that reaches beyond the employment relationship. First, individuals are more mobile, whether by choice or through imposed contingent arrangements. Individuals will have employment relationships with a number of different employers over their working life, as well as relationships with various labor market intermediaries such as government agencies, community organizations, and temporary help firms. As such, there is today a broader spectrum of relationships that are more fully reflected in the term 'employment relations' than the term 'industrial relations.'

Further, there are a growing number of instances where relations among stakeholders in various networks or 'engineered systems' have become more salient than relations within traditional organizational, market or institutional boundaries. This includes the webs of relationships that exist across supply chains, the complex mix of stakeholders involved in regional innovation networks, and key parts of our societal infrastructure (transportation systems, the power grid, and so on).

Many principles developed by IR scholars apply in these complex systems. For example, there is an adage in collective bargaining that 'it takes three agreements to get one – an agreement within labor, and agreement within management, and an agreement between labor and management.' Moreover, as Walton and McKersie (1965) first documented, the 'intra-organizational' bargaining is often more challenging than the negotiations between the parties. In complex systems, the same principle holds, with the additional consideration that the internal negotiations are now within each of many stakeholders in a complex system (Cutcher-Gershenfeld *et al.*, 2005). This can be thought of as collective bargaining times 'n' – the principles apply, but instead of two parties (labor and management), there are 'n' stakeholders. Similarly, we know from labor-management relations that innovative labor-management partnerships are only sustainable if they deliver results for each party separately and for the relationship as a whole. In the context of complex, engineered systems, the same principle applies – each stakeholder needs to see valued results, as well as the delivery of results for the system as a whole. Here there is a connection to the growing focus on what are termed 'double bottom line' approaches to business, which involve accounting and governance mechanisms that track delivery of results to shareholders and to society (in various forms).

Of course, relations among stakeholders in a complex, engineered system are similar, but not the same as relations among labor and management in an employment relationship. The legal context is different and the connections to product and other markets are also distinct. Indeed, research on these new forms of 'lateral' stakeholder relations represents an emerging area of research that is documenting and assessing new institutional forms. While the phenomena are distinct, the mindset that comes from the study of IR is particularly valuable in this new domain. Not only must we as a field expand the scope of employment relations that are now relevant to study, but we must ask ourselves whether a broader array of stakeholder relations are within scope for the field. The center of the field is likely to remain on employment relations (a more encompassing term than IR), but the utilization of applied social science methods to address these additional types of stakeholder relations may represent an important additional area of expertise for the field.

Ultimately, it is possible that the very nature of employment will change as a result of these emerging lateral institutional arrangements. The development of rigorous social science models, methods and theory to understand relations in this context will build on the comparative perspective that has been a part of IR from its inception, resulting in a mix of qualitative field observation, mathematical modeling (using a mix of graph theory, game theory and network modeling methods), institutional analysis, and other forms of expertise. It will go beyond the popular observation that 'the world is flat' (Friedman, 2005) into a more systematic analysis of which relations are taking place in a more lateral way, which ones are not, and what the implications are in both cases.

CONCLUSION: EMPLOYMENT RELATIONS IN THE KNOWLEDGE ECONOMY

A close consideration of the terms 'industrial' and 'relations' allows for reflection on the future directions of the field itself. We see that the word 'industrial' has connotations that have not survived as a central defining term in the emerging global, knowledge-driven economy. While a focus on 'industry' has expanding utility, it is the employment relationship that remains at the center of the field and it is 'employment' that has replaced 'industrial' as a defining term for the field. While relations between labor and management are of continued importance, there is a web of additional relationships that represent promising domains for scholars in this field. The word 'relations' continues to be appropriate, even if it is defined in broader ways.

Certain key principles codified in the establishment of schools, institutes and departments have continued value. These include attention to the principle of interweaving theory, policy and practice, as well as the principle of taking a multi-disciplinary, problem-centered approach. The principle of balance between labor and management also still holds, but it has expanded to include a balance across other stakeholders as well. All three principles can be found in varying degrees in business schools, law schools, and departments of economics, psychology or sociology. As well, these principles are valued to some degree in professional associations outside the LERA. But it is in the programs and professional association formerly known as 'industrial relations' where there is the most complete value placed on theory, practice and policy together; where there is the most complete embodiment of a multi-disciplinary, problem-centered approach; and where there is the most complete appreciation of the need for balance among labor, management and other stakeholders.

Although some universities and states did not look behind the words 'industrial relations' and judged the programs under this banner as outdated, in other cases there is recognition that labor and employment relations is, if anything, more important in a global, knowledge-driven economy. In this sense, the pivotal choice on the part of a number of states to establish these academic programs over a half century ago provides society with a unique, new opportunity to address the ways people matter when it comes to employment and stakeholder relations in the emerging, global knowledge economy.

NOTES

1. Among developments that did not warrant celebration were the use of thugs, injunctions and yellow-dog contracts by management, and the use of violence during strikes and at other times by workers and union representatives.
2. Carnegie Mellon stands out as an early exception, charting its path to prominence by focusing at the intersection of the disciplines.

REFERENCES

Abernathy, Frederick H., Dunlop, John T., Weil, David and Hammond, Janice H. (1999), *A Stitch in Time: Lean Retailing and the Transformation of Manufacturing*, New York: Oxford University Press.

Commons, John R. and Andrews, John B. (1916), *Principles of Labor Legislation* (revised edition), New York: Harper and Brothers (1927 edition).

Commons, John R., with Saposs, David J., Sumner, Helen L., Mittleman, E.B., Hoagland, H.E., Andrews, John B. and Perlman Selig (1918), *History of Labour in the United States, Volume II*, New York: The Macmillan Company.

Cutcher-Gershenfeld, Joel (1988), *Tracing a Transformation in Industrial Relations: A Case Study of Xerox and ACTWU*, Washington, DC: US Department of Labor.
Cutcher-Gershenfeld, Joel, Barrett, Betty and Lawson, Christopher (2005), 'Building the internal organization to support lateral alignment: a case study of the Office of Environment and Energy, Federal Aviation Administration,' Cambridge, MA: MIT Project on Lateral Alignment in Complex Systems.
Cutcher-Gershenfeld, Joel, Nitta, Michio, Barrett, Betty, Belhedi, Nejib, Chow Simon, Inaba, Takashi, Ishino, Iwao, Lin, Wen-Jeng, Moore, Michael, Mothersell, William, Palthe, Jennifer, Ramanand, Shobha, Strolle, Mark and Wheaton, Arthur (with Cheryl Coutchie, Seepa Lee and Stacia Rabine) (1998), *Knowledge-Driven Work: Unexpected Lessons from Japanese and United States Work Practices*, New York: Oxford University Press.
Dunlop, John (1958), *Industrial Relations Systems*, New York: Henry Holt.
Friedman, Thomas L. (2005), *The World Is Flat: A Brief History of the Twenty-First Century*, New York: Farrar, Straus and Giroux.
Gershenfeld, Gladys, Gershenfeld, Walter and Cutcher-Gershenfeld, Joel (2008), 'LERA/IRRA then and now,' *Perspectives on Work* **11**: 2 (Winter), 9–12.
Harbison, Frederick and Myers Charles A. (1959), *Management in the Industrial World: An International Analysis*, New York: McGraw Hill.
Kaufman, Bruce E. (1993), *The Origins and Evolution of Industrial Relations in the United States*, Ithaca, NY: ILR Press.
Kochan, Thomas, Katz, Harry and McKersie, Robert (1984), *The Transformation of American Industrial Relations*, New York: Basic Books.
Murman, Earll, Allen, Tom, Bozdogan, Kirkor, Cutcher-Gershenfeld, Joel, McManus, Hugh, Nightingale, Debbie, Rebentisch, Eric, Shields Tom, Stahl, Fred, Walton, Myles, Warmkessel, Joyce, Weiss, Stanley and Widnall, Sheila (2002), *Lean Enterprise Value: Insights from MIT's Lean Aerospace Initiative*, New York: Palgrave/Macmillan.
Patterson, S. Howard (1929), *Social Aspects of Industry: A Survey of Labor Problems and Causes of Industrial Unrest*, New York: McGraw-Hill.
Piore, Michael J. and Sabel, Charles F. (1984), *Second Industrial Divide: Possibilities for Prosperity*, New York: Basic Books.
Rezler, Julius (1968), 'The place of the industrial relations program in the organizational structure of the university,' *Industrial and Labor Relations Review* **21** (2) 251–61.
Rynes, Sara. (2007), Editor's forward: tackling the 'Great Divide between research production and dissemination in human resource management', *The Academy of Management Journal* **50** (5), 985–6.
Taylor, Frederick W. (1911), *The Principles of Scientific Management*, New York: Harper Bros.
Walton, Richard and McKersie, Robert (1965), *A Behavioral Theory of Labor Negotiations*, New York: McGraw-Hill.
Weber, Max (1947), *The Theory of Social and Economic Organization*, New York: Oxford University Press.
Whyte, William Foote (1959), *Human Relations in the Restaurant Industry (Work, Its Rewards and Discontents)*, New York: American Hotel Association Educational Institute.
Womack, James, Jones, Daniel and Roos, Daniel (1991), *The Machine that Changed the World*, New York: Harper-Collins.

J53

2. The original industrial relations paradigm: foundation for revitalizing the field

Bruce E. Kaufman

INTRODUCTION

The field of industrial relations (IR) is in decline across most nations of the world. The reasons for this pronounced decline are numerous. Arguably the most important factor, however, is the steady and increasingly severe erosion in union density in most countries. To a large degree, most scholars regard trade unionism, collective bargaining and labor-management relations, and the national labor policy and labor law within which they are embedded, as the core subjects of the field (Adams, 1993; Strauss and Whitfield, 1998).

Admittedly, these subjects are examined from a variety of disciplinary perspectives, theoretical points of view and national experiences, giving IR research a rich diversity. In addition, one certainly must recognize that other subjects, such as contingent work, work–family balance, and dispute resolution, are also important parts of the intellectual dialogue in the field. Nonetheless, the indisputable fact remains that the study of trade unions and labor–management relations forms the heart of IR, through the observation of Keller (1996: 202) that, 'Discussions of the future of IR always tend to turn into a debate on the future of trade unions.' Since union density has declined for several decades in a slow but cumulatively significant way across nearly all regions of the world, the field of IR has suffered its own long-term decline (Kaufman, 2006).

Is there any way out for IR? One option is to hope for a union resurgence or emergence of some alternative form of collective worker voice. At the present time, however, the prospects do not look encouraging (Bennett and Kaufman, 2002; Fiorito, 2007; Willman and Bryson, 2007).

The second option is to fundamentally restructure and reposition IR in terms of subject matter, theories, and policy issues so that it occupies a larger and more prosperous intellectual place in the study of the work

31

world and, at the same time, also decreases its dependence on the trade union movement. This repositioning cannot just take any form or direction for much of the territory of the world of work is already claimed by other disciplines and fields of study, such as management, labor economics, organizational sociology and labor law. Likewise, such a repositioning cannot go so far so as to abandon certain fundamental intellectual and ethical principles that lie at the heart of IR for then the field would lose its very identity and intellectual coherence. Nonetheless, if scholars, operating within these broad constraints, could successfully redefine the intellectual territory of IR so it is more inclusive and relevant with respect to labor issues and policy debates, then the field might also have a brighter future. This repositioning, I should note, does not mean abandoning the subject of trade unions or taking on the full neo-liberal agenda, but it does imply that trade unions would move from the core subject of the field to only one of several equally important subjects and that unions would likewise be subjected to more objective and critical analysis than has heretofore been the norm.

In this chapter, I take up the challenge of developing the second strategic option – a broadened and reconfigured vision of the paradigm of IR. My argument is that the contemporary union-centered version of IR is not a faithful representation of the original IR paradigm that first emerged in the late 1910s and early 1920s in the field's birth country, the United States. To develop this argument, I provide a brief review of this original IR paradigm and then describe in more detail what I have elsewhere called the 'three faces of industrial relations' (Kaufman, 2004a). These three faces collectively represent the field's core subject matter and ideological value statement, at least as originally enunciated in the USA. I next examine the core intellectual and ethical principle that underlies these three faces and ties them together as a unified whole. This common denominator, I argue, is rejection of the competitive labor market model of demand and supply. This position can also be stated as the assertion that labor is not a commodity. The chapter ends with conclusions and implications. Although written largely from an American perspective, the hope is that the general ideas and principles developed here are relevant to the study of IR in all countries.

THE DEFINITION AND INTELLECTUAL BOUNDARIES OF INDUSTRIAL RELATIONS

The field of IR has largely Anglo-American roots. The work of the English duo Sidney and Beatrice Webb, particularly their landmark book *Industrial*

Democracy (1897), was foundational. The field did not emerge as a consciously self-identified subject of research and practice in England, however, but rather in the United States in the late 1910s and early 1920s (Kaufman, 2004a). In the academic world, the American 'father' of IR is institutional labor economist John R. Commons, who along with colleagues of what is called the 'Wisconsin School' largely defined and developed the early model of IR. In an earlier book (op. cit.), I have claimed that industrialist John D. Rockefeller Jr. also deserves to be considered a 'father' of IR, given his great influence in spreading the study and practice of IR in American corporations and universities and through the International Labor Organization.

The original paradigm of IR cannot be found in any one article or book. I nonetheless claim it is possible to canvas this early work and distill from it a synthetic portrait of the key ideas and principles that collectively define the original vision of IR.

The place to start in describing the original IR paradigm is to first define the subject matter and intellectual boundaries of IR. The most authoritative source on this matter is a 1928 report prepared by the Social Science Research Council (US) entitled *Survey of Research in the Field of Industrial Relations*. It states (p. 19, emphasis added): 'the focal point of the field is *the employer–employee relationship*.' Also relevant is a report by the National Industrial Conference Board a few years later that states (p. 31): 'the term "industrial relations" comprises every incident that grows out of employment.' The breadth of the IR term is also indicated in a Russell Sage Library publication, *Industrial Relations: A Selected Bibliography* (1919), which states that the field covers both personnel management and alternative systems of workforce governance (e.g., trade unions, employee representation plans, and so on).

Based on this and other evidence, I conclude that the core subject of the original IR paradigm is the employer–employee relationship and, in particular, all the behaviors, outcomes, practices and institutions that emanate from or impinge on the employment relationship. Viewed from this perspective, IR could more accurately be called employment relations. It is also evident from this definition that the subject area of IR, as initially defined and conceived, is much broader than the study of trade unions, labor law or any other such topic. Rather, the original paradigm of IR covers all aspects of the employment relationship, thus including within the field employment relationships of all types (for example union and non-union, private and public, formal and informal) and a large number of related subject areas, such as labor economics, human resource management, industrial psychology, industrial sociology, labor law, labor history and political science.

Although the original IR paradigm was centered on the employment relationship, it was not a unitary construct in terms of research and practice. Rather, IR was part of an intellectual project, part an applied program of problem solving and labor reform, and part of a moral and ideological commitment. I call these three dimensions of the original IR paradigm the 'three faces' of industrial relations. Each is briefly described below.

THE THREE FACES OF ORIGINAL INDUSTRIAL RELATIONS

The original paradigm of IR had three different dimensions or 'faces.' In practice they substantially overlapped; in theory they are distinct and separate.

Science-building

Science-building is largely an academic endeavor aimed at explaining behavior and expanding knowledge through theory building and empirical investigation. The focus of science-building in original industrial relations (OIR) was on explaining the behaviors, institutions and outcomes associated with the *employment relationship*. I have already quoted two sources from the 1920s that clearly state the employment relationship is the central subject of IR. With regard to science-building, J. Douglas Brown, first director of the Princeton IR Section, provides a concise statement of three characteristics of the original paradigm: a focus on the employment relationship, coverage of all forms of employment relationships (private/public, union/non-union), and a multidisciplinary approach in recognition that the employment relationship contains economic, organizational, psychological, social, legal, political, and historical dimensions. With reference to the founding of the Section, he states (1976: 5, emphasis in original):

> It was the intention of the founders to broaden the scope of the field studied to *all* factors, conditions, problems and policies involved in the employment of human resources in organized production or service. It was not to be limited to any single academic discipline. Nor was the term 'industrial relations' limited to activities within *private* enterprise but was assumed to cover the relations of government and all other institutions with those people who constituted the working forces of the country.

Science-building in IR was a modest and somewhat diffuse activity in the 1920s but, nonetheless, had a visible and organized presence. It was carried on by a diverse range of people both inside and outside academe. Included within the original IR, for example, were not only the institutional labor economists famous in the field (Commons, Selig Perlman, Sumner Slichter, and so on), but also members of the human relation school (for example, Elton Mayo), industrial psychologists (for example, Arthur Kornhauser), post-Taylor writers on scientific management (for example, Morris Cooke, Harlow Person), writers in personnel management (for example, Ordway Tead), business executives (for example, Henry Dennison, Sam Lewisohn), consultants (for example, Mary Follett), and trade unionists (for example, Leo Wolman).

The clearest evidence of the expansive nature of IR research in this period, as well as the fact that IR research was a recognized activity, comes from the aforementioned 1928 Social Science Research Council report. For more than 100 pages, it describes employment-related research being done in more than a dozen disciplines and fields of study. Admittedly, however, the large bulk of this research was relatively applied and theoretical work was spotty.

Problem-solving

The second face of OIR is the application of science and knowledge to solving practical problems and devising public policy. In its problem-solving dimension, the focus of early IR was on solving the Labor Problem, which eventually evolved into 'labor problems' in the plural form. Illustratively, Dale Yoder (1931) states, 'The most widely accepted approach to the study of IR is one which involves an examination of the phenomena that are usually described as Labor Problems.'

The central point of view was that the free-market capitalist system of that era was composed of a variety of institutions that collectively malperformed in the labor/employment area; the task of IR is to discover and design new or reformed institutional arrangements that solve these labor problems and thereby increase efficiency and human welfare. This process of institutional reform must be evolutionary and adaptive in light of changes in the economy and the nature of social/economic problems; certainly it is not a one-way street to ever-greater market regulation. Commons (1934), in particular, was insistent that maximum opportunity be allowed for individual economic autonomy (what he called 'progressive individualism') and that the profit–motive should be relied on wherever possible, as long as self-interest and profit-making are guided by rules that channel them toward socially constructive purposes and the outcomes fall within minimal bounds of equity (what he called 'reasonable value').

Within these broad boundaries, by the end of the 1920s the proponents of original IR had developed four different institutional instruments for

solving labor problems and improving the efficiency and fairness of the
employment relationship. These were, respectively, professional/progressive
labor management, labor law and social insurance, trade unions and collective bargaining, and macroeconomic stabilization/full employment
policy (Kaufman, 2003).

The duality between labor problems and IR is revealed in the university
textbooks used in the 1920s and 1930s to teach IR (for example, Watkins,
1922). Titled 'Labor Problems' (or some variant), the front part was
devoted to a survey of various labor problems (long hours, child labor, and
so on), followed by sections on the different institutional solutions to these
problems, with emphasis on the first three instruments mentioned above.

Ethical/ideological

The third face of OIR expressed the ethical values and ideological position
of the field regarding work and employment. Early industrial relationists
were frank that the field was based on certain fundamental values. Sumner
Slichter (1928: 287) acknowledged such, for example, when he said 'To the
vast majority of people, however, even to the economists and sociologists,
the labor problem is more than this [an object of scientific inquiry]. It is also
a matter of ethics, a matter not simply of what is or what might be, but of
what should be.'

What were the ethical and ideological commitments of early IR? Slichter
states on this matter, 'From the ethical point of view, therefore, the labor
problem is concerned with two principal things: with the effect of the prevailing institutions . . . upon the conflict between life and work, and with
the institutional change needed to harmonize men's activities as laborers
with their interests as men' (Slichter, 1928: 288). Explicit in this statement
is the recognition that labor is embodied in human beings; as a result, the
conditions, performance and outcomes of work carry a higher moral
significance than is true for inanimate factor inputs such as capital and
land.

Less clearly revealed, but an animating conviction nonetheless, is
the contention that the prevailing labor markets and institutions of early
twentieth-century American capitalism were systematically slanted in favor
of property owners and consumers and against the interests and wellbeing
of workers. Thus, values that are central to OIR are enshrined in propositions such as: the conditions and outcomes of work should meet
minimum social standards; workers who provide the labor input should not
be viewed solely as a means to greater production or a cost to be minimized
but also as human beings with legitimate interests in reasonable and
rewarding conditions and outcomes of work; human rights should have

precedence over property rights; and the workplace, like other spheres of society, should provide stakeholders with democratic rights, provisions for due process and opportunities for voice and representation. Also explicit in Slichter's statement is recognition that attainment of these ethical objectives requires institutional change led through the collective action of government and other social actors.

The normative commitments of OIR can be summarized in a social welfare function (Kaufman, 2005). Analytically, this welfare function is quasi-lexicographic; conceptually it is analogous to Maslow's 'hierarchy of needs' theory. The IR social welfare function begins with first-order survival needs and then, as these are minimally satisfied, brings in successively higher-order needs (or social goals). The first argument of the IR social welfare function is production of goods and services (or economic efficiency), for a reasonable and progressing standard of living is a prerequisite for human survival and happiness. Once a minimum level of goods and services is produced (with observance of core human rights), the second argument in the IR welfare function is fairness, equity and social justice. IR is committed to fairness and social justice, partly because they are fundamental moral values subscribed to by all human beings and partly because they are prerequisites to efficiency and, thus, a stable and economically advancing society. The third and yet higher-order argument of the IR social welfare function is that the conditions and experience of work enhance (and certainly do not retard) the opportunity of workers for self-development and self-actualization.

THE CORE PRINCIPLE OF INDUSTRIAL RELATIONS

Having described the three faces of the original IR paradigm, the question emerges: is there any common principle that unites these three faces and ties them together? I believe the answer is yes. This core principle provides, I assert, the intellectual and normative common denominator that unites all scholars and practitioners of IR and gives IR its unique reason for being as a social science field of study and practice. Stated another way, without this core principle a separate and intellectually/socially relevant field of IR cannot exist.

The core principle of IR can be stated in two ways (Kaufman, 2007a). They perfectly match, like opposite sides of the same coin.

The first version of the core principle is rejection of the orthodox competitive demand/supply labor market model as the appropriate framework for analyzing and understanding the key features and outcomes of the

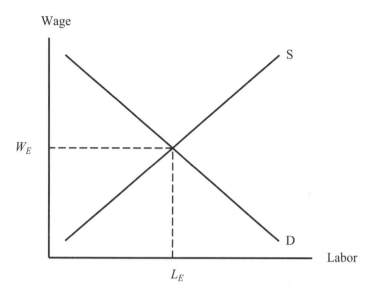

Figure 2.1   Wage/employment determination in a competitive labor market

employment relationship. This model is depicted in Figure 2.1. It shows the demand curve for labor (D), the supply curve (S), and the determination of the equilibrium wage and quantity of labor (W_E, L_E). It is fair to say that this diagram is the single most important theoretical construct in neoclassical labor economics, provides the starting point and frame of reference for practically all analyses of labor and employment issues by orthodox economists, and is the core idea behind the neoclassical/neo-liberal attack on labor market institutions and regulation. It is also the model of the labor market and employment relationship that the founders of IR rejected – or, more correctly, wished to substantially revise. As described below, this diagram and the theory it represents may well describe certain specific, broad, or long-run tendencies regarding labor, but must nonetheless be rejected by industrial relationists as an appropriate theoretical foundation for the field.

The second version of the core principle is the proposition that labor is embodied in human beings, which can be alternatively stated as labor is not a commodity. In the early twentieth century, many writers made this distinction by calling labor the 'human factor' (Kaufman, 2008).

This version of the core principle applies to both the positive and normative sides of IR. As a positive statement, the core principle asserts that in the scientific study of IR it is essential for a proper understanding and explanation of employment-related phenomena to recognize that labor is embodied in living human beings. The implication of this proposition is that models and theories that treat labor similarly to inanimate factor inputs, such as capital and land, are likely to be biased and incomplete tools for IR research. As a normative statement, the proposition that labor is not a commodity asserts the fundamental moral/ethical belief that since labor is embodied in human beings, the terms, conditions and treatment of labor cannot be evaluated by the same efficiency criterion used for inanimate inputs (e.g., maximum productivity, minimum cost). The implication of this normative proposition is that society has a legitimate and compelling rationale for using laws and institutions to modify or replace terms and conditions of employment that are inhumane, anti-social or in violation of basic human rights.

DEEPER ANALYSIS: ECONOMIC THEORY

These two versions of the core principle of IR, I maintain, are mirror images of each other. That is, the competitive demand/supply model only has theoretical coherence when labor is treated akin to a commodity. The essence of a commodity is that it is a homogeneous good and each unit is identical. Neoclassical theory recognizes in a very limited way that labor is embodied in human beings, since workers are modeled as maximizing agents with a set of preferences. Nonetheless, this theory necessarily treats workers as commodities for purposes of deriving the demand/supply model and the determination of equilibrium wages and employment. It must also make the same assumption to reach the conclusion that a perfectly competitive labor market maximizes efficiency. Elucidating these points requires a brief foray into basic economic theory.

If workers are not treated as commodities, several crucial aspects of the competitive labor demand/supply model collapse. One, for example, is a well-defined downward sloping labor demand curve (Kaufman, 2007b). The labor demand curve is equivalent to the competitive firm's marginal product of labor schedule, derived by adding homogeneous units of labor to the production function. For the labor demand curve to take the form of a unique one-to-one mapping between the wage rate and quantity demanded of labor, it is crucial that labor be a commodity, such as a ton of coal, since then the marginal product of each unit of labor is entirely technologically determined by the production function. But if labor is not a commodity, then the marginal product schedule and labor demand curve in Figure 2.1 transform from a line to an ill-defined band of values that is consistent with a number of alternative wage/labor combinations. The reason is that the amount of productive services supplied by inanimate inputs is fixed by nature, but the amount of labor services (or 'labor power' in Marxian terminology) provided by workers is volitionally supplied and can take a very large range of values (from zero when the worker sleeps on the job to the maximum amount the person is capable of performing) depending on a host of non-technological variables, such as morale, perceived fairness of pay, and treatment by the employer. Thus, any given wage rate is consistent with a large range of possible marginal products coming out of the production function, making it impossible to draw the determinate, well-defined labor demand curve in Figure 2.1.

The labor supply curve also changes shape (or form) if labor is not a commodity-like entity. A crucial assumption in deriving the market labor supply curve in Figure 2.1 is that each individual firm faces a perfectly elastic (horizontal) labor supply curve, indicating it is a 'wage taker.' But a firm is a wage taker only of if labor is a homogeneous commodity, for otherwise labor is differentiated and with differentiated labor the firm's supply curve becomes upward sloping (just as a firm's product demand curve becomes downward sloping when the good is differentiated). One factor that differentiates labor is when the employer and employee have a personal relationship, which is almost universal since the labor services are embodied in the worker and the worker must therefore have personal contact with the employer (or management representatives). For whatever reason, when the labor supply curve of individual firms is upward sloping then the labor market is no longer perfectly competitive but transforms into some version of monopsony (Manning, 2003). A monopsony labor market, in turn, does not resemble Figure 2.1 since it has three curves (marginal revenue product, supply curve and marginal cost of labor), yields an equilibrium wage below the competitive wage, results (potentially) in some measure of labor exploitation, and does not have a well-defined labor demand schedule.

Labor must also be a commodity-like entity for the model depicted in Figure 2.1 to determine a unique equilibrium wage and clear the labor market in the case of excess supply. Neither is likely to happen if labor is embodied in a human being. Demand and supply do not yield a competitive equilibrium wage, for example, because the wage rate performs two functions – it allocates labor but is also used by firms to motivate labor (Solow, 1990) – and the wage rate that meets one objective will most likely not meet the other (a condition in macroeconomic theory of more 'targets' than 'instruments'). In commodity markets, by way of contrast, demand/supply are able to determine a unique equilibrium since price performs only the allocative function and not the motivational function (e.g., a barrel of oil does not have to be motivated to supply a certain amount of energy). Likewise, wage rates seldom fall in situations of excess labor supply (i.e., generalized unemployment) because firms consciously avoid imposing wage cuts, knowing that wage cuts can actually raise labor costs through the negative effect on employee morale, cooperation and productivity. But if wage rates do not fall in response to excess labor supply, the labor market will remain out of equilibrium and involuntary unemployment may persist for a long period.

In response, a neoclassical economist could argue that the model of perfect competition assumes a world of perfect information and complete contracts and with complete contracts all of the above-cited anomalies disappear. For example, with a complete contract (i.e., a contract negotiated prior to the exchange that specifies in perfect detail every aspect of the good/service to be delivered) the firm knows the exact value of the worker's marginal product; the amount of work effort of the employee is locked-in by a contractual agreement prior to any personal contact in the workplace; and the issues of motivation is moot since the contract stipulates in advance how much labor is to be supplied.

But this argument fails because of its own internal contradiction. As Ronald Coase (1937) first argued, complete labor contracts can only exist in a world of zero transaction cost (i.e., zero costs of transferring property rights). But, as Coase and other 'new institutional' economists show, in an environment of zero transaction cost firms have no reason to hire employees but instead obtain labor services from independent contractors (since control of labor – the principal legal criterion defining the status of employee – has no economic value in a world of perfect information and zero transaction cost). The net outcome, argued Coase, is that all firms dissolve into single person proprietorships, obtain labor from independent contractors through buying and selling labor services in product markets, and the labor market and employment relationship disappear. The contradiction, therefore, is that the neoclassical demand/supply model in Figure 2.1 can only be saved by assuming labor services are traded in complete contracts, but this very assumption logically implies that the labor market and employment relationship do not exist (Kaufman, 2007b). One invalidates the other. Conversely, if labor contracts are incomplete (which real world labor contracts most surely are), then all the anomalies cited above that arise from the human essence of labor reappear, again causing the competitive demand/supply model in Figure 2.1 to deconstruct.

A FOUNDATION FOR THE FIELD

Although perhaps not obvious at first, these conclusions are of fundamental importance to IR and, indeed, in my opinion provide the foundation for the field. To appreciate why, we must return to the three faces of IR described above. The essential point to establish is that each of the three faces gains intellectual power and moral credibility in direct proportion to the extent the demand/supply model in Figure 2.1, and the commodity theory of labor underlying it, are shown to be false.

I earlier argued that the science-building face of IR is centered on explaining the existence and principal characteristics and outcomes of the employment relationship. The insight of institutional economics is that the neoclassical competitive labor market model of demand/supply by its very assumptions precludes the existence of an employment relationship. As described above, the demand/supply diagram in Figure 2.1 can exist only in a world of zero transaction cost, but in such a world economic theory predicts all firms are single-person proprietorships and buy labor services in the product market from independent contractors, not from employees in the labor market. As an illustration, this would mean that to build its cars the Ford Motor Company does not hire from the labor market several hundred thousand people working as employees for a wage, but goes to the product market and hires for a price the business services of several hundred thousand people who work for the company as independent contractors and do all the jobs otherwise performed by employees. But note that in this zero transaction cost (complete contract) world, since all labor services come from independent contractors, no employees or employment relationship exist, precluding by the logic of the model a place for the field of IR since its object of study – the employment relationship – disappears. The study of labor, in this case, might be called 'commercial relations' rather then industrial (employment) relations.

Even if an employment relationship exists in a competitive labor market, the demand/supply model is still fatally flawed as a foundation for science-building. The reason is that it eliminates most of the interesting things to study in IR. In this model, for example, all terms and conditions of employment are entirely market determined, obviating the possibility of negotiation and bargaining. Also obviated is the existence of internal labor markets, and all the human resource practices and institutional rules that accompany internal labor markets (e.g., training programs, promotion by seniority). Since a competitive labor market presumes zero transaction cost, all labor contracts are complete and terms and conditions of employment, once agreed upon, are fully and faithfully executed. This feature also eliminates numerous important subjects in IR having to do with principal–agent problems and moral hazard (e.g., harassment by supervisors, employee shirking on the job). And, finally, the perfect information assumption in the model eliminates yet other important IR subjects, such as strikes. A strike would never occur in a perfectly competitive labor market since both parties to the dispute could foresee the eventual wage outcome and would rationally agree to this settlement beforehand, thus saving both sides the costs of striking.

Given this reasoning, the conclusion stated above seems inescapable. That is, scholars doing science-building cannot rely on the competitive/commodity model of labor markets as the foundation for theorizing since this model eliminates most, if not all, of the core subjects that are central to the field. In reaching this conclusion, I am *not* saying that the competitive demand/supply model is completely useless and should be abandoned, as it is my opinion that for textbook exposition of basic market forces and empirical investigation of certain trends and developments of an aggregated or long-run nature (e.g., changes in the skilled/unskilled wage differential over two or three decades) the model provides useful insights and predictions. What I do claim is that for the study of most issues relevant to IR, particularly in the short run and at the level of the firm, a substantially revised and reconfigured model that takes into full account the human essence of labor and the imperfect nature of labor markets is an undoubted necessity.

Next, consider the implications of the competitive/commodity labor model for the second face of IR, problem-solving. Just as the competitive model eliminates most of the subjects central to the analytical study of IR, so too does the model eliminate most of the employment problems that provide the focus for practice and policy-making. As noted earlier, the concept of labor problems is central to IR. The essence of a labor problem is some maladjustment, defect or shortcoming that emanates from the labor market and employment relationship, and the *raison d'être* of IR is to provide a solution to the labor problem. Note, however, that with a competitive model of the labor market not only does an employment relationship not exist, but also neither do labor problems. The second face of IR also disappears!

The competitive model banishes labor problems by the assumptions it makes. At its core level, the theory is a model of perfect people exchanging goods and services in perfect markets operating within a web of seamless contract laws enacted and enforced by a perfect government. As enshrined in the fundamental welfare theorem of neoclassical microeconomics, the operation of this perfect people/market/government economy leads to a 'best of all possible worlds' in which the invisible hand of free markets leads to a production and allocation of resources that is Pareto optimal – that is, the most efficient possible. In this efficient world, all resources are fully utilized so no labor problem known as 'unemployment' (or at least involuntary unemployment) exists. Likewise, in a competitive labor market all workers are paid the value of labor's marginal product so labor problems of exploitation and discrimination are also non-existent. As another example, labor problems such as excessive work hours, inadequate workplace safety and sexual harassment cannot persist in a competitive labor market because workers can easily quit and find a job elsewhere.

Based on this reasoning, I again conclude that the competitive/ commodity model of labor markets must be rejected, in this case since it eliminates most, if not all, of the real world labor problems that provide the focus for applied problem-solving in IR and, likewise, renders a 'guilty verdict' – guilty of serving as a deleterious market interference, rather than as a social cure – on all proposed institutional interventions (e.g., unions, minimum wages) to solve these problems (Kaufman, 2007c).

The argument is equally strong for the third dimension of IR, the ethical/ideological face. On ethical/ideological grounds, proponents of IR maintain that labor should not be treated like a commodity. In practice, this means that the terms and conditions of employment should meet reasonable social and ethical standards with regard to humanly satisfying work conditions, workplace fairness, social justice and fundamental human rights. The competitive demand/supply model eliminates all of these ethical/ ideological propositions. In the competitive model, the only social criterion used to evaluate the terms and conditions of labor is efficiency. Efficiency, in turn, is promoted by unrestricted trading of labor in free markets where competition sets all terms and conditions of employment. If efficiency is enhanced by child labor, 12-hour workdays, or poverty-level wages, the demand/supply model gives no room to object on social or ethical grounds. Indeed, in this model any institutional intervention to change market-determined outcomes, say by a trade union or protective labor law, is an unwise interference that disturbs an otherwise optimal allocation of resources.

The competitive demand/supply model is claimed to be ideologically neutral. Yet, in practice, this model is constructed with a set of assumptions that promotes the interests of consumers and employers over workers (Stiglitz, 2000). Workers are, after all, treated as a commodity input and factor cost in this theory; they have no higher purpose than creating the most goods possible for consumers (and firms) at the lowest possible cost. The ethical/ideological proposition of IR is that workers are human beings, not commodities, and social welfare is promoted by not only producing goods cheaply and in quantity but also having them produced in a way that promotes a satisfying and rewarding work experience (Budd, 2004).

The third face of IR also requires, therefore, rejection of the competitive/ commodity model of labor. This model is intrinsically and inherently antagonistic to the core ethical and moral principles that guide research, practice and policy-making in IR. Adherence to the competitive/ commodity model of labor would not only eliminate the rationale for the field of industrial relation, so too would it eliminate the rationale for government bodies such as the International Labor Organization (ILO).

In summary, I claim the field of IR and the competitive demand/supply model are mutually incompatible and cannot logically or ethically co-exist.

The core principle that forms the foundation of IR as a field of study and practice, therefore, must be rejection of the demand/supply (commodity) labor model.

CONCLUSION: BUILDING ON A UNIFIED FRAMEWORK

In this chapter, I have outlined and described the original paradigm of IR, as developed in the United States in the 1910s–1920s. I do not claim it is the only paradigm, as the conception and articulation of IR differs across countries and all have merit and interest. The early American paradigm commands attention, however, because it was in the United States that IR as a formal concept and institutionalized entity first appeared in the academic and business worlds.

As noted in this chapter's introduction, the field of IR has suffered a significant decline in many countries of the world in recent years. One reason, I allege, is that over time IR has increasingly become associated (not exclusively but predominantly) with a relatively narrow set of subjects related to trade unions and collective bargaining, and the labor law and policy regimes that regulate them. As national labor movements have declined across most countries, the field of IR has inevitably suffered the same fate. The message of this chapter is that one strategy available to cope with this problem is to go back to the broader conception of IR contained in the original paradigm. That is, in this original paradigm the core topic of IR is the employment relationship – a subject that certainly includes trade unions and labor law/policy but that also includes many other employment-related topics.

To say that IR covers the broad subject of the employment relationship is not enough, however. The field also has to bring to the analysis of the employment relationship a unified, productive intellectual and normative framework in order to give the field coherence and value-added. Another contribution of this chapter is to suggest an outline of such a framework (elaborated in Kaufman, 2004b, 2007b). This framework begins with a core principle: rejection of the orthodox model of a competitive demand/supply labor market and its complementary proposition that labor is a commodity. In its place, IR must substitute an alternative theory of the employment relationship. My suggestion is that a fruitful place to look is the theory of institutional economics, along with complementary theories (e.g., socio-economics, post-Keynesian economics, the French regulation school). This body of theory provides an insightful explanation for the existence of the employment relationship that neoclassical economics lacks and also explains the existence of numerous labor and employment problems that neoclassical economics denies or minimizes.

Finally, institutional economics also provides a theoretical and policy rationale for a selective, balanced and cost-effective regime of institutional regulation of the employment relationship, including collective bargaining and protective labor laws, in contrast to the neo-liberal policy of orthodox economics that views such regulation and institutions as undesirable impediments to efficiency. Most certainly labor market regulation and institutional interventions can be carried to excess (and in some cases have been), but IR theory predicts that capitalism and free markets would nonetheless self-destruct without an institutional infrastructure that humanizes, stabilizes, professionalizes, democratizes and balances the marvelous but flawed operation of demand and supply. IR, therefore, is the study and practice of finding a balance between market forces and institutions and the social objectives of efficiency, fairness and human self-development in the employment relationship.

REFERENCES

Adams, Roy (1993), ' "All aspects of people at work": Unity and division in the study of labor and labor management,' in R. Adams and N. Meltz (eds), *Industrial Relations Theory: Its Nature, Scope and Pedagogy*, Metuchen, NJ: Scarecrow Press, pp. 119–60.

Bennett, James and Kaufman, Bruce (2002), 'Conclusion: the future of private sector unionism in the US – assessment and forecast,' in J. Bennett and B. Kaufman (eds), *The Future of Private Sector Unionism in the United States*, Armonk, NY: M.E. Sharpe, pp. 359–86.

Brown, J. Douglas (1976), *The Industrial Relations Section of Princeton University in World War II: A Personal Account*, Princeton, NJ: Princeton University.

Budd, John (2004), *Employment with a Human Face: Balancing Efficiency, Equity, and Voice*, Ithaca, NY: Cornell University Press.

Coase, Ronald (1937), 'The nature of the firm,' *Economica* **4** (November), 386–405.

Commons, John (1934), *Institutional Economics: Its Place in Political Economy*, New York: Macmillan.

Fiorito, Jack (2007), 'The state of unions in the United States,' *Journal of Labor Research* **28** (1), 43–68.

Kaufman, Bruce (2003), 'John R. Commons and the Wisconsin School on industrial relations strategy and policy,' *Industrial and Labor Relations Review* **57** (1), 3–30.

Kaufman, Bruce (2004a), *The Global Evolution of Industrial Relations: Events, Ideas, and the IIRA*, Geneva: International Labour Organization.

Kaufman, Bruce (2004b), 'Employment relations and the employment relations system: a guide to theorizing,' in B. Kaufman (ed.), *Theoretical Perspectives on Work and the Employment Relationship*, Champaign, IL: Industrial Relations Research Association, pp. 41–75.

Kaufman, Bruce (2005), 'The social welfare objectives and ethical principles of industrial relations,' in J. Budd and J. Scoville (eds), *The Ethics of Human Resources and Industrial Relations*, Champaign, IL: Labor and Employment Relations Association, pp. 23–59.

Kaufman, Bruce (2006), 'Labor institutionalism and industrial relations: a century of boom and bust,' *Labor History* **47** (August), 295–318.

Kaufman, Bruce (2007a), 'The core principle and fundamental theorem of industrial relations,' *International Journal of Comparative Labor Law and Industrial Relations* **23** (1), 5–34.

Kaufman, Bruce (2007b), 'The impossibility of a perfectly competitive labor market,' *Cambridge Journal of Economics* 31 (September), 775–88.

Kaufman, Bruce (2007c), 'What unions do: insights from economic theory,' in J. Bennett and B. Kaufman (eds), *What Do Unions Do?: A Twenty Year Perspective*, New Brunswick: Transaction Press, pp. 12–45.

Kaufman, Bruce (2008), *Managing the Human Factor: The Early Years of Human Resource Management in American Industry*, Ithaca, NY: Cornell University Press.

Keller, Berndt (1996), 'The German approach to industrial relations: a literature review,' *European Journal of Industrial Relations* **2** (2), 199–210.

Manning, Alan (2003), *Monopsony in Motion*, Princeton, NJ: Princeton University Press.

National Industrial Conference Board (1931), *Industrial Relations: Administration of Policies and Programs*, New York: NICB.

Russell Sage Foundation Library (1919), *Industrial Relations: A Selected Bibliography*, New York: Russell Sage.

Slichter, Sumner (1928), 'What is the labor problem?' in J. Hardman (ed.), *American Labor Dynamics in Light of Post-War Developments*, New York: Harcourt Brace, pp. 287–91.

Social Science Research Council (1928), *Survey of Research in the Field of Industrial Relations*, New York.

Solow, Robert (1990), *The Labor Market as a Social Institution,* New York: Basil Blackwell.

Stiglitz, Joseph (2000), 'Democratic development as the fruits of labor,' *Perspectives on Work* **4** (1), 31–7.

Strauss, George, and Whitfield, Keith (1998), 'Research methods in industrial relations,' in G. Strauss and K. Whitfield (eds), *Researching the World of Work*, Ithaca, NY: ILR Press, pp. 5–29.

Watkins, Gordon (1922), *An Introduction to the Study of Labor Problems*, New York: Thomas Crowell.

Webb, Sidney, and Webb, Beatrice (1897), *Industrial Democracy*, London: Longman, Greens.

Willman, Paul and Bryson, Alex (2007), 'Union organization in Great Britain,' *Journal of Labor Research* **28** (1), 93–116.

Yoder, Dale (1931), 'Introductory courses in industrial relations,' *Personnel* **7** (February), 123–7.

USA

J53
123

3. A meta-paradigm for revitalizing industrial relations

John W. Budd

INTRODUCTION

The decline of the academic field of industrial relations (IR) has been well chronicled (Kaufman, 1993, 2004). This decline is the product of myriad factors, including issues relating to academic scholarship inside and outside of IR, university enrollments and administrative structures, national political climates, and the weakening of labor unions. Revitalizing IR as an academic enterprise is therefore a complex task, and I will focus only on one piece of the puzzle: a revitalized vision for the field of IR that charts a new course between two extremes that have contributed to the field's decline. An earlier generation of IR scholars emphasized the need for a single, integrative theory to successfully define the field. This drive for a single theory pushed out alternative theoretical perspectives. And when a grand theory failed to materialize, subsequent scholarship became excessively focused on the operation of IR processes and largely devoid of explicit theoretical discussions (Budd, 2004).

A middle course can help revitalize IR. First, the field does not need a single, overarching theory, but it does need a common vision of its core subject, a unifying symbol (Adams, 1993), or an axis of cohesion (Abbott, 2001). IR should not be defined by a paradigm, but by a meta-paradigm – an organizing map that defines the field's parameters (Masterman, 1970; Ritzer, 1980). This broader vision paves the way for a return to the inclusive approach of the field's early decades nearly 100 years ago in which multiple theoretical perspectives were welcomed.[1] A revitalized, inclusive field of IR should include scholars from today's IR, human resource management (HRM), and other related disciplines, including economics, psychology, sociology, history, law, political science, and elsewhere.[2]

Second, charting a middle course requires enriching the process focus of contemporary IR. In most industrial-relations scholarship, unions and other labor-market institutions are treated as self-evidently good, so research and teaching largely seek to understand how these institutions work in practice.

For many years, most labor relations textbooks have focused uncritically on the labor relations processes – how unions are organized, contracts negotiated, and disputes resolved. HRM research and teaching proceeds in largely the same process-oriented manner. Such approaches produce incomplete understandings (a process cannot be fully understood without knowing what it is trying to accomplish), bind scholars to particular institutional forms (witness the parallel decline of unions and academic IR), and leave fields open to criticisms of emphasizing facts over theory (such as Coase's (1984: 230) attack that the early IR scholars simply accumulated 'a mass of descriptive material waiting for a theory, or a fire'). Revitalizing the academic study of work requires explicitly rooting scholarship in the fundamental objectives of the employment relationship and in multiple theoretical perspectives on how the employment relationship works.

In fact, it is this explicit attention to the objectives of the employment relationship and the multiple theoretical perspectives on this relationship that should serve as the meta-paradigm for the field. The core subject of IR is the objectives or interests of the various parties to the employment relationship (Budd, 2004; Budd and Bhave, forthcoming). IR scholarship analyzes – sometimes in a positive fashion, sometimes in a normative fashion – the composition, determinants, and effects of these objectives in alternative (but typically unstated) theories of the employment relationship. Recognizing this meta-paradigm as the intellectual distinguishing feature of the field provides the umbrella for embracing a variety of theoretical and methodological perspectives and, therefore, making significant advances in knowledge and revitalizing the field. This approach necessitates re-considering how we think about an academic field and demands being explicit in both the objectives of the employment relationship and our theoretical approaches. These requirements are the focus of the remainder of this chapter.

WHAT IS A FIELD OF STUDY?

Historically, there was a very strong sense that IR needed a singular, integrative theory to define itself as a field. As one of the participants in this quest for what Kaufman (1993: 150) characterizes as 'the holy grail of IR,' Somers (1969b: 39) concisely captured the driving need: 'the survival of IR as a separate discipline and its growth as a respectable field of study require a broad conceptual or theoretical framework.'[3] This theme is also echoed among HRM scholars as evidenced by the following lament: 'the science of HRM has been marked by an absence of an integrative theory or general conceptual system' (Ferris *et al.*, 1995: 3).

While this search for the 'holy grail of IR' pre-dates Kuhn's (1962) seminal book on scientific revolutions, Kuhn's theory is useful for understanding this search. Kuhn defined normal science as a discipline in which there was nearly universal acceptance of a single paradigm. Pre-paradigmatic or immature science is characterized by 'nearly random' fact-gathering and 'one somehow hesitates to call the literature that results scientific' (Kuhn, 1962: 15–16). This captures the mindset that underlies the preoccupation with finding a single theory. There are two counterarguments, however. One, the meaning of 'paradigm' can be quite varied. In fact, Masterman (1970) identifies 21 different usages of 'paradigm' in Kuhn (1962). The broadest usage, the meta-paradigm, refers to an organizing map that defines the parameters of a field (Masterman, 1970; Ritzer, 1980). As already noted in the introduction, this is the type of 'paradigm' needed by the field of IR.

Two, even with a definition of paradigm that equates to a general theory, it is questionable whether Kuhn's (1962) framework accurately applies to the social sciences (Thomas, 1979). Economics studies the allocation of scarce resources. While marginal analysis is dominant, alternative major paradigms include classical, neoclassical, institutional, Keynesian, and Marxist economic thought. While sharing the domain of trying to understand human behavior, the field of psychology includes cognitive, biological, psychoanalytical, humanistic, behavioral, and socio-cultural approaches. The discipline of law includes the oft-conflicting views of the law and economics school and critical legal studies. These disciplines all include competing theoretical frameworks about the most compelling way to understand the central questions of the field (Rosenberg, 1995). Sociology has at least three major paradigms, each with at least two major theories and its own dominant methodology (Ritzer, 1980). The revitalized field of IR envisioned here would be no different from many disciplines that include multiple theoretical perspectives.

If social science disciplines are not defined by a single theory, what does define a discipline or field? Most definitions include both content and social aspects (Abbott, 2001; Becher, 1989; Dorson, 1976; Nissani, 1995; Toulmin, 1972; Whitley, 2000). Of particular relevance here is that the content aspect does not require a single discipline-defining theory. Rather, it requires 'a distinction in style or emphasis' (Becher, 1989: 38). The distinct emphasis in IR is the employment relationship. No other field so thoroughly focuses on the world of work. That studying the world of work is not unique to IR is not problematic. The existence of a discipline does not require exclusivity (Abbott, 2001; Becher, 1989; Whitley, 2000); economics, for example, clearly overlaps with mathematics, statistics and sociology. Nor does a discipline have to have unique theories or methodologies

(Abbott, 2001; Adams, 1988; Becher, 1989; Ritzer, 1980; Rosenberg, 1995; Whitley, 2000); many disciplines today share theories and methodologies.

Therefore, common objections to IR as a field because it lacks a unique, general theory and methodology are overly strict. Other social, and even natural, science disciplines do not meet this mythic standard. Moreover, it is arguable that the drive for a single theory has weakened rather than strengthened the discipline by degrading important intellectual schools.[4] Rather, what is needed is a strong common vision, or axis of cohesion (Abbott, 2001), of the core topics of the field, which is inclusive, not exclusive. Within this vision, or meta-paradigm, diverse research based on careful theories – plural – can revitalize and advance the field.

EXPLICIT OBJECTIVES

The starting point for scholarship on the employment relationship should be the objectives of this relationship. Elsewhere I have championed a trilogy of objectives for modern IR: efficiency, equity and voice (Budd, 2004; Befort and Budd, 2007; Budd and Zagelmeyer, forthcoming). Because of the clear implications for competitiveness, economic development, jobs and economic prosperity, the effective use of scarce resources is an important objective of the employment relationship. This class of concerns can be grouped under the heading of efficiency. Contemporary discourse emphasizes the supremacy of competitive markets – supported by common law protections for property rights and the freedom to contract – in promoting efficiency. Even setting aside the controversial debates over the extent to which markets are competitive, however, a sole focus on efficiency reduces the employment relationship to a purely economic transaction that workers endure solely to earn income.

In actuality work is a fully human activity. In addition to being an economic activity with material rewards undertaken by selfish agents, work is also a social activity with psychological rewards undertaken by human beings in a democratic society. For this reason, employees are entitled to fair treatment (equity) and opportunities to have input into decisions that affect their daily lives (voice). So the objectives of the employment relationship are efficiency, equity, and voice. However, this is not to say that all IR scholars have a singular vision of efficiency, equity, and voice.

Equity entails fairness in the distribution of economic rewards (such as wages and benefits), the administration of employment policies (such as nondiscriminatory hiring and just-cause discharge), and the provision of employee security (such as safety standards and unemployment insurance). In IR, the particular concern with equity is rooted in the sometimes abusive and exploitive employment practices of the early twentieth century, such as long hours at low wages in dangerous working conditions (Kaufman, 1993). As such, equitable employment outcomes include minimum standards – minimum wages, maximum hours, minimum safety standards, and protections against arbitrary discharge and favoritism. In HRM, the emphasis on equity focuses on general fairness and distributive justice (Folger and Cropanzano, 1998). HRM also advocates fair treatment of employees to enhance organizational welfare. Equity in the employment relationship can also be approached from political theories of liberty and democracy, moral views of human dignity, psychological theories of human nature, and religious beliefs about the sanctity of human life.

Voice is similarly multi-dimensional. As the ability to have meaningful employee input into decisions, it includes both individual and collective forms. In IR, employee voice is largely conceived as industrial democracy rooted in political theories of liberty and democracy and is premised on the belief that workers in a democratic society are entitled to the same democratic principles of participation in the workplace as in the political arena (Derber, 1970). In HRM, voice is closely related to procedural justice – the extent to which procedures are fair (Thibaut and Walker, 1975). Forms of employee voice are also an important part of many recent corporate efforts to improve competitiveness and quality via employee involvement programs and the creation of high performance work systems (Appelbaum and Batt, 1994). Individual voice can also be approached from self-determination theories in theology, moral philosophy and psychology.

Later in this chapter I will show the power of this efficiency, equity and voice framework, but at this point, my key point for creating a meta-paradigm (rather than a single theory) is the embracing of explicit objectives, not necessarily the objectives of efficiency, equity and voice. As alternatives to equity and voice, other scholars have conceptualized employee interests as survival and income, fulfillment and social identity, and power and control (Budd and Bhave, forthcoming). Employer objectives might also include enhancing stakeholder value or maintaining dominance over labor; the interests of the state could also include maintaining freedom and the rule of law, promoting equitable outcomes, or supporting the domination of the elite (Budd and Bhave, forthcoming). Debates over these interests should be an integral part of the core vision of IR as explicit objectives of the employment relationship are the foundation for a meta-paradigm in an inclusive, revitalized field of IR.

These objectives provide a common set of core topics for IR scholars and also distinguish IR from other disciplines. Mainstream economics focuses on narrow conceptions of efficiency, not equity and voice (or equity and voice are conveniently conceptualized in market-based terms: voluntary transactions are equitable because they are not coerced; and voice occurs through individual choice of what transactions to engage in). Sociology and psychology are often focused on equity, and political science on voice, but not with efficiency.

EXPLICIT THEORIES

Scholars of the employment relationship also differ in the theoretical models they apply to this relationship; four models are instructive: the egoist, unitarist, pluralist and critical employment relationships (Budd, 2004; Budd *et al.*, 2004; Budd and Bhave, forthcoming). The egoist model, favored by scholars influenced by neoclassical economics, emphasizes self-interested, rational agents in competitive markets searching for transactions that maximize their utility. Labor is conceptualized as a commodity like any other useful resource and work is a conceptualized as a lousy activity that individuals endure only to earn income.

The unitarist model rejects the narrow conceptions of labor as a commodity and workers (and employers) as perfectly rational agents and instead embraces a psychological conception of the human agent. Equity and voice are largely seen in terms of individual perceptions of fairness, justice and input into decision-making, especially in the form of distributive and procedural justice (Folger and Cropanzano, 1998). This model further assumes that the objectives of employers and employees are completely consistent with each other. This unitarist view of conflict therefore predicts that the right employment policies and practices will align the interests of employers and employees (Fox, 1974; Lewin, 2001). This model underlies the HRM school of thought, which focuses on analyzing and creating policies that simultaneously benefit employers and employees. Given its theoretical basis, unitarist research generally centers on individual rather than collective identities, behaviors and practices.

The pluralist model of the employment relationship further enriches the conception of employees by also seeing them as human beings with rights in a democratic society. As such, equity goes beyond perceptions of individual fairness to include minimum standards such as living wages that all human beings should be entitled to; voice goes beyond narrow task-related input to include industrial democracy – the right of human beings to widely participate in informed decision-making (Budd, 2004). Pluralist IR scholars (mainstream IR in the United States) further model the employment relationship as characterized by a variety of competing interests – higher wages versus lower labor costs, employment security versus flexibility – as well as shared interests – productive workers, profitable employers, a healthy economy. In other words, employment relationship conflict is theorized to be pluralist (Clegg, 1975; Fox, 1974) or mixed-motive (Kochan, 1998; Walton and McKersie, 1965). The pluralist IR model also assumes that because of market imperfections, employers have greater bargaining power than individual employees.

Lastly, the critical employment relationship model is rooted in the power and control interests of employers and employees (Hyman, 1975). The schools of thought emphasizing this theoretical perspective can be grouped together under the umbrella of critical IR and encompass Marxism, feminism, and other sociological theories based on the division and control of labor. Marxist applications theorize that employer-employee conflict is one element of unequal power relations between the capitalist and working classes throughout society. Feminist models focus on unequal power relations between men and women; critical race theories are concerned with segregation and control along racial lines. In critical theories, the employment relationship is not a voluntary exchange, but rather a contested exchange (Bowles and Gintis, 1990).

The extent to which all four schools of thought are welcome within the current field of IR is debatable. For some, views on labor unions are a particular flashpoint of controversy with adherents to the egoist and unitarist models being skeptical or even hostile to unions and adherents to the pluralist and critical models being more supportive (for reasons discussed in the next section). Other dividing lines include views on high performance work practices (Kochan, 2000) and debates over models of economic versus behavioral man (Kaufman, 1999). What is clear, however, is that a revitalized field of IR should include all of these theoretical perspectives, and should encourage cross-fertilization of ideas and methodologies. This will be difficult to achieve if the key models of the employment relationship continue to linger unstated below the surface of our research, teaching, and discourse.

EXPLICIT INDUSTRIAL RELATIONS

A critic might argue that the objectives and four models of the employment relationship outlined in the previous sections have implicitly underlain research on work in IR and related disciplines for decades. Even if this is true, the central contribution of my argument remains: these objectives and models need to be made explicit.[5] A deep understanding of all aspects of work will only come from this explicitness, and this explicitness further forms the basis for productive dialogue across scholars and practitioners with differing perspectives. In short, we need a more 'explicit' IR. (Indeed, to drive home the point in dramatic fashion, one might even argue we need 'Industrial Relations XXX' – a revitalized field where, as in XXX-rated movies, everything is explicit and fully revealed.) Several examples can be used to demonstrate the power of explicit IR.

Debates over public policy intervention in the employment relationship are ultimately rooted in the intersection of the objectives and theories of the employment relationship (Befort and Budd, 2007; Budd and Zagelmeyer, forthcoming). With narrowly-defined objectives – especially a particular focus on economic efficiency – and an egoist theory in which the employment relationship is modeled as voluntary transactions among well-informed, self-interested actors in perfectly-competitively markets, there is little role for work-related public policies. Abuses and exploitation are prevented by the invisible hand of perfectly-competitively markets, while other aspects of work are private affairs best left to individual choice. But if one defines the objectives of the employment relationship more broadly – for example, to include equity and voice – and if the employment relationship is modeled in a more nuanced fashion in which workers with human needs and possibly democratic rights are not the equals of their employers because of imperfect markets and other real-world complexities, then public policies are seen in a different light.

The unitarist model predicts that government policies can encourage cooperative relations between employers and employees while also preventing destructive competition by shortsighted employers. In the pluralist theory, government policies to create minimum labor standards and social safety nets are an important element of balancing efficiency, equity and voice in imperfect markets. In critical theories of the employment relationship, employment and labor laws are predicted to imperfectly protect workers' interests because power imbalances between employers and employees are deeply embedded in the socio-political system, and predicted to perpetuate the dominance of the powerful group, whether it be capitalists, men or a dominant ethnic group.

Similar differences can be derived for the theoretical conceptualizations of labor unions (Budd, 2008; Budd *et al.*, 2004). The assumptions of the egoist model – namely that employers and employees are equals interacting in competitive markets pursuing self-interested financial objectives – imply that labor unions are monopolies that reduce economic welfare by impeding the operation of competitive markets. In the unitarist model, the assertion that employer and employee interests can be aligned results in unions being seen as unnecessary, outside third parties. Since the pluralist theory models the employment relationship as a bargaining problem between individuals with shared and conflicting objectives, labor unions are seen as a welfare-enhancing solution to the imbalance between employees and employers. In critical scholarship, the structural inequalities that are assumed to pervade the workplace and the greater socio-political context yield the prediction that labor unions cannot completely balance the power of employers.

It is important for IR scholarship to make these different theoretical assumptions and predictions explicit. Otherwise, scholars from different perspectives largely talk past each other. Egoist and unitarist research is seen as cynically anti-union by pluralist and critical scholars; pluralist and critical research is seen as blindly pro-union by egoist and unitarist scholars. Similar issues are apparent in the large research literature on high-performance works practices in which pluralist and critical scholars have difficulty understanding the egoist and unitarist emphasis on the success of these programs in increasing organizational performance, and in which egoist and unitarist scholars have difficulty understanding the reservations of the pluralist and critical scholars. When key theoretical differences are unstated, others dismiss the research as descriptive, or, even worse, as normative. For decades, economists have dismissed IR research in this way. This dismissiveness stems from the failure to see the theoretical foundations of the pluralist IR model – a failure of vision that even afflicts many IR scholars.[6] Failing to explicitly identify objectives and theories also leaves various groups tied to the fortunes of specific institutions, whether they are markets, human resources policies or labor unions. More explicit recognition of the assumed objectives and theories would help these different camps understand each other better, and thereby help create a more inclusive, revitalized field.

This lack of productive scholarly discourse spills into the policy arena. There is a longstanding lack of consensus on reforming US labor policy (Dunlop, 1961). More explicit discussion of the objectives of the employment relationship and the alternatives for their achievement is not a magic bullet that would easily break this political gridlock, but it would certainly create a more constructive policy dialogue. This approach would help us move beyond traditional discourse in which free markets or labor unions are seen as self-evidently good. Should policymakers be troubled by the decline in union density, the increase in income inequality, or a lack of true participation or democracy in some employee involvement initiatives? These questions can only be answered against standards for the objectives of the employment relationship. Policymakers should be troubled by the decline in union density, for example, if it causes greater imbalances between efficiency, equity, and voice. This is the basis for reasoned policy debates.

Only with an explicit recognition of the theories of the employment relationship can we also appreciate the contradictory mess of the current state of US employment and labor laws (Befort and Budd, 2007). The underlying importance of the employment-at-will doctrine reflects egoist thinking, the labor law protections of union activity are rooted in pluralist theorizing, and the body of US employment laws is generally based on a unitarist model in which the determination of the terms and conditions of employment are left in the hands of employers, but subjected to minimal standards of good human resources practices such as nondiscrimination. These inconsistent theoretical foundations have created an incoherent body of laws and policies that lack doctrinal consistency, but the roots of this confusion go unnoticed because the relevant theoretical foundations are left unstated.

Moreover, individual features of the world's IR systems rarely serve efficiency and equity and voice (or other objectives) equally (Budd, 2004). Looking at German works councils in isolation fails to promote the equity standard; an exclusive focus on German-style industrywide bargaining leaves significant gaps in workplace efficiency and voice. In combination, these two features are perhaps stronger than the sum of the individual parts and can balance efficiency, equity and voice as a complementary system. In other words, wholesale rather than piecemeal reform of the US system is warranted. But only with standards for the objectives of the employment relationship can researchers, practitioners and policymakers turn their attention to crafting institutions, policies and practices that achieve the desired objectives.

As another example, the importance of a more explicit approach to IR research and policy discourse is also apparent in the domain of the resolution of rights disputes.[7] Much of this research traditionally focused on unionized grievance systems, but the rise of nonunion dispute resolution systems and the mandatory arbitration of employment law claims in the past two decades have considerably broadened the debates (Colvin, 2004; LeRoy and Feuille, 2001). Some research strongly champions nonunion grievance and arbitration procedures, while other research is quite critical of them. But with the current process-based approach of IR research, it is difficult to compare different systems of workplace dispute resolution. We know a lot about the number of steps in different procedures, how long it takes to process grievances, and who files grievances, but these procedural elements do not reflect the fundamental purposes of dispute resolution procedures. It is admittedly common for the literature to refer to a dispute resolution procedure's 'effectiveness,' but the dimensions of effectiveness are typically unclear. As such, appropriate metrics for workplace dispute resolution procedures are greatly needed (Bemmels and Foley, 1996; Lewin, 1999; Lipsky *et al.*, 2003). The efficiency, equity, and voice framework can be applied to dispute resolution procedures to provide a rich analytical framework in which researchers can analyze and compare dispute resolution systems (Budd and Colvin, forthcoming). In short, this is another example where greater attention to explicit objectives is needed to promote not only a deeper understanding of key employment issues, but also a more meaningful dialogue across scholars of differing perspectives.

EXPLICIT COMPARATIVE STUDIES

A central aspect of a revitalized field of IR should be the analysis of the contributions of individuals, markets, institutions, organizational strategies, and public policies toward fundamental employment relationship objectives. To see how this might work, Figure 3.1 summarizes an analysis of the degree to which elements of comparative IR provide efficiency and/or equity and/or voice (Budd, 2004).

There seems to be little debate that efficiency is well served in Japanese-style enterprise unionism, as it is congruent with other dimensions of HRM strategies such as lifetime employment, company loyalty and worker participation. Critiques of the Japanese system of enterprise unionism on the basis of impairing efficiency or quality are therefore rare. However, the

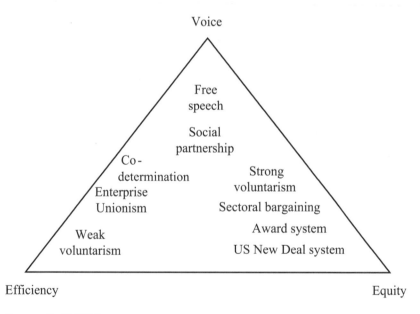

Source: Budd (2004).

Figure 3.1   Analyzing comparative industrial relations systems

extent to which equity is fulfilled is questionable. Responsiveness to firm profitability and the lack of inter-firm labor solidarity undermine the establishment of minimum work standards. Moreover, the exclusion of large numbers of non-core employees within the enterprise is not consistent with the provision of equity. Evaluating the ability of enterprise unions to provide employee voice is more difficult. The extent of employee involvement and joint consultation provides employee input into a wide range of topics. Enterprise unions are legally distinct from the companies and also have the right to strike to support their use of voice. On the other hand, the legitimacy of employee voice in this system is diminished by the extent to which consultation over managerial topics is voluntary and by the degree to which enterprise unions are dependent on a single company.

In contrast, European-style sectoral bargaining best serves the equity dimension of the employment relationship objectives. Because of extension procedures, contract coverage can be very high – often over 80 percent and sometimes over 90 percent of the workforce – even if union membership is low. Moreover, these contracts provide uniform, minimum standards for a range of employment terms and conditions. Thus, equity is well-served. The voice standard is fulfilled to some degree because terms and conditions of employment are being established through collective bargaining, not unilateral management action. But this fulfillment is limited because collective bargaining is very centralized and largely removed from rank and file participation (for example, contract ratification votes are rare). Lastly, sectoral bargaining is consistent with efficiency when stability is valued, but contemporary corporate IR strategies emphasize decentralized relationships to enhance competitiveness and efficiency (Katz and Darbishire, 2000). As such, sectoral bargaining serves efficiency and voice to a limited degree, but is weighted towards equity in Figure 3.1.

Or consider voluntarism. In a voluntaristic IR system, the balance between efficiency, equity, and voice depends on the vagaries of markets and public policies. When labor markets are tight, as in Britain in the 1960s, labor has sufficient power to compel a richer standard of equity and voice ('strong voluntarism' in Figure 3.1). But this leads to concerns with efficiency, as illustrated by the reform agenda of the Conservative government targeting union power as a perceived roadblock to efficiency and competitiveness (Towers, 1997). When labor markets are loose, as in Britain and New Zealand in the 1980s and 1990s, the evidence suggests that employers' leverage translates, as expected, into domination of efficiency over equity and voice ('weak voluntarism' in Figure 3.1). To wit, in a weak British labor market, the Japanese auto plants in Britain conceded union recognition on the conditions that broad managerial prerogatives remain in management's unilateral control, that wages and terms and conditions of employment will be established not through bargaining, but through a joint employee-management company council in which the union has no formal role, and that strikes are not allowed. Katz and Darbishire (2000: 97) label this 'quasi-nonunionism.'

Other examples are also presented in Figure 3.1 (see Budd, 2004), but note carefully that the purpose here is not to provide a convincing case that Figure 3.1 contains the correct evaluations of these elements. Rather, the intent is to demonstrate the usefulness of this analytical framework. Disagreements with the placement of any element in Figure 3.1, in fact, reinforce the usefulness of this framework and provide the basis for richer discourse within IR. This is another example where the more explicit incorporation of employment relationship objectives into IR scholarship can help revitalize the field.

IMPLICATIONS FOR TEACHING

Teaching about labor unions and labor relations in the United States is dominated by processes – how unions are organized, how contracts are negotiated, and how interest and rights disputes are resolved. From Dunlop's (1949) *Collective Bargaining: Principles and Cases* to Holley *et al.*'s (2005) aptly titled *The Labor Relations Process*, this is most visibly illustrated by the generations of textbooks that focus uncritically on labor relations processes. Because US unions typically use these processes to negotiate detailed work rules, the subject of labor relations is furthermore typically equated to the study of these rules. In other words, thick descriptions of the how, what, and where of the major labor relations processes and the resulting work rules drive traditional labor relations courses and textbooks.

What's missing is 'why?' (Budd, 2008). Labor relations processes and work rules are means to more fundamental ends or objectives, not ends in their own right. What are these ends? When are union-negotiated work rules a desirable or undesirable method for achieving these objectives? Are there better ways of pursuing these objectives in the twenty-first-century employment relationship? These should be the central labor relations questions – questions ignored by courses and textbooks that narrowly focus on how the existing labor relations processes and detailed work rules operate in practice.

While the process-based approach fits with the golden age of IR in which collective bargaining was viewed by many as self-evidently good, we are no longer in that golden age. Rather, the US labor relations system is roundly criticized by many observers and participants. Demonstrating the continued relevance of independent employee representation and other labor market checks and balances requires an intellectual framework that is rooted in the objectives of the employment relationship. Moreover, a description of how the current processes work without any discussion of what the processes are trying to achieve fails to provide the basis for determining whether the processes are working, and fails to supply metrics for judging alternative strategies, policies and processes. In short, when the presentation of the labor relations processes is divorced from their underlying reasons, it is difficult to develop a complete appreciation and understanding of the processes specifically, and of the nature of work more generally.

A renewed focus on the objectives of the employment relationship can fill these critical gaps in IR instruction. Labor law and the current labor relations processes are best understood through their linkages to the goals of efficiency, equity and voice. Labor history is not simply a chronicling of the rise of institutions; it is a richer history of employers' and workers' attempts to achieve efficiency, equity and voice against the backdrop of the changing nature of work (Budd, 2008). In the final analysis, the extent to which efficiency, equity, and voice are achieved provide the metrics for evaluating whether the current system needs reforming and for analyzing alternative reform proposals. Budd (2008) therefore uses a dynamic paradigm of 'labor relations equals balancing workplace goals and rights' to replace the tired paradigm of 'labor relations equals detailed work rules.' This requires making both the objectives and the theories of the employment relationship explicit. Such explicitness is therefore important not only for research future of the IR, but for the teaching future as well.

CONCLUSION: TOWARD A COMMON INTELLECTUAL VISION

It is well known that the world of work has changed greatly over the last two or more decades. At an organizational level, intense competitive pressures have resulted in an increased emphasis on flexible and sometimes participative forms of work organization and greater levels of contingent compensation. At the same time, labor unions and other labor market institutions have declined in strength while job security has decreased and labor market inequalities have increased. Policies and institutions need to be redesigned. To be a viable academic enterprise and to be relevant for informing practice and policy, research on employment must respond to these realities (Kochan, 2000).

But scholars from IR and HRM have been moving apart for a couple of decades (Kaufman, 1993, 2001, 2004). Given the complexity and diversity of the patterns of employment systems engendered by the changing nature of work, future research must draw on the complementarities of the differing schools of thought on the employment relationship (Kaufman, 2001). Rather than seeking a single defining theory for an academic field about work, what is needed is a common intellectual vision – a meta-paradigm – for an inclusive and revitalized field of IR. I have argued here that this meta-paradigm can be created by explicit attention to the objectives of the employment relationship and the multiple theoretical perspectives on this relationship in IR research and teaching. Explicit recognition of differing theoretical assumptions across different schools of thought will not make these differences evaporate, but it can facilitate productive dialogue (Kaufman, 2001).

Putting the objectives of employment back into IR also provides the basis for greater dialogue with other groups. IR scholars often advocate for adding checks and balances to the labor market, such as labor unions and government laws, to ensure that market-based competition among workers and employers is beneficial and not abusive. Similarly, the United Nations and the International Labour Organization are strong advocates for adding checks and balances to markets to help them achieve a richer set of objectives than pure economic efficiency (International Labour Organization, 1999; United Nations Development Programme, 1999). Through papal encyclicals such as Pope Leo XIII's famous *Rerum Novarum* ('On the Condition of Workers,' 1891) and Pope John Paul II's *Centesimus Annus* ('The Hundredth Year,' 1991), the Catholic Church also advocates improving markets with checks and balances to achieve human dignity. Scholars who focus on business ethics (Bowie, 1999), human rights (Lauren, 1998), theology (Alford and Naughton, 2001), the natural environment (Esty, 2001), and governance of international organizations (Stiglitz, 2002), all embrace the underlying principle of adding checks and balances to economic markets to achieve more fundamental aims. Unions have successfully created stronger linkages with churches, immigrant rights groups, environmentalists, and other advocacy organizations in recent years. But the avenue for creating greater synergies with these groups is not through the narrow promotion of specific processes or institutions, it is through embracing the nature of work and creating shared dialogue over common views of the objectives of the employment relationship.

It will probably take a number of efforts to revitalize the academic field of IR. Creating a meta-paradigm such that the objectives of the employment relationship provide a common vision for the scholarship of diverse scholars is one important element that should not be overlooked.

NOTES

1. Because the term 'industrial relations' today is frequently seen as meaning unionized employment relationships, a return to the early conception of industrial relations would perhaps be better served by a new label of 'human resources and industrial relations.' But for convenience, I will continue to use 'industrial relations.' As is evident elsewhere in this volume, the term 'employment relations' is also being used as a replacement for 'industrial relations,' but 'human resources and industrial relations' is explicitly more inclusive and has greater continuity with the traditional labels, at least in the United States. To wit, 'employment relations' can be a synonym for a narrow conception of 'industrial relations' to the exclusion of human resource management. The Washington State Public Employment Relations Commission, the Wisconsin Employment Relations Commission, and other similarly-named state agencies handle union-related issues, not human resource management problems. Moreover, in academic circles, 'employment relations' does not always include human resource management (Edwards, 1995).
2. Nothing in this chapter should be interpreted as a movement away from understanding and valuing labor unions. A broadened meta-paradigm in which IR research is rooted explicitly in the objectives and theories of the employment relationship should, in fact, provide a richer framework for understanding the broad scope of the employment relationship including labor unions. Moreover, this meta-paradigm should not be interpreted as a movement away from the field's longstanding attention to solving labor problems and fostering social justice. In fact, the proposed meta-paradigm is intended to provide a stronger analytical framework for understanding the role of labor unions and other institutions in promoting social justice. In a world dominated by a neoliberal market paradigm, revitalizing both the IR field and the IR institutions for providing social justice requires a strong analytical framework rooted in fundamental objectives and theories. This should be seen as a movement toward, not away from, enhanced social justice.
3. Dunlop's (1958) IR systems model is the most well-known attempt at formulating a general theory of IR; other works include Somers (1969a), Barbash (1984), Barbash and Barbash (1989), Adams and Meltz (1993) and Hills (1995).
4. In particular, Kaufman (1993, 2004) argues that Dunlop's (1958) systems model emphasizes the external environment over the internal, unionized situations over nonunion, and institutional labor economics over behavioral sciences.
5. I am not alone in this approach. Barbash (1984) highlighted the objectives of cost discipline and PEEP (price, equity, effort, and power). Osterman (1999) explicitly identifies efficiency, equity, opportunity, voice, and security as employment-related public policy objectives. Osterman *et al.* (2001) and Dannin (2006) articulate the case for values-based approaches to employment issues. And Kaufman (1993) shows how the founders of IR rooted their scholarship in the objectives of efficiency, equity, and self-actualization.
6. For example, in his eloquent descriptions of the theoretical foundations of the pluralist model, one of the strongest advocates of the pluralist perspective refers to these assumptions as *normative* foundations (Kochan, 1998, 2000). In reality, these foundations reflect beliefs about how the employment relationship works as much as how it should work; they are no more normative than the neoclassical economics assumptions of rational economic agents and competitive markets (Budd *et al.*, 2004).
7. Rights disputes are conflicts over whether an employee's rights granted through an employee handbook, a union contract, or an employment law have been violated.

REFERENCES

Abbott, Andrew (2001), *Chaos of Disciplines*, Chicago, IL: University of Chicago Press.

Adams, Roy J. (1988), 'Desperately seeking industrial relations theory,' *International Journal of Comparative Labour Law and Industrial Relations*, **4** (1), 1–10.

Adams, Roy J. (1993), ' "All aspects of people at work": unity and division in the study of labor and labor management,' in Roy J. Adams and Noah M. Meltz (eds), *Industrial Relations Theory: Its Nature, Scope, and Pedagogy*, Metuchen, NJ: IMLR Press/Rutgers University, pp. 119–60.

Adams, Roy J. and Meltz, Noah M. (eds) (1993), *Industrial Relations Theory: Its Nature, Scope, and Pedagogy*, Metuchen, NJ: IMLR Press/Rutgers University.

Alford, Helen J. and Naughton, Michael J. (2001), *Managing as if Faith Mattered: Christian Social Principles in the Modern Organization*, Notre Dame: University of Notre Dame Press.

Appelbaum, Eileen and Batt, Rosemary (1994), *The New American Workplace: Transforming Work Systems in the United States*, Ithaca, NY: ILR Press.

Barbash, Jack (1984), *The Elements of Industrial Relations*, Madison, WI: University of Wisconsin Press.

Barbash, Jack and Barbash, Kate (eds) (1989), *Theories and Concepts in Industrial Relations*, Columbia, SC: University of South Carolina Press.

Becher, Tony (1989), *Academic Tribes and Territories: Intellectual Enquiry and the Cultures of Disciplines*, Milton Keynes, England: Open University Press.

Befort, Stephen F. and Budd, John W. (2007), 'Invisible hands, invisible objectives: bringing workplace law and public policy into focus,' unpublished manuscript, University of Minnesota.

Bemmels, Brian and Foley, Janice R. (1996), 'Grievance procedure research: a review and theoretical recommendations,' *Journal of Management*, **22** (3), 359–84.

Bowie, Norman E. (1999), *Business Ethics: A Kantian Perspective*, Malden, MA: Blackwell.

Bowles, Samuel and Gintis, Herbert (1990), 'Contested exchange: new microfoundations for the political economy of capitalism,' *Politics and Society*, **18** (2), 165–222.

Budd, John W. (2004), *Employment with a Human Face: Balancing Efficiency, Equity, and Voice*, Ithaca, NY: Cornell University Press.

Budd, John W. (2008), *Labor Relations: Striking a Balance*, 2nd edn, Boston, MA: McGraw-Hill/Irwin.

Budd, John W. and Bhave, Devasheesh (forthcoming), 'Values, ideologies, and frames of reference in employment relations,' in Nick Bacon, Paul Blyton, Jack Fiorito and Edmund Heery (eds), *Sage Handbook of Industrial and Employment Relations*, London: Sage.

Budd, John W. and Colvin, Alexander J.S. (forthcoming), 'Improved metrics for workplace dispute resolution procedures: efficiency, equity, and voice,' *Industrial Relations*.

Budd, John W., Gomez, Rafael and Meltz, Noah M. (2004), 'Why a balance is best: the pluralist industrial relations paradigm of balancing competing interests,' in Bruce E. Kaufman (ed.), *Theoretical Perspectives on Work and the Employment Relationship*, Champaign, IL: Industrial Relations Research Association, pp. 195–227.

Budd, John W. and Zagelmeyer, Stefan (forthcoming), 'Public policy and employee participation,' in Adrian Wilkinson, Paul Gollan, David Marsden and David Lewin (eds), *The Oxford Handbook of Participation in Organizations*, Oxford: Oxford University Press.

Clegg, H.A. (1975), 'Pluralism in industrial relations,' *British Journal of Industrial Relations*, **13** (3), 309–16.

Coase, R.H. (1984), 'The new institutional economics,' *Journal of Institutional and Theoretical Economics*, **140** (1), 229–32.

Colvin, Alexander J.S. (2004), 'Adoption and use of dispute resolution procedures in the nonunion workplace,' *Advances in Industrial and Labor Relations*, **13**, 71–97.

Dannin, Ellen (2006), *Taking Back the Workers' Law: How to Fight the Assault on Labor Rights*, Ithaca, NY: Cornell University Press.

Derber, Milton (1970), *The American Idea of Industrial Democracy, 1865–1965*, Urbana, IL: University of Illinois Press.

Dorson, Richard M. (1976), *Folklore and Fakelore: Essays Toward a Discipline of Folk Studies*, Cambridge, MA: Harvard University Press.

Dunlop, John T. (1949), *Collective Bargaining: Principles and Cases*, Chicago, IL: Irwin.

Dunlop, John T. (1958), *Industrial Relations Systems*, New York: Holt.

Dunlop, John T. (1961), 'Consensus and national labor policy,' in Gerald G. Somers (ed.), *Proceedings of the Thirteenth Annual Meeting of the Industrial Relations Research Association*, Madison, WI: Industrial Relations Research Association, pp. 2–15.

Edwards, P.K. (1995), 'From industrial relations to the employment relationship: the development of research in Britain,' *Relations Industrielles*, **50** (1), 39–63.

Esty, Daniel C. (2001), 'Bridging the trade–environment divide,' *Journal of Economic Perspectives*, **15** (3), 113–30.

Ferris, Gerald R., Rosen, Sherman D. and Barnum, Darold T. (1995), 'Toward business–university partnerships in human resource management: integration of science and practice,' in Gerald R. Ferris, Sherman D. Rosen and Darold T. Barnum (eds), *Handbook of Human Resource Management*, Cambridge, MA: Blackwell, pp. 1–16.

Folger, Robert and Cropanzano, Russell (1998), *Organizational Justice and Human Resource Management*, Thousand Oaks, CA: Sage.

Fox, Alan (1974), *Beyond Contract: Work, Power and Trust Relations*, London: Faber and Faber.

Hills, Stephen M. (1995), *Employment Relations and the Social Sciences*, Columbia, SC: University of South Carolina Press.

Holley, William H., Kenneth M. Jennings and Roger S. Wolters (2005), *The Labor Relations Process*, 8th edn, Mason, OH: Thomson/South-Western.

Hyman, Richard (1975), *Industrial Relations: A Marxist Introduction*, London: Macmillan.

International Labour Organization (1999), *Decent Work*, Geneva.

Katz, Harry C. and Darbishire, Owen (2000), *Converging Divergences: Worldwide Changes in Employment Systems*, Ithaca, NY: ILR Press.

Kaufman, Bruce E. (1993), *The Origins and Evolution of the Field of Industrial Relations in the United States*, Ithaca, NY: ILR Press.

Kaufman, Bruce E. (1999), 'Expanding the behavioral foundations of labor economics,' *Industrial and Labor Relations Review*, **52** (3), 361–92.

Kaufman, Bruce E. (2001), 'Human resources and industrial relations: commonalities and differences,' *Human Resource Management Review*, **11** (4), 339–74.

Kaufman, Bruce E. (2004), *The Global Evolution of Industrial Relations: Events, Ideas, and the IIRA*, Geneva: International Labour Office.

Kochan, Thomas A. (1998), 'What is distinctive about industrial relations research?,' in George Strauss and Keith Whitfield (eds), *Researching the World of Work: Strategies and Methods in Studying Industrial Relations*, Ithaca, NY: ILR Press, pp. 31–45.

Kochan, Thomas A. (2000), 'On the paradigm guiding industrial relations theory and research: comment on John Godard and John T. Delaney, "Reflections on the 'High Performance' Paradigm's Implications for Industrial Relations as a Field,"' *Industrial and Labor Relations Review*, **53** (4), 704–11.

Kuhn, Thomas S. (1962), *The Structure of Scientific Revolutions*, Chicago, IL: University of Chicago Press.

Lauren, Paul Gordon (1998), *The Evolution of International Human Rights: Visions Seen*, Philadelphia, PA: University of Pennsylvania Press.

LeRoy, Michael H. and Peter Feuille (2001), 'Private justice in the shadow of public courts: the autonomy of workplace arbitration systems,' *Ohio State Journal on Dispute Resolution*, **17**, 19–93.

Lewin, David (1999), 'Theoretical and empirical research on the grievance procedure and arbitration: a critical review,' in Adrienne E. Eaton and Jeffrey H. Keefe (eds), *Employment Dispute Resolution and Worker Rights in the Changing Workplace*, Champaign, IL: Industrial Relations Research Association, pp. 137–86.

Lewin, David (2001), 'IR and HR perspectives on workplace conflict: what can each learn from the other?,' *Human Resource Management Review*, **11** (4), 453–85.

Lipsky, David B., Seeber, Ronald L. and Fincher, Richard D. (2003), *Emerging Systems for Managing Workplace Conflict*, San Francisco, CA: Jossey-Bass.

Masterman, Margaret (1970), 'The nature of a paradigm,' in Imre Lakatos and Alan Musgrave (eds), *Criticism and the Growth of Knowledge*, Cambridge: Cambridge University Press, pp. 59–89.

Nissani, Moti (1995), 'Fruits, salads, and smoothies: a working definition of interdisciplinary,' *Journal of Educational Thought*, **29** (2), 121–8.

Osterman, Paul (1999), *Securing Prosperity: The American Labor Market: How It has Changed and What to Do about It*, Princeton, NJ: Princeton University Press.

Osterman, Paul, Kochan, Thomas A., Locke, Richard and Piore, Michael J. (2001), *Working in America: A Blueprint for the New Labor Market*, Cambridge, MA: MIT Press.

Ritzer, George (1980), *Sociology: A Multiple Paradigm Science*, Boston, MA: Allyn and Bacon.

Rosenberg, Alexander (1995), *Philosophy of Social Science*, Boulder, CO: Westview Press.

Somers, Gerald G. (ed.) (1969a), *Essays in Industrial Relations Theory*, Ames, IA: Iowa State University Press.

Somers, Gerald G. (1969b), 'Bargaining power and industrial relations theory,' in Gerald G. Somers (ed.), *Essays in Industrial Relations Theory*, Ames, IA: Iowa State University Press, pp. 39–53.

Stiglitz, Joseph (2002), *Globalization and its Discontents*, New York: W.W. Norton.

Thibaut, John and Laurens Walker (1975), *Procedural Justice: A Psychological Analysis*, Hillsdale, NJ: Lawrence Erlbaum Associates.

Thomas, David (1979), *Naturalism and Social Science: A Post-Empiricist Philosophy of Social Science*, Cambridge: Cambridge University Press.

Toulmin, Stephen (1972), *Human Understanding*, Princeton, NJ: Princeton University Press.

Towers, Brian (1997), *The Representation Gap: Change and Reform in the British and American Workplace*, Oxford: Oxford University Press.

United Nations Development Programme (1999), *Human Development Report 1999*, New York: Oxford University Press.

Walton, Richard E. and McKersie, Robert B. (1965), *A Behavioral Theory of Labor Negotiations*, New York: McGraw-Hill.

Whitley, Richard (2000), *The Intellectual and Social Organization of the Sciences*, Oxford: Oxford University Press.

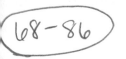

Canada
UK, USA

JS3
B52

4.   An institutional environments approach to industrial relations

John Godard

INTRODUCTION

The study of industrial relations (IR) in the United States is rooted in the work of the early institutionalists (for example, Kaufman, 1993, 2004). Born largely in reaction to liberal economics, this work was substantially influenced by both the German historical and the British Fabian traditions. As such, it was sensitive to the historical foundations of institutional arrangements and studied these arrangements from a broad, economy and society perspective (Kaufman, 2004: 107). If there was a defining core, it may be argued to have been the institutions of labor and employment and their implications for the nature, relations and outcomes of employment.

The loss of this tradition in the decades after World War II is attributable to a number of factors. These include the growth in popularity of method-ological individualism and behavioralism in the social sciences and the establishment of formal industrial relations programs that came increas-ingly to consist of relatively independent subject areas, none of which addressed broader issues of economy and society and at least two of which (organizational behavior, human resource management) came to have little to do with the core concerns of the field. The mainstream of the field became increasingly isolated, focusing on narrow issues and practical prob-lems having to do with collective bargaining and contract administration (Godard, 1994).

The introduction of behavioral research methods in the 1970s (Kochan, 1980) and of management theory in 1980s (Kochan et al., 1986) helped to bring new life to the field, but they were controversial (for example, Hyman, 1982; Strauss, 1982; Godard and Delaney, 2000, 2002; Delaney and Godard, 2001). They seemed to move the field further away from its insti-tutional tradition and closer to the fields of organizational behavior and human resource management, both of which had come to be dominated by an ahistorical and institutionally blind, managerial orientation. The con-sequence has been a field of study most defined by its seemingly endless search for revitalization, yet often with little clearly stated rationale for why it should be revitalized or even why it should continue to exist.

The field's loss of intellectual bearings is not the only (or even primary) reason for its current state. Rather, this state is largely a reflection of a number of trends over which IR scholars have had little control (see Kaufman, 2004: 331–80). Of particular importance have been the weakening of labor institutions and a general ideological shift to the right, with workers coming to accept their positions of subordination, and concerns about inequality, injustice, and autocracy at work largely falling out of fashion.[1] Barring some sort of dramatic reversal in these trends, it is not likely that a major revitalization of the field can occur, especially if one uses the conventional criterion of membership size. Yet in view of the developments of the past few decades (for example, Freeman, 2007), there is now, perhaps more than ever, need of an area of study that addresses in some systematic way the institutions of labor and employment *as* institutions and the implications of these institutions for the nature, relations, and outcomes of employment, proceeding from a broad, economy and society perspective.

The central premise of this chapter is that, in order to effectively realize this potential, there is a need for the field to regain its intellectual bearings. This does not require a shift backwards, to the work of Commons and the early institutionalists, but rather a shift forwards, to a 'new institutionalist' approach that both draws from and contributes to the 'new institutionalism' emergent over the past few decades in socio-economics, political studies, and historical sociology. As reviewed elsewhere (Godard, 2002; 2004: 235–44; 2007a: 3–9), this literature may be seen as in the same tradition as its early institutional counterpart; it is sensitive to the historical foundations of institutional arrangements and proceeds from a broad, economy and society perspective. But it advances it in a number of ways. Below, I elaborate on what can be referred to as an 'institutional environments' approach to IR that draws from this literature, rather than seeking to review it once again. I then illustrate its possible value with reference to two research examples: the role of unions in Canada and England, and the exceptional decline of the US labor movement.

THE INSTITUTIONAL ENVIRONMENTS APPROACH

The institutional environments approach does not represent a specific theory. Rather, it is a 'way of thinking,' much in the same way as is conventional economics, but without its a priori theoretical assumptions and methodological individualism. Indeed, if there is a defining characteristic of the new institutionalism, it is the tendency to go beyond these assumptions and reject methodological individualism in favor of a more nuanced, historically informed analysis, one that focuses on the importance of often taken-for-granted rules that underpin economic, social and political institutions. For present purposes, it is possible to identify seven tenets of a new institutionalist or 'institutional environments' approach to industrial relations, as developed elsewhere.[2]

The first tenet is recognition that actors do not behave as isolated entities, rationally pursuing innate needs or interests in an institutional vacuum, but are instead part of a broader community of actors subject to institutionalized rules (for example, DiMaggio and Powell, 1983). Rules are defined broadly, to include norms, understandings, and expectations, as well as laws and formal incentive structures. These rules can be so taken for granted that actors may be unaware of them. However, they tend to be embedded in the decision-making processes and ultimately in the behavior of actors. In effect, they tend to set the parameters for what is considered to be rational, in both an instrumental and a normative sense (that is, Weber's calculative versus value rationality). Thus, for example, intensive anti-union behavior has historically been the rational choice for employers in the United States, but not in Great Britain, where informal 'rules of the game' have meant a greater tolerance for union representation (Jacoby, 1991; Adams, 1994).

The second tenet is that rules are embedded not just in behavior, but also in the economic, social, and political institutions or arrangements that constitute and are constituted by this behavior, including market and financial structures, state agencies, legal structures, education and training systems, and others. These institutions, and the rules undergirding them, may be seen to comprise the institutional environment within which workers, their unions, and their employers act. They are produced and reproduced through processes of social action and in fact are what make such action possible. They are also often the product of extensive experimentation, learning and negotiation. To the extent that this is the case, they can be highly complex and sophisticated, involving substantial layering and self-reinforcing feedback processes, rendering them difficult to alter in any substantial way without risking institutional collapse.

The third tenet is that institutions tend to be complementary, comprising distinctive variants of capitalism. The most common distinction in the new institutional literature is found in the 'varieties of capitalism' thesis developed by Hall and Soskice (2001). They distinguish between 'coordinated' market economies and their 'liberal' market counterparts (for example, Hall and Soskice, 2001). Coordinated market economies are best represented by Germany, but are often considered to include other continental European nations and Japan. In the case of Germany, this model consists of coordinated inter-firm relations, strong business associations, bank financing and extensive cross-holding across firms, highly developed and coordinated training, strong social and labor market programs, high union coverage, industry level bargaining, and codetermination. In combination, these institutions are (in theory) associated with a form of 'stakeholder capitalism,' in which banks and large firms are considered social institutions, and firms are managed so as to maximize long-term growth without sacrificing the interests of particular stakeholders (especially workers). Coupled with high levels of formal training, this gives rise to an economy that (in theory) can be inflexible and slow to adapt, but that also supports high skill levels, high wages, and high value-added, quality production.

Liberal market economies are best represented by the United States, but are often considered to include Canada, the United Kingdom, and sometimes Australia. In the case of the United States, this model consists of pretty much the opposite of the German economy, giving rise to 'shareholder capitalism,' in which banks (which play a lesser role) and firms are considered economic institutions with few if any social obligations, and firms are managed so as to maximize profits with little regard for particular stakeholders other than investors. Coupled with low levels of formal training, this gives rise to an economy that is flexible and quick to adapt, but which tends to be characterized by low skill levels, low wages, and low value-added, low quality production.

The coordinated versus liberal market economy distinction is overstylized and suffers from numerous possible limitations (see Crouch, 2005), at best providing two ideal types against which economies can be compared; even Germany and the United States may in this respect not conform all that well to the models associated with them (for example, Allen, 2006). But it, at minimum, sensitizes us to systematic differences in the institutional environments to which workers, their unions, and their employers tend to be subject, and it underscores how these differences can be expected to matter. In this regard, it may be useful to think not in terms of general types, but rather of national variants of capitalism and differences in the logic governing work and employment relations within these variants.

The fourth tenet is that institutional environments shape (and are shaped by) the orientations and identities of the actors and the relationships between them. In the United States, employer, worker and union orientations tend to be short-term and opportunistic. Employers do not just seek to maximize short-term profit, they also believe in unilateral control deriving from property rights doctrine. They therefore tend to be hostile to legal systems of employee representation. Unions in turn seek to maximize their members' immediate economic interests, in part reflecting membership preferences and in part reflecting historical barriers to the development of an alternative role. The resulting relationship is largely adversarial.

In Germany, employer, worker and union orientations tend to be long-term and cooperative. Employers do not just incorporate worker interests into their decision making, they also accept as legitimate a substantial role for worker representatives in making decisions and tend to be more receptive to legal systems of employee representation. Unions in turn seek to maximize social interests, serving as 'social partners' in matters of economic and social policy and constraining economic gains so that they do not have negative economic or social consequences. The resulting relationship is largely collaborative. Again, these distinctions may be over-stylized, but this approach suggests that assumptions that may apply (more-or-less) in one country (for example, the United States) may not apply in another (for example, Germany). In essence, workers, unions and employers can be expected simply to think differently, with important consequences for the relations between them.

The fifth tenet is that nation state paradigms play an important role in shaping institutional environments and the rules that underpin them. For example, the US state paradigm may be characterized as primarily liberal (the military sector notwithstanding) in the classical sense associated with *laissez-faire* economics. It tends to support high levels of competition, weak labor and employment laws, and strong shareholder governance rights, with limited direct involvement in the economy, and weak social and labor market programs.

In contrast, the German state paradigm may be characterized as corporatist and social democratic, supporting high levels of coordination, strong labor and employment laws, strong stakeholder governance rights, substantial state involvement in the economy (albeit through the social partners), and strong social and labor market programs. Although these depictions may be viewed as caricatures, it is apparent that the policies adopted in each are consistent with (and essential for) a liberal market and a coordinated market economy, respectively. To an extent, they may be a reflection of as much as a precursor to each, but in either case, they provide the core organizing principles from which economic institutions derive.

Sixth, national paradigms reflect and can to a considerable extent be explained by the conditions under which a modern nation was formed as a modern nation.[3] These conditions and discourses around them give rise to deeply embedded 'institutional norms,' or beliefs, values, and principles as to the role, rationale for, and legitimacy of established institutions. Institutional norms are much 'deeper' than, and underpin, the everyday formal and informal rules through which institutions of the political economy are produced and reproduced over time. They give institutions (and the rules that comprise them) meaning and legitimacy and are drawn on by interested actors in attempting to influence institutional rules and designs.

These norms help both to explain institutional complementarities and to account for the tendency for nations to follow along historical 'path trajectories.' Thus, as discussed more fully below, the liberal market paradigm that has tended to be dominant within the United States may ultimately be attributable to the conditions under which the United States was formed, especially its individualist development, lack of formal class traditions (and conflicts), revolutionary birth, and Protestant religious traditions. The corporatist paradigm that has tended to be dominant in Germany may be attributable to its founding conditions, especially its formation as an exercise in state building, its state driven industrial development, its feudal and class traditions (and hence more radical labor movement), and its significant social-Catholic influences (Lehmbruch, 2001: 56–7).

Seventh, institutional norms and the arrangements associated with them may be seen to give rise to and perpetuate mobilization biases (to borrow from Bachrach and Baritz, 1962) that privilege one or more groups or institutions over others. This is so in two respects. First, institutional norms and arrangements have implications for the distribution of resources (for example, property) and for the rights and obligations that attach to those resources. Thus, they can give rise to power imbalances. Second, and more fundamentally, the structural embedding of norms within institutional designs means that dominant groups' interests and values are more likely to be served by the institutional status quo, often in ways that are hidden from view or taken for granted.

Mobilization biases may be strengthened over time, especially if dominant groups are able to effectively control the agenda and achieve ideological hegemony (Bachrach and Baratz, 1962; Lukes, 1974), thereby strengthening norms and interpretations of these norms that serve their interests. This does not mean that opposing groups (for example, unions) can never 'win.' But effective mobilization and change require successful appeals to particular institutional norms and/or the ability to demonstrate that established arrangements do not serve these norms satisfactorily. Even here, historically ingrained mobilization biases may be too strong over the long run, allowing dominant groups to undermine institutional changes that conflict with their interests and with more deeply ingrained norms that support them. In the case of the United States, this helps explain why the liberal paradigm has become so dominant, despite some apparent departures from it in the New Deal and World War II eras (see below).

ILLUSTRATING THE INSTITUTIONAL ENVIRONMENTS APPROACH

The tenets identified above cannot be viewed as statements of fact, nor can they be viewed as forming a theory in the formal sense of this term. But they do provide an intellectual grounding for the field, one that can have important implications for research and ultimately policy issues. They also suggest a series of propositions that can inform specific research projects. In this regard, the varieties of capitalism thesis is especially useful, providing a starting point for thinking about institutional environments and two 'ideal types' against which nations might be compared. Yet the institutional environments approach allows us to go beyond this thesis, with important potential implications for the study of industrial relations within as well as across nations.

First, the institutional environments approach suggests that the rules and norms underpinning action are historically constituted and vary across nations. These rules and norms may in turn have implications for the orientations and roles of the parties, even though they are often so taken for granted that neither the parties nor those who study them are explicitly aware of their importance. This may be most evident across different varieties of capitalism, but it may also be the case across nations associated with a particular variety, with implications not only for the assumptions that are most appropriate in analyzing these relations, but also for whether theory and research can be expected to generalize across borders.

Second, the argument that there are deeply ingrained institutional norms that underpin institutional environments allows for an approach to explaining work and employment relations that is less empiricist and more consistent with theoretical realism (Godard, 1994). The new institutionalism not only makes it possible to go beyond 'surface' explanations; it also suggests that sustainable institutional change within a particular nation may be difficult or misguided unless it is consistent with long-established institutional norms and traditions and the mobilization biases to which they give rise.

The first of these implications can be illustrated by addressing differences in the institutional environments and traditions of Canada and England. A comparison between Canada and England is especially useful in this respect given that both are liberal market economies with similar union density levels (roughly 30 percent) and with workplace level, majority-based legal recognition systems. Yet these countries have quite different institutional traditions, as reflected in potentially important legal and normative differences.

The second is illustrated by the exceptional decline of the US labor movement in comparison to other western labor movements. An analysis of the US labor movement's decline is especially interesting given the paradox that it, or at least a large segment of it, is perhaps the most innovative in the world, as reflected by the myriad of strategies adopted over the past quarter century in order to reverse decline.

Example I: Canada versus England[4]

As has been the case in the United States, Canada is characterized by a tradition of employer unilateralism and hostility towards unions. Canadian labor law is also based primarily on the Wagner Act model and premised on the assumption of adversarial relations between the parties, although it is stronger than in the United States (reflecting different state traditions and structures: see Godard, 2007f), in large part explaining Canada's higher union density (roughly 30 percent compared to 12 percent) (Godard, 2003).

In contrast, England, and Britain in general, has a tradition of informality, trust, and 'mutuality' in the workplace (for example, Hyman, 1997, 2003: 41–4), with employers historically relying more on worker consent and cooperation than on autocratic supervision or Tayloristic work design (as in North America). It also has a tradition of voluntary union recognition, under which employer resistance to unions has been muted both by historical conditions encouraging industry bargaining (Howell, 2005) and by established 'rules of the game' to which employers have been expected to adhere if they wish to be accepted by the upper classes (Jacoby, 1991). To some extent, this tradition was eroded during the Thatcher years, but the New Labour government has sought to rekindle it, enacting labor laws and policies designed to encourage voluntary recognition and collaborative relationships at work. The government has provided unions with relatively weak bargaining rights (Smith and Morton, 2001), but it has also provided for a statutory recognition process should employers fail to voluntarily grant recognition where a union has majority support (see Wood and Godard, 1999). In contrast to the US and Canadian systems, the British system actually encourages employer involvement in the recognition process, in theory increasing the likelihood of employer acceptance of union recognition, but also providing employers with greater say in the terms under which a union is recognized.

The result is a system in which unions tend to be weaker and more dependent on employer goodwill (Brown *et al.*, 1997; Bryson *et al.*, 2004), but in which employer unilateralism and anti-unionism are also less pervasive (Oxenbridge *et al.*, 2003; Oxenbridge and Brown, 2004) and unions are perceived as less of a threat. While the former means that unions are encouraged to place greater emphasis on collaborative, performance-enhancing strategies than on traditional collective bargaining as a means to achieve gains (Hyman, 1997; Brown *et al.*, 2000; Terry, 2004: 205), the latter means that employers are more willing to provide them with such a role and, more generally, to provide workers and their representatives with meaningful input to workplace change initiatives. Indeed, the history of mutuality may mean that the effectiveness of change is also more dependent on worker 'consent' and hence collaboration with worker representatives than is the case in Canada (or the United States).[5] In effect, the institutional environment of labor and employment relations in England would appear as a result to be conducive to a more collaborative, 'partnership' model than has been the case in Canada (and the United States), although one in which the union may be a much weaker, 'junior' partner.

These differences are illustrated by a recent study drawing on data from random telephone surveys of 750 Canadian and 450 English workers conducted in 2003–4 (Godard, 2007b, c, d, e). This study reveals that alternative work practices (AWPs) associated with the high-performance paradigm have consistently positive implications for workers in England, but not Canada, which suggests that employers provide workers and their representatives more input into their implementation in the former country (Godard, 2007e). It also finds that AWPs are associated with higher levels of satisfaction and commitment in the union sector in England, but not in the non-union sector or in either sector in Canada, suggesting that unions may play a proactive role where these practices are adopted in England (but not Canada) (Godard, 2007e). Moreover, AWPs are positively associated with political participation in England, but only in union firms, suggesting that the combination of unions and AWPs creates a more genuinely participative environment, with spillovers outside of the workplace (Godard, 2007b). There is no such finding for Canada.

The findings from this study further reveal a negligible union wage premium in England yet a strong positive interaction between union coverage and high-commitment human resource management (HRM) practices (but not AWPs) with respect to pay (Godard, 2007c), consistent with the argument that unions in England achieve gains through performance-enhancing strategies rather than collective bargaining. Finally, in the English sample, union representation bears a strong positive association with the adoption of high-commitment HRM practices, suggesting that unions are complementary with more collaborative, high commitment workplaces; in the Canadian sample, union representation bears a strong positive association with traditional bureaucratic practices, consistent with a more adversarial labor relations model (Godard, 2007d).

There is always danger of over-emphasizing differences at the expense of similarities. It is also debatable as to which system is to be preferred. But these findings suggest that although a more collaborative, 'mutual gains' approach appears to have met with some success in England, this is largely because it is consistent with British institutional norms and traditions. It is not consistent with Canadian (or US) norms and traditions, and this is why it has met with only limited success in Canada (and the United States). To be sure, these norms and traditions are not omnipotent, so it is always possible to find examples where alternative labor relations approaches appear to be effective. But such examples can be found only among a small minority of employers and are unlikely to become more widespread. Moreover, attempts to change this by transferring the British system of labor law to Canada (or the United States) would likely be disastrous, especially because it allows so much opportunity for employers to undermine a union's attempt to gain recognition. Where British institutional norms and traditions discourage employers from taking advantage of this opportunity, Canadian and US norms and traditions encourage it.

More generally, it would appear that any attempt to develop universalistic theory or policy prescriptions is likely to be misguided even within liberal market economies if it does not explicitly account for differences in institutional environments. These extend beyond more obvious differences in labor law regimes to include informal and often taken-for-granted rules and understandings that have become embedded through historical processes and may be alterable only over the long run. A similar caution applies to any attempt to generalize research findings across borders. This may be especially true with regard to the implications of work and HRM practices for unions, which some researchers have treated as generalizable from the British to the North American context (Godard, 2008).

Example II: The Decline of the US Labor Movement[6]

Although unions have faced decline in a number of developed nations, the decline of the US labor movement has been exceptional in the sense that it predates and has been more severe than that of other western labor movements. What makes this decline especially startling is the widespread belief in the postwar era that labor unions were an integral part of the US economic, social, and political fabric on the one hand (for example, Kerr *et al.*, 1960), and the seemingly endless revitalization strategies that have been advanced in order to reverse their decline over the past three decades on the other hand.

A variety of explanations have been advanced for the exceptional decline of the US labor movement. These include problems of 'bureaucratic conservatism' (Voss and Sherman, 2000), economic forces (Troy, 2000), social developments (Heckscher and Carré, 2006: 616), the weakening of labor law (Human Rights Watch, 2000), and/or the very model on which US labor law is based (Adams, 1993). But the institutional environments approach provides for a deeper explanation, suggesting that these and other possible explanations ultimately reflect the founding conditions of the United States, the dominant institutional norms they generated, and the embedding of these norms within the broader institutional environment of which unions are part.

The importance of the historical conditions under which the United States was founded has been addressed by numerous scholars, beginning with Tocqueville (1998 [1835]) but also including Hartz (1955), Lipset (1963, 1964) and, in the field of industrial relations, Perlman (1949 [1928]) and Jacoby (1991). This literature does not bear repeating at length in this chapter. But it generally argues that the conditions under which the United States was formed (for example, its individualist, frontier development, with little state involvement; its initial settlement by Puritans fleeing persecution; its birth out of a revolution against the tyranny of the British state; and its lack of feudal and class/elite traditions) and the discourses surrounding these conditions (see Frege, 2007: 161–71) came to be reflected in a number of norms that render the United States 'exceptional.' These include a strong, Lockean conception of the sanctity of property and of ownership rights deriving from property; a belief that property and wealth are attributable to the achievements of the individual and so do not carry with them the same duties or obligations as would be the case if they derived from inherited status (Hutton, 2002); a corresponding belief that authority deriving from property rights should not be interfered with and entails few if any obligations to either workers or society (Hutton, 2002); a distrust of centralized state power and hence administrative law (Taras, 1997); an emphasis in law on freedom of contract and hence both 'free' labor and 'free' markets (Brody, 2005); and a belief in the legitimacy of 'possessive individualism' and hence of the unfettered pursuit of economic self-interest.

These arguments are over-stylized and provide a rather one-dimensional depiction of American cultural values. But from a new institutionalist perspective they are important because the conditions and norms they identify have become structurally embedded within institutions over the course of US history. As such, they largely explain the US institutional environment as it has developed over this time. The result has been a variant of capitalism in which employer property rights have been particularly strong and the interests of capital particularly dominant (Jacoby, 1991). They have meant that, alongside a long tradition of formal democracy in political affairs, there has been a long tradition of managerial autocracy in economic affairs (Frege, 2007: 171). They (regardless of ethnic divisions) have also meant a conservative working class and a political system in which employers (that is, capital), partly as a result, have never had to make the sorts of accommodations characteristic of other developed nations (Jacoby, 1991). Finally, they have meant a minimal role for the state in economic affairs, other than to protect property rights and promote competition in labor and product markets.

This environment in turn helps to explain a number of the factors commonly blamed for the US labor movement's exceptional decline. For example, exceptional employer hostility towards unions can be explained by a strong belief in property rights and individualistic competition and by a system in which these beliefs have been largely institutionalized within the governance of both firms and markets. The much-criticized conservative and bureaucratic orientation of the US labor movement is attributable in part to employer beliefs and hostility, but also (compare Voss, 1993) to a conservative working class, a general public distrust of strong unions and labor laws despite its support for the right to join unions (Bok and Dunlop, 1970: 12–14), a state that is anti-corporatist and hence offers little role for unions beyond collective bargaining, and a legal system that has historically placed sharp restrictions on collective action (Hattam, 1993). Perhaps even more significant, however, have been the implications of US institutional norms for the Wagner Act, which has been at the core of the US system of IR and (arguably) of its decline (Godard, 2003).

From the very beginning, it was necessary to sell the Wagner Act not as a means to enhance democracy at work or to reduce inequality, but rather as a means to enhance the economic well-being of Americans by boosting worker spending power and thereby helping to end the Great Depression (Kaufman, 1996). It was also drafted in a way that defined labor rights largely in terms of individual rights and 'liberty of contract,' largely to finesse longstanding judicial norms that favoured 'free labor' over collective bargaining (Woodiwiss, 1990: 162–4; Brody, 2005: 110–37). Even still, it was widely considered to represent an unconstitutional intrusion of state power into economic affairs, and the 1937 Supreme Court decision upholding it was unexpected (Dubofsky, 1994: 142–6). Support for labor rights was pretty much undermined by 1940 (Harris, 1982: 37), and the Wagner Act was substantially weakened over the ensuing decade. From an institutional environments perspective, the model on which it was based was just too out of step with dominant institutional norms and the broader institutional environment they underpinned.

There can be little doubt that successful employer resistance and politics also played a significant role in this regard, yet it is arguable that institutional norms have in any case been of major importance in accounting for employer success. A system in which state intervention, and especially administrative law, has traditionally been weak and distrusted has meant that the National Labor Relations Board was given only weak powers so as to guard against employer challenges to its constitutionality (Woodiwiss, 1990: 160–77) and that it has been easy for employers to frustrate its decisions (Taras, 1997). A distrust of state intervention along with norms supporting 'free' markets and 'free' contracts have helped employers to ensure weak provisions for good-faith bargaining and the absence of first contract arbitration; norms giving primacy to private property and to free speech have enabled employers to win substantial rights with which to undermine organizing drives; a tradition of formal democratic processes helps explain their success in obtaining the elimination of card certification in the 1940s; and the notion of 'free' labor and personal liberty help to account for their success in obtaining provision for open shops.

These arguments have been developed more fully elsewhere (Godard, 2007a), as have their implications for the future prospects of the US labor movement. Within the context of the present analysis, however, the main implication is that a new institutionalist analysis can help scholars to move beyond the litany of competing explanations that have been advanced to account for the US labor movement's decline and to develop a deeper and more institutionally informed understanding of why this decline has occurred. It also suggests an important lesson: many of the nostrums that have been advanced for reversing this decline are likely to be misguided or at least unduly optimistic unless they account for dominant institutional norms and the mobilization biases they engender.

This may be especially true with respect to the Employee Free Choice Act (as it also was for the Labor Law Reform Act of 1978), defeated in the Senate in 2007. This act contained a number of provisions found in Canadian labor law and widely considered to have been of some effectiveness in that country (Godard, 2003). Yet too many of these provisions were the very ones identified above as at odds with US institutional norms. These norms and the mobilization biases they have engendered mean that, even if the labor movement succeeded in disproving many of the canards advanced by opponents, winning passage of the Act would be much more difficult than otherwise, and that, if it had passed, it could very well have suffered much the same fate as the original Wagner Act.

PROSPECTS FOR NEW INSTITUTIONALIST INDUSTRIAL RELATIONS

The institutional environments approach advocated in this chapter offers a potential direction for the field. It may be especially inviting because it provides for an intellectual grounding that on the one hand resonates with the field's institutionalist tradition, yet on the other hand locates it within an emergent literature on the economy, state and society. This approach suggests a need to dig beneath the everyday assumptions that underpin the behavior of actors and are often taken for granted by scholars, and in so doing to develop an understanding of how institutional norms and traditions matter for both policy and practice. It also suggests a need to locate IR analysis within a broader analysis of the economy and society.

Yet, paradoxically, there may be institutional barriers to the field's successful adoption of this approach – especially in the United States. First, dominant institutional norms may engender biases not only against labor unions, but against institutional analysis as well, helping to explain why behavioral, rational choice models have been especially predominant in that country (Schorske, 1997; Frege, 2005, 2007). Although there is indeed a significant institutionalist tradition in the United States, it largely emerged in antithesis to free market economics, as has the new institutionalism discussed in this chapter; and while it may have thrived in the New Deal and early post-World War II eras this may have been largely an aberration, as may have been the case for the enactment of New Deal labor laws and the growth of labor unions in the late 1930s and 1940s. Thus, as has been the case for the US labor movement, the decline of institutionally oriented research in IR was earlier and has been more severe in the United States than elsewhere.[7]

Second, the institutional structure and location of the field itself could prove to be a barrier. The field would need not only to embrace an institutional environments approach, but also to develop ties with new institutionalist associations and areas of study, thereby achieving some level of integration with the new institutionalist literature.[8] Yet this would likely require a substantial realignment of the field. The main US association (the Labor and Employment Relations Association) has, by historical design, a large non-academic component, often concerned with narrow practitioner issues, and it has long held its annual meetings in conjunction with the American Economics Association. Moreover, IR scholars have increasingly come to be located within business schools, which may not prove to be as conducive to new institutionalist analysis as social science departments, where it has flourished most. Thus, whether such realignment can occur is an open question.

To the extent that such barriers do indeed exist, it may mean that, barring an upheaval similar to that of the New Deal era, the new institutionalism may hold limited promise for the field (at least in the United States). Yet it at minimum provides an alternative to the neoliberal and managerialist dogma that has come to dominate social thought over the past quarter century or more. In this regard, the problem may not be one of whether or how IR as a field is revitalized or even survives, but rather one of whether and how the study of work and the institutions associated with it can be strengthened. The argument of this chapter has been that, whatever the barriers to its adoption within the field of IR may be, an institutional environments approach can serve this objective.[9]

NOTES

1. These issues may have grown in importance in organizational behavior, but, even if so, only from an institutionally naive managerial perspective, with their attainment considered important largely as a means to maximizing employer outcomes.
2. This section draws from Godard (2002), Godard (2004) and Godard (2007a).
3. This is difficult to define with clarity, but what I have in mind includes all developments up to and including the formation of an industrial economy (for example, the late 1880s in the United States) and the state structures that support it.
4. This section (Canada versus England) draws extensively from Godard (2007d).
5. This is borne out, for example, by analysis of the 2001–2 World Values Survey data set, which reveals that only 44 percent of British respondents believed in following instructions at work without question, compared to 58 percent in Canada and 65 percent in the United States. These data are available from Inglehart *et al.* (2004).
6. This section (The decline of the US labor movement) draws extensively from Godard (2007a).
7. For example, the traditional institutionalist approach has remained far more prevalent in Britain (see, Gospel, 2005).
8. In particular, it might make sense to establish ties (for example, joint conference sessions) with the Society for the Advancement of Socio-Economics (SASE), which has been perhaps the primary 'home' for new institutionalist analysis and has a substantial membership in both North America and Europe. At present, it has streams for both IR and HRM. Neither is well developed, thus providing an ideal opening for the field.
9. I thank Bruce Kaufman, Carola Frege and Charles Whalen for comments and suggestions on earlier versions of this chapter.

REFERENCES

Adams, Roy (1993), 'The North American model of employee representational participation: a hollow mockery,' *Comparative Labor Law Journal*, **15** (4), 4–14.

Adams, Roy (1994), 'Union certification as an instrument of labor policy: a comparative perspective,' in Sheldon Friedman, Richard W. Hurd and Rudolph A. Oswald (ed.), *Restoring the Promise of American Labor Law*, Ithaca, NY: ILR Press, pp. 260–69.

Allen, M. (2006), *The Varieties of Capitalism Paradigm – Explaining Germany's Comparative Advantage*, Basingstoke: Palgrave Macmillan.

Aronowitz, Stanley (2005), 'On the AFL-CIO split', *ZNet*, Friday, 19 August.

Bachrach, P. and Baratz, M. (1962), 'The two faces of power,' *American Political Science Review* **56**, 947.

Bok, Derek and Dunlop, John (1970), *Labor and the American Community*, New York: Simon and Schuster.

Brody, David (2005), *Labor Embattled*, Urbana, IL: University of Illinois Press.

Brown, William, Deakin, Simon and Ryan, Paul (1997), 'The effect of British industrial relations legislation, 1979–97,' *National Institute Economic Review*, **161**, 69–83.

Brown, William, Nash, D. and Oxenbridge, Sarah (2000), 'The employment contract: from collective procedures to individual rights,' *British Journal of Industrial Relations*, **38** (2), 611–29.

Bryson, Alex (2005), 'The size of the union membership wage premium in Britain's private sector,' unpublished manuscript, The Policy Studies Institute (London).

Bryson, Alex, Gomez, Rafael and Willman, Paul (2004), 'The end of affair? The decline in employers' propensity to unionize,' in John Kelly and Paul Willman (eds), *Union Organization and Activity*, London: Routledge, pp. 72–91.

Crouch, Colin (2005), *Capitalist Diversity and Change*, Oxford: Oxford University Press.

Delaney, John and Godard, John (2001), 'An industrial relations perspective on the high performance paradigm,' *The Human Resource Management Review*, **11**, 395–429.

DiMaggio, Paul J. and Powell, Walter (1983), 'The Iron Cage revisited: isomorphism and collective rationality in organizational fields,' *American Sociological Review*, **48**, 147–60.

Dubofsky, Melvin (1994), *The State and Labor in Modern America*, Chapel Hill, NC: University of North Carolina Press.

Freeman, Richard (2007), *America Works. The Exceptional US Labor Market*, New York: Russell Sage.

Frege, Carola (2005), 'Varieties of industrial relations research,' *British Journal of Industrial Relations*, **43** (2), 179–208.

Frege, Carola (2007), *Employment Research and State Traditions*, Oxford: Oxford University Press.

Godard, John (1994), 'Beyond empiricism: toward a reconstruction of IR theory and research,' *Advances in Industrial and Labor Relations*, (US), **6**, 1–35.

Godard, John (2002), 'Institutional environments, employer practices, and states in liberal market economies,' *Industrial Relations*, **41** (2), 249–86.

Godard, John (2003), 'Does labor law matter? The density decline and convergence thesis revisited,' *Industrial Relations*. **42** (3), 458–92.

Godard, John (2004), 'The new institutionalism, capitalist diversity, and industrial relations,' in Bruce Kaufman (ed.), *Theoretical Perspectives on Work and the Employment Relationship*, Urbana-Champaign: IL: Industrial Relations Research Association, pp. 229–64.

Godard, John (2007a), 'Institutional norms, mobilization bias, and the exceptional decline of the American labor movement,' unpublished working paper, the University of Manitoba Faculty of Management.

Godard, John (2007b), 'Is good work good for democracy? Work, change, and political participation in Canada and England,' *British Journal of Industrial Relations*, **45** (4), 760–90.

Godard, John (2007c), 'Unions, work practices, and wages under different institutional environments: the case of Canada and England,' *Industrial and Labor Relations Review*, **60** (4), 457–76.

Godard, John (2007d), 'The implications of work and human resource practices for unions in Canada and England: an institutional environments approach,' working paper, the Faculty of Management, the University of Manitoba.

Godard, John (2007e), 'Consistent inconsistencies? Estimating the implications of alternative work practices for workers,' working paper, the Faculty of Management, the University of Manitoba.

Godard, John (2007f), 'Institutional norms and the survival of the collective bargaining in Canada,' unpublished manuscript.

Godard, John (2008), 'Union formation,' in Paul Blyton *et al.* (eds), *Handbook of Industrial and Employment Relations*, London: Sage Publications, pp. 375–405.

Godard, John and Delaney, John (2000), 'Reflections on the high performance paradigm's implications for IR as a field,' *Industrial and Labor Relations Review*, **53** (3), 482–502.

Godard, John, and Delaney, John (2002), 'On the paradigm guiding industrial relations theory and research: reply to Thomas A. Kochan,' *Industrial and Labor Relations Review*, **55** (3), 542–4.

Gospel, Howard (2005), 'Markets, firms and unions. a historical-institutionalist perspective on the future of unions in Britain,' in Sue Fernie and David Metcalf (eds), *Trade Unions: Resurgence or Demise?* London: Routledge.

Hall, Peter A. and Soskice, David (2001), 'An introduction to varieties of capitalism,' in Peter A. Hall and David Soskice, *Varieties of Capitalism: The Institutional Foundations of Comparative Advantage*, Oxford: Oxford University Press, pp. 1–70.

Harris, Howell (1982), *The Right to Manage*, Madison, WI: University of Wisconsin Press.

Hartz, Louis (1955), *The Liberal Tradition in America*, New York: Free Press.

Hattam, Victoria (1993), *Labor Visions and State Power*, Princeton, NJ: Princeton University Press.

Heckscher, Charles and Carré, Francoise (2006), 'Strength in networks. Employment rights organizations and the problem of co-ordination,' *British Journal of Industrial Relations*, **44** (4), 6505–28.

Howell, Chris (2005), *Trade Unions and the State*, Princeton, NJ: Princeton University Press.

Human Rights Watch (2000), *Unfair Advantage*, New York: Human Rights Watch.

Hutton, William (2002), *The State We're In*, London: Little Brown.

Hyman, Richard (1982), untitled comment on Thomas Kochan, 1980, *Collective Bargaining and Industrial Relations*, in 'A Review Symposium,' *Industrial Relations*, **21** (1), 100–14.

Hyman, Richard (1997), 'The future of employee representation,' *British Journal of Industrial Relations*, **35** (3), 309–36.

Hyman, Richard (2003), 'The historical evolution of British industrial relations,' in Paul Edwards (ed.), *Industrial Relations Theory and Practice in Britain,* 2nd edn, Oxford: Blackwell, pp. 37–57.

Inglehart, Ronald, Basanez, Miguel, Diez-Medrano, Jaime, Halman, Loek and Luijkx, Ruud (2004), *Human Beliefs and Values: A Cross-Cultural Sourcebook Based on the 1999–2002 Values Surveys*, Mexico: Siglo XXI.

Jacoby, Sanford (1991), 'American exceptionalism revisited: the importance of managers,' in Sanford Jacoby (ed.), *Masters to Managers: Historical and Comparative Perspectives on American Employers*, New York: Columbia University Press, pp. 173–200.

Kaufman, Bruce (1993), *The Origins and Evolution of the Field of Industrial Relations in the United States*, Ithaca, NY: ILR Press.

Kaufman, Bruce (1996), 'Why the Wagner Act? Re-establishing contact with its original purpose,' in David Lewin, Bruce Kaufman and Donna Sockell (eds), *Advances in Industrial and Labor Relations*, Greenwich, CT: JAI Press, pp. 15–68.

Kaufman, Bruce (2004), *The Global Evolution of Industrial Relations*, Geneva: International Labor Office.

Kerr, Clark, Dunlop, John, Harbison, Frederick and Myers, Charles (1960), *Industrialism and Industrial Man*, New York: Oxford University Press.

Kochan, Thomas (1980), *Collective Bargaining and Industrial Relations*, Homewood, IL: Irwin.

Kochan, Thomas (2005), *Restoring the American Dream*, Cambridge, MA: MIT Press.

Kochan, Thomas, Katz, Harry and McKerzie, Robert (1986), *The Transformation of American Industrial Relations*, New York: Basic Books.

Lehmbruch, Gerhard (2001), 'The institutional embedding of market economies: the German "Model" and its impact on Japan,' in Wolfgang Streeck and Kozo Yamamura (eds), *The Origins of Nonliberal Capitalism*, Ithaca, NY: Cornell University Press.

Lipset, Seymor Martin (1963), *The First New Nation: the United States in Historical and Comparative Perspective*, New York: Basic Books.

Lipset, Seymor Martin (1964), 'Canada and the United States – a comparative view,' *Canadian Review of Sociology and Anthropology*, **1**, 173–85.

Lukes, Stephen (1974), *Power: A Radical View*, London: Macmillan.

Oxenbridge, Sarah and Brown, William (2004), 'Achieving a new equilibrium? The stability of cooperative employer–union relationships,' *Industrial Relations Journal*, **35** (5), 388–402.

Oxenbridge, Sarah, Brown, William, Deakin, Simon and Pratten, Cliff (2003), 'Initial response to the statutory recognition provisions of the Employment Relations Act 1999,' *British Journal of Industrial Relations*, **41** (2), 315–34.

Perlman, Selig (1949 [1928]), *A Theory of the Labor Movement*, New York: Augustus M. Kelley.

Schorske, C.E. (1997), 'The new rigorism in the human sciences. 1940–1960,' in T. Bender and C.E. Schorske (eds), *American Academic Culture in Transformation*, Princeton, NJ: Princeton University Press pp. 309–30.

Smith, Paul and Morton, Gary (2001), 'New Labour's reform of Britain's employment law: the devil is not only in the detail but in the values and policy too,' *British Journal of Industrial Relations*, **39** (1), 119–38.

Strauss, George (1982), untitled comment on Thomas Kochan, 1980, *Collective Bargaining and Industrial Relations*, in 'A Review Symposium,' *Industrial Relations*, **21** (1), 95–9.

Taras, Daphne (1997), 'Collective bargaining regulation in Canada and the United States: divergent cultures divergent outcomes,' in Bruce Kaufman (ed.), *Government Regulation of the Employment Relationship*, Madison, WI: Industrial Relations Research Association, pp. 295–342.

Terry, Mike (2004), ' "Partnership": a serious strategy for UK trade unions?' in Anil Verma and Tom Kochan (eds), *Unions in the 21st Century: An International Perspective*, Basingstoke: Palgrave Macmillan.

Tocqueville, Alexis de (1998 [1835]), *Democracy in America*, Ware: Wordsworth.

Troy, Leo (2000), 'US and Canadian industrial relations: convergent or divergent?' *Industrial Relations*, **39** (4), 695–713.

Voss, Kim (1993), *The Making of American Exceptionalism: Knights of Labor and Class Formation in the Nineteenth Century*, Ithaca, NY: Cornell University Press.

Voss, Kim and Sherman, Rachel (2000), 'Breaking the iron law of oligarchy: union revitalization in the American labor movement,' *American Journal of Sociology*, **106** (2), 303–49.

Wood, Stephen J. and Godard, John (1999), 'The statutory union recognition procedure in the Employment Relations Bill: a comparative analysis,' *British Journal of Industrial Relations*, **37** (2), 203–45.

Woodiwiss, Anthony (1990), *Rights vs. Conspiracy: A Sociological Essay on the History of Labor Law in the United States*, New York: Berg.

PART 2

Reconstructing institutions

5. Social capital and the labor movement

David B. Lipsky and Ronald L. Seeber

INTRODUCTION

The causes and consequences of the decline of the American labor movement over recent decades have been examined in countless books and articles. Scholars and commentators, however, have virtually ignored one critical dimension. In this chapter, we focus on the social capital implications of the relative decline of the labor movement. There are several definitions of the term social capital. For our purposes, a relevant definition has been provided by the World Bank: 'Social capital refers to the institutions, relationships, and norms that shape the quality and quantity of a society's social interactions . . . Social capital is not just the sum of the institutions which underpin a society – it is the glue that holds them together.'[1] The concept of social capital can be traced to the early part of the twentieth century and was implicitly used by philosophers as early as the eighteenth century. But recent research on social capital has been triggered largely by the work of Robert Putnam, especially his seminal books, *Making Democracy Work* (Putnam, 1993) and *Bowling Alone* (Putnam, 2000; Coleman, 1990; Adler and Kwon, 2002; Portes, 1998).

In *Bowling Alone*, Putnam examined long-term trends in civic and social institutions in the United States and concluded that there had been a significant decline in political, civic, religious and philanthropic participation in our society. 'The ebbing of community over the last several decades,' Putnam writes, 'has been silent and deceptive. We notice its effects in the strained interstices of our private lives and in the degradation of our public life . . . Weakened social capital is manifest in the things that have vanished almost unnoticed – neighborhood parties and get-togethers with friends, the unreflective kindness of strangers, the shared pursuit of the public good rather than a solitary quest for private goods' (Putnam, 2000: 402–3).

Putnam devotes a chapter in *Bowling Alone* to the decline of the labor movement and other workplace associations. He concludes, 'Americans at the beginning of the twenty-first century are demonstrably less likely than our parents were to join with our co-workers in formal associations . . . The workplace is not the salvation for our fraying civil society' (Putnam, 2000: 92). In Putnam's examination of workplace institutions, he confines his analysis to unions and an array of professional associations. Neither Putnam nor any other researcher that we have discovered has examined the decline of the union movement within the context of labor's social network.[2] The creation and development of the American labor movement led to establishment of other institutions and associations allied with unions, opposed to unions or (in the case of government agencies) designed to regulate unions and collective bargaining, and the elements of this network are what we examine in this chapter.

The initial premise for our research was the belief that the weakening of the labor movement must have caused collateral damage to organizations and institutions that have a close relationship to unions. In our research we have sought to track the effects of the growth and relative decline of American unions on a large sample of organizations that arguably owe their own existence entirely or in large part to the existence and survival of the union movement. We collected data for a sample of workplace organizations, institutions and agencies in five categories: federal agencies, neutral organizations and associations, organizations allied with unions, organizations allied with the business community and opposed to unions, and university and college programs in labor relations. Analysis of the trends in the membership, staffing and revenue of these organizations and institutions largely confirms the hypothesis (there are important exceptions) that there appears to be a pronounced relationship between these trends and union membership. Whereas union density – union membership as a proportion of the workforce – peaked in the 1950s and has continued to decline, for many of the organizations we examined comparable measures peaked in the 1970s or 1980s and declined thereafter. In other words, there appears to have been roughly a 20- to 30-year lag between the labor movement's zenith and that of organizations and institutions in the labor movement's social network.

We do not argue here that there is a direct cause-and-effect relationship between the relative decline of the labor movement and the relative or absolute decline in allied organizations. The chain of factors that leads from the decline of the labor movement to the decline of each of these other organizations is usually a complex one. In the 1970s and 1980s, there were many forces affecting both unions and organizations in labor's orbit: globalization and growing international competition, deregulation of many industries, and a growing conservative political climate in the nation are only some of the relevant factors. For example, the size of the staff and the so-called 'real budget' (the budget adjusted for the cost of living index) of the Federal Mediation and Conciliation Service (FMCS) reached a historic high in the late 1970s and then declined. Arguably, several factors explain the decline of the FMCS: the decline of strikes and other work stoppages and budget cuts during the Reagan administration are two proximate causes. But we maintain that the FMCS's decline can ultimately be traced to the decline of the labor movement. Imagine, for a moment, that the union movement had doubled in size between the mid-1950s and the mid-1970s: under those contra-factual circumstances, it is unlikely that work stoppages would have declined in the 1970s or that the Reagan administration could have targeted the FMCS for budget cuts.

We conclude that the stock of social capital that had been built by the rise of the union movement and collective bargaining has been severely damaged by the shrinkage of American unions. In the final section of our chapter, we discuss the implications of our findings. For example, can proponents of unions hope for the revitalization of the labor movement if the social network needed to support unionism has significantly withered? Can a vibrant union movement be built in the face of the widespread erosion of civic participation in the United States? If Americans are too busy (with work and family obligations) or too distracted (by the Internet and other diversions) to become members of political parties, religious organizations and other voluntary associations, what are the prospects of persuading them to join a union?

THE THEORY OF SOCIAL CAPITAL

The concept of social capital can be compared with the concepts of physical capital and human capital. Human capital refers to the level of skills, knowledge and productive abilities embodied in the workforce. Presumably, investment in the education and training of workers increases the stock of human capital (see, for example, Mincer, 1958; Becker, 1993; Rosen, 1977). Physical capital, the traditional concept of capital in economics, refers to the stock of factories, plants, machines and other facilities used in the production of goods and services and includes the technology embodied in these physical assets. Presumably, financial investment in physical assets increases the stock of physical capital. Social capital, as noted, refers to the relationships between and among individuals and institutions in society – and not only those relationships but also the trust, commitment and tolerance that is built as a consequence of those relationships. Presumably, creating and developing institutions and fostering connections between and among them increase the stock of social capital.

Putnam and other scholars have linked social capital to both civic virtue and pluralistic democracy. In linking social capital to civic virtue, Putnam writes, 'The difference is that "social capital" calls attention to the fact that civic virtue is most powerful when embedded in a dense network of reciprocal social relations. A society of many virtuous but isolated individuals is not necessarily rich in social capital' (Putnam, 2000: 19). Many researchers have also postulated a link between social capital and pluralistic democracy, arguing that a high level of social capital was virtually a necessary condition for democracy to thrive (see, for example, Putnam, 2000: 336–49). Some of America's founders, however, thought that political parties, voluntary associations and other special interest groups were antithetical to the cause of democracy. In one of *The Federalist Papers* (Number 10), James Madison called such groups 'mischiefs of faction' and argued that in a democracy they needed to be tolerated but carefully controlled (Madison, 1788). By contrast, Alexis de Tocqueville, America's most famous visitor, believed that the success of our democracy was rooted in the willingness of our citizens to participate in a multitude of civic activities and societies (Tocqueville, 2000 [1835]). Contemporary political theorists continue to debate the question of whether voluntary associations and civic societies are essential elements of a successful democracy (see, for example, Lowi, 1969).

Social capital can be analyzed at both the individual and the institutional level; it is accumulated and maintained by the interactions between individuals, between institutions and between individuals and institutions. (For a recent study of social capital at the individual level, see Avgar, 2007.) Putnam found that there has been a significant decline in the number of individuals who are active members of groups like the PTA (the National Parent Teacher Association), the American Legion, the Red Cross and other voluntary associations. Americans seem to have turned from organized group activities to more personal leisure activities. For example, Putnam found that there had been a significant decline in the number of people participating in bowling leagues and an increase in individual bowling (hence, the title of his book, *Bowling Alone*).

But there may be two explanations for the declining number of members in voluntary organizations. First, as Putnam emphasizes, the decline may be attributed to waning interest in such groups (and growing interest in watching television and surfing the Internet). Second, the decline may be at least partly the consequence of barriers individuals face in gaining access to groups and organizations they would otherwise like to join. There may be limitations on the ability of organizations to offer their services to potential members – limitations created by an organization's lack of resources, legal constraints or other factors. The first explanation suggests that declining membership is the result of declining demand by individuals for the services and benefits that voluntary associations deliver. The second explanation, by contrast, suggests that declining membership is a supply phenomenon – the result of constraints on the ability of voluntary associations to attract and retain members.

This discussion has obvious connections to the analysis of trends in union membership. For several decades, industrial relations scholars have debated whether the relative decline in union membership has been principally a supply or a demand phenomenon (Dickens and Leonard, 1985; Farber, 1985; Freeman and Medoff, 1984; Troy, 1986). In the case of unions, however, employers and the government play a much more significant role in affecting membership than they do in the case of the PTA, the Elks and other voluntary associations. Our purpose here is not to enter into the debate about the causes of union membership decline, but rather to assess the effects of that decline on the stock of social capital in the United States.

The concept of social capital has had its critics (see for example DeFilippis, 2001; Durlauf, 1999, 2002). Not all researchers agree that 'hyper-individualism' has taken the place of community ties in American society. Some researchers have responded to Putnam and his allies 'by repeatedly showing the persistence of contemporary neighborhood communities. Driven by data, ethnographers and survey analysts have documented the persistence of supportive relations' (Quan-Haase and Wellman, 2006: 283). Critics of the concept of social capital point out a number of its limitations. For example, a pronounced normative element affects the work of social capital researchers. Although Putnam maintains that social capital is a neutral term, his belief that civic virtue and democracy are highly dependent on the stock of social capital is not always supported by hard evidence. Such evidence is especially difficult to gather because there is no consensus on how to measure social capital.

A basic assumption of social capital research is that organizations with larger memberships contribute more to the stock of social capital than organizations with smaller memberships. Membership data alone, however, cannot adequately account for the relationship aspects of social capital, including trust, reciprocity, commitment and tolerance. The assumption that large organizations contribute more to social capital than small organizations ignores the fact that it is possible for a small group to create (or destroy) a significant amount of social capital if the group consists of highly active, committed and influential members. One has only to think of al-Qaeda to understand that it is possible for a relatively small but fanatic group of individuals to have a highly significant effect – positive or negative – on the stock of social capital. As Putnam acknowledges, 'Social capital . . . can be directed toward malevolent, antisocial purposes, just like any other form of capital' (Putnam, 2000: 22).

METHODOLOGY

We will follow Putnam's lead and rely heavily on membership trends in voluntary organizations in our analysis. In addition to membership, where appropriate we will also use data on revenue and the size of an organization's staff. In assessing the effects of the decline of the union movement on social capital, we had to make some fundamental judgments about the organizations, institutions and associations we needed to study. Conceptually, the universe of organizations we needed to consider should include all of those in the union movement's social network – potentially thousands of organizations.

In choosing the sample of organizations we wanted to study, we needed to consider the size, shape and nature of the union movement's social network. We started by considering organizations closely allied with the labor movement – ones that fundamentally share the values, goals and objectives of unions. But as we proceeded, we realized that an accurate assessment of the labor movement's social network had to include federal and state agencies, neutral organizations, professional associations, college and university programs in labor relations and even organizations that did not share labor's values and actively opposed the union movement. Table 5.1 provides a list of the organizations we studied: 16 agencies, associations and institutions as well as all colleges and universities that offer degrees in labor relations and human resource management. We used two key criteria to select our sample. First, we sought to include as many member-based organizations as we possibly could so that we would be able to make a direct comparison between union membership trends and the membership trends of other organizations in the union network. Second, our desire to examine trends obviously meant that we needed to confine our sample to organizations that had been in existence for several decades. We did not include in our analysis organizations and associations that have come into existence within the last decade or so. We also excluded from consideration countless think tanks, research institutions and Internet blogs of recent origin with programs that include either pro- or anti-union perspectives.

Two organizations on our list, the National Policy Association and the Work in America Institute, have gone out of existence. The fact that these two organizations, which only a few years ago were thriving entities, no longer exist helps to substantiate our hypothesis, as we will point out later. In the case of government agencies, of course it was not possible to collect membership data, so we relied in our analysis on revenue, budget and staffing data. In the case of college and university programs, we relied on the number of students enrolled in these programs and the number of degrees granted.

Table 5.1   Types and names of organizations in the study

Federal agencies
Federal Mediation and Conciliation Service
National Labor Relations Board

Neutral and professional associations
American Arbitration Association
Association for Labor Relations Agencies
Labor and Employment Relations Association
National Academy of Arbitrators
National Policy Association
Work in America Institute

Organizations allied with unions
Americans for Democratic Action
Association for Union Democracy
National Coordinating Committee for
  Multiemployer Plans

Organizations allied with business
American Manufacturing Association
Business Roundtable
National Association of Manufacturers
National Right-to-Work Committee
US Chamber of Commerce

**College and university programs in labor
 relations and human resource management**
All degree-granting institutions in higher
  education

Collecting historical data for some of the organizations in our sample was relatively easy, but for others it was difficult or impossible. The data for federal agencies, for example, is readily available in annual reports and other documents. Our personal association with some of the organizations facilitated the collection of the data we needed; for example, we had access to all the data the Labor and Employment Relations Association had available. The M. P. Catherwood Library at the School of Industrial and Labor Relations is the repository for the records of many organizations in labor's orbit, including the National Academy of Arbitrators, and so we had access to all the data we sought for the Academy. Voluntary nonprofit associations are required to file Form 990s with the Internal Revenue Service, which provide information on the filing organization's mission, programs and finances. A commercial website called Guidestar collects and provides Form 990s to users who pay a subscription fee (see www.guidestar.org). We subscribed to Guidestar and obtained the data we needed for some organizations, but for others we discovered that we could only obtain the organizational data we needed for the last three or four years. Another source for data on voluntary associations is the *Encyclopedia of Associations: National Organizations of the US*. Although helpful in some respects, the *Encyclopedia* can only report data organizations choose to submit, and we soon realized that some of the organizations of interest did not supply the *Encyclopedia* with accurate or reliable data. We confirmed our suspicions in some cases by comparing data reported in the *Encyclopedia* with the data reported for the same organization on Form 990.

In sum, we started with an ambitious plan to collect comprehensive historical data for a large sample of organizations that, in our judgment, depended to some degree on the labor movement for their existence and vitality. In the course of our research, we faced the reality that the data we needed for some of the organizations we hoped to study simply was not available or not reliable.

FINDINGS

In this section we report our findings on the organizations listed in Table 5.1. Our principal objective is to determine whether the long-term trend in union density is followed by similar relative trends in membership, revenue or staffing for the organizations listed in the table. We do not purport that the relative decline in the union movement over the last 50 years is the only factor explaining the trends in organizations in labor's network. For each organization we examined, its growth or decline has arguably been the consequence of several factors, some related directly or indirectly to the decline of the labor movement and some unique to the organization itself. In this chapter we cannot provide a detailed narrative for each of the organizations we have studied. In some cases a change in strategy helps explain trends in the organization. In others effective (or ineffective) leadership accounts for the organization's fate. Some of the organizations seem to be excellent examples of goal displacement – the development of new goals that replace or supplement the goals the organization was established to serve (Selznick, 1949).

Federal Agencies

As Table 5.1 indicates, we examined two federal agencies, the Federal Mediation and Conciliation Service (FMCS) and the National Labor Relations Board (NLRB). The FMCS, established by the Taft-Hartley Act

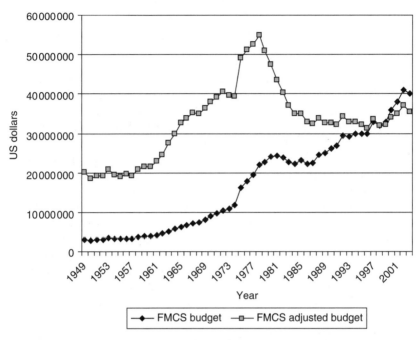

*Figure 5.1   Federal mediation and conciliation service total revenue in
nominal and real terms, 1949–2003*

of 1947, is the principal federal agency assigned the responsibility of using
mediation to resolve collective bargaining disputes, including work stoppages that fall within the jurisdiction of the Taft-Hartley Act. Figure 5.1
shows FMCS budget figures for the period 1949 through 2003. The figure
shows that the budget for the FMCS grew from approximately $3 million
to $40 million over that period. However, when the FMCS's budget is
adjusted for a cost-of-living index (in the calculation we used the consumer
price index (CPI), with the CPI equal to 100 in 1997), the figure shows that
in real dollars the agency's budget peaked in 1978 and steadily declined
through 1996; in recent years there has been a slight upturn in the budget
(in constant dollars, from $31.2 million in 1996 to $37.1 million in 2002),
but the agency's budget in recent years has in real terms been about 35
percent lower than it was in the late 1970s.

Similarly, the size of the FMCS's staff peaked at nearly 600 in 1979 and
declined steadily thereafter to 274 in 1997; there was a slight upturn to 290
in 2003. The number of mediators on the FMCS's staff peaked at 315 in
1977 and declined to less than 200 in recent years. As noted earlier, the relative decline in the funding and staffing of the FMCS appears to be related,

with a lag, to the relative decline of the labor movement, but it also seems to be even more closely related to the decline of work stoppages in the United States. There are several measures of strike activity and some of the key measures reached historic highs in the 1970s and then trended downward. For example, there were more than 5000 strikes in the United States in 1975 and the trend has been steadily downward since that peak year. The number of work stoppages involving 1000 workers or more ranged from 200 to over 400 from the 1950s through the 1970s, but in recent years the number has been between 15 and 40 (Katz and Kochan, 2004: 202–5).

The relative weakening of the labor movement in the United States resulted in the 'withering away' of the strike (see Ross and Hartman, 1960: 42–61) and lower demand by unions and employers for the mediation services provided by the FMCS. In recent years, the agency has reexamined its mission and objectives. For example, the rise of alternative dispute resolution offered new opportunities for the agency, including the mediation of land disputes between Indian tribes. During the Clinton administration, the director of the FMCS, John Calhoun Wells, undertook a strategic planning exercise to examine new directions the agency might take. During the administration of George W. Bush, the directors of the agency (Peter Hurtgen and Arthur Rosenfeld) continued to search for new directions, expanding the agency's activities in both nonunion and non-workplace disputes (see FMCS: Who We Are: Our History at http://www.fmcs.gov/internet/itemDetail.asp?categoryID=21&itemID=15810 accessed on 5 July 2007).

Turning to the NLRB, the budget for the agency in nominal dollars steadily expanded from about $4.2 million in 1946 to $233 million in 2003. But adjusting the agency's budget by the CPI shows that, in 1997 dollars, the budget for the agency in real dollars peaked at $227 million in 1978 and in recent years has hovered around $200 million, a decline of about 14 percent. In earlier decades, the NLRB's budget increased during both Republican and Democratic administrations, doubling during the Eisenhower years and doubling again during the Kennedy–Johnson years. The relative decline in the budgets of the FMCS and the NLRB began during the Reagan administration, but continued during the Clinton years. We have not examined budget and staffing for other federal agencies that play a role in labor and employment relations, but we speculate that the pattern we have uncovered for both the FMCS and the NLRB exists for other federal agencies as well.

Neutral and Professional Associations

We turn our attention now to several neutral and professional associations. The American Arbitration Association (AAA), for example, was

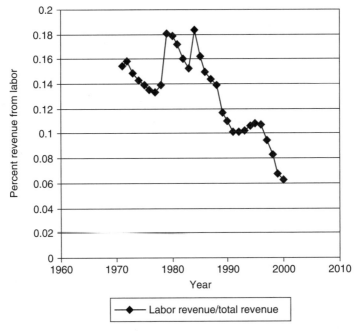

Figure 5.2   The American Arbitration Association: revenue from labor relations activities as a proportion of total revenue, 1971–2000

established in 1925 and provides parties in disputes with the services of neutrals, including principally arbitrators but also mediators. From the start, the AAA was a principal provider of arbitrators in commercial disputes, but beginning especially in the 1930s the AAA became the principal provider of arbitrators in grievance disputes arising under collective bargaining agreements (http://www.adr.org/aaa_mission). We examined several measures of the AAA's relative activity in disputes arising in labor relations.

Whereas total revenue for the AAA steadily increased over the decades and now stands at about $90 million, the revenue the AAA derives from its labor activities reached a plateau in the 1980s in nominal terms. In inflation-adjusted terms, the AAA's labor revenue increased at a slow but steady rate through the mid-1990s, but has declined over the past ten years. Among arbitrators it is well known that the AAA shifted the focus of its activities from labor relations to other dispute arenas, including construction and international. This shift is illustrated in Figure 5.2, which shows AAA's labor revenue as a proportion of its total revenue. The figure shows that this ratio reached a peak in the early 1980s (in 1985 labor revenue was over 18 percent of the AAA's total revenue). But the ratio has, with the exception of a few years, steadily decreased over the past 20 years. Labor revenue now accounts for less than 6 percent of the AAA's total revenue.

The National Academy of Arbitrators (NAA) is an honorific professional society that restricts membership to individuals who have 'substantial and current experience as an impartial arbitrator of labor–management disputes sufficient to demonstrate general acceptability by both labor and management.' A threshold requirement for membership in the Academy 'is at least five years of labor–management arbitration experience and a minimum of 50 "countable" arbitration awards' (http://www.naarb.org/member_guidelines.html). On the one hand, in some respects the data for the NAA do not conform to our central hypothesis. For example, since its founding in 1947, membership in the NAA has steadily increased and now stands at approximately 600. On the other hand, trends in dues and revenue show that in real terms both measures have declined since reaching a high point in 1989. The NAA is a graying organization: when the authors conducted a survey of NAA members in 1999, the average age of members was 62, and almost certainly it must be higher now. Also, diversity is not a hallmark of the organization: our survey revealed that only 12 percent of the members were female and 2.5 percent were African-American (Picher *et al.*, 2000: 11–13). There is much concern within the Academy about the relative decline of collective bargaining, and over the years members have debated – often with intensity – the steps that need to be taken to ensure the NAA's survival. Some members have argued that the Academy needs to broaden its mandate and include arbitrators and other neutrals who take cases in the nonunion sector, while other members object to these proposals and argue that the NAA needs to be faithful to its original purpose and mission (Picher *et al.*, 2000: 7–9).

The Labor and Employment Relations Association (LERA), formerly the Industrial Relations Research Association (IRRA), is a professional association with a membership consisting of academics, union representatives, managers, neutrals and government officials. An association that was also founded in 1947, LERA is a two-tiered organization: there is both a national organization and about 60 local chapters. An individual can choose to belong to the national organization, to a local chapter or to both. LERA also offers organizational memberships to corporations, unions and others. At the national level, individual membership in LERA peaked at about 5000 in the mid-1970s and thereafter decreased steadily to about 3100 in the early 1990s. Membership in the national organization then grew for a few years, reaching 3338 in 2001 but has since declined, falling to 2700 in 2005. The records containing membership information for the local chapters are incomplete, but LERA officers believe total membership in the local chapters is currently between 6000 and 8000.

Members of LERA have debated for years the reasons for the association's decline. In part, the declining membership in the association may be a reflection of the general decline in voluntary associations identified by Putnam and others. In part, declining LERA membership is clearly related to the decline in unions and labor relations in the United States. The officers and active members of the association have consistently emphasized LERA's broader mission – to focus on the workplace more generally and not simply on the union sector. But the association continues to be identified as a forum for individuals and organizations that have a special interest in union–management relations.

We attempted to gather relevant information for the Association for Labor Relations Agencies (ALRA), which is 'an association of impartial government agencies in the United States and Canada responsible for administering labor–management relations laws or services' (http:// www.alra.org/about.htm). The government agencies belonging to ALRA operate principally in the public sector, and in the public sector (in contrast to the private sector) union membership expanded in the 1960s and 1970s and has remained stable in recent years. We thought it would be instructive to compare the experience of a public sector professional association with other organizations in our sample; we expected membership in an organization like ALRA to be stable, rather than declining, and our hypothesis was confirmed by the information we were able to gather. Currently, about 75 government agencies are members of ALRA, a slightly lower number than the 79 agencies that were members a few years ago (phone interview with Dan Nielsen, 4 April 2007).

We list two other organizations in this particular category that had close ties to the labor movement: the National Policy Association (NPA) and the Work in America Institute (WAI). Both are now defunct. Founded in 1924, the NPA had been an important forum for 'senior business, labor, agricultural and academic leaders [to] come together on an ongoing basis to focus on economic and social issues of mutual concern and national significance' (http://nationalcherryblossomfestival.org/html/npa.html). But the NPA encountered successorship problems when its senior business and labor leaders left the organization.

The WAI was founded by Jerome M. Rosow in 1971, who served as its chair for most of its existence. The institute became well known for studies and conferences it sponsored on workplace innovations, such as autonomous work teams, labor–management partnerships and quality of work-life programs. When Rosow retired, the institute encountered a successorship problem similar to the NPA's and the institute shut down in 2003.[3]

Organizations Allied with Unions

The National Coordinating Committee for Multiemployer Plans (NCCMP), founded in 1974, is 'an organization of national, regional and local multiemployer pension and health and welfare plans, International, and Local Unions, national and local employer associations, individual local employers, and multi-employer fund professionals' (http://www.nccmp.org/, accessed on 19 June 2007). The major purpose of the NCCMP is to represent the interests of Taft-Hartley (multiemployer) benefit plans in the legislative and regulatory process. Both authors of this chapter have participated in NCCMP conferences, which bring together an interesting mix of union representatives and Wall Street investment managers. Contrary to our central hypothesis, membership in the NCCMP has been relatively stable over the years principally because of the relative stability of the number of Taft-Hartley plans.

The two remaining organizations listed in this category in Table 5.1 are venerable organizations that have always been independent of the labor movement but closely related to it. The Americans for Democratic Action (ADA) bills itself as 'America's most experienced independent liberal lobbying organization' (http://www.adaction.org/about.htm, accessed on 19 June 2007). Founded in 1947 by Eleanor Roosevelt and other leading liberals of the era, the ADA has always been a champion of civil rights and civil liberties. But it has also been a strong advocate for the labor movement and collective bargaining. One of its founders was Walter Reuther, then president of the United Auto Workers, and in the 1990s Jack Sheinkman, at the time the president of UNITE, served a term as the ADA's president. The ADA currently claims 65 000 members nationwide. We were not able to obtain a continuous series of membership or revenue data for the organization, but fragmentary evidence suggests that the ADA's fortunes have waxed and waned over time. As best we can determine, variation in the ADA's membership is not a function of trends in labor union membership but more a consequence of changes in the popularity of liberal causes. Form 990 for the ADA suggest its public support and total revenues declined just before and after the election of George W. Bush.

The Association for Union Democracy (AUD), founded in 1969, has always been one of the principal advocates for democratic unionism and the individual rights of union members. According to AUD's website, '[I]nternal democracy makes unions stronger and better able to fight for the rights and interests of working people. No other organization is dedicated solely to advancing the democratic rights of union members' (http://www.uniondemocracy.org/, accessed on 28 June 2007). Since he founded the organization nearly 40 years ago, Herman Benson has been its moving force (see http://www.blogger.com/profile/159922302828445776 82). In addition to examining Form 990s for AUD we conducted a telephone interview with Kurt Richwerger, AUD's program and development director, who confirmed that the organization's membership (AUD prefers the term 'associates') peaked about 20 years ago and has modestly declined to its current level of about 800. 'We have an extremely small base of support because of the nature of our work,' Mr Richwerger said. 'We are an organization for union members having problems with their unions.'

Organizations Allied with Business

Of the five organizations in Table 5.1 that we list as allied with business, only one, the National Right to Work Committee (NRTWC), has a mission entirely devoted to opposing the union movement. On its website, the NRTWC says it 'is the only national organization devoted solely to promoting the right of an individual to work, without being forced to join a labor union or pay union dues' (http://www.right-to-work.org/about/ history.php, accessed on 28 June 2007). The NRTWC claims that it has 2.2 million members, but we were unable to verify that claim. Nor were we able to construct time-series data on the organization's membership that we believe are reliable. However, the organization did provide us with time-series data on its revenue, which shows an increase in public contributions from under $1 million in the 1960s to $9.6 million in 1998 and thereafter a decline to $5.5 million in 2005. The size of the NRTWC's staff peaked at 300 in 1997 and stood at 227 in 2005. We speculate that the recent decline of the NRTWC may have some relationship to the state of the labor movement, but it may also be related to the policies of the second Bush administration; if the policies of that administration have been markedly pro-business and anti-union, as many union proponents have maintained, then arguably those policies could have reduced the demand for the NRTWC's services.

To confirm our impressions, we conducted a telephone interview with Mark Mix, president of the NRTWC. Mr Mix said he rejected our hypothesis that the relative decline in the labor movement might have led to a decline in the viability of his organization. He told us 'the National Right to Work Committee is actually doing better than ever.' Mr Mix also rejected the view that declining union membership implied that unions are less powerful today than they were in the past: 'Unions have become more active because they're more desperate. Their decline has made them busier in the public policy process' (telephone interview, 23 April 2007).

Three of the other business organizations listed in Table 5.1 (AMA, Business Roundtable, and US Chamber of Commerce) have not suffered a notable decline in either membership or budget resources. Membership in the NAM, however, has declined over the long term. This decline appears to be largely the consequence of the decline in the manufacturing sector in the US and not necessarily a consequence of the decline of the labor movement. The business organizations we examined pursue multiple objectives and so it is difficult to isolate the effect of the decline of the labor movement on their activities. Moreover, it is quite possible that our hypothesis that labor's decline contributes to the erosion of business organizations opposed to labor's interests is wrong and, on the contrary, the growth of social capital associated with business-allied organizations has contributed to the decline of the labor movement.

University Programs in Labor Relations and Human Resource Management

Many academics believe that labor relations as a field of study has been in decline for a number of years at most universities and colleges. At the same time, most academics believe that the fields of human resource management and organizational behavior have been in the ascendancy (see, for example, Kaufman, 1992; Whitfield and Strauss, 2000).

We wanted to find objective data that would either confirm or refute these views. Time-series data on bachelor's, master's and doctor's degrees granted in labor relations, human resource management (HR) and organizational behavior (OB) are published by the federal government in the *Digest of Educational Statistics*. Figure 5.3 shows the number of bachelor's degrees and master's degrees granted in labor relations as a proportion of the total number of such degrees granted in labor relations, human resource management and organizational behavior from 1970 through 2001, the latest year for which these types of data are available. In 1970, there were 2353 bachelor's degrees awarded in these three fields; by 2001, the number had increased to 7944. But the number of bachelor's degrees in labor relations declined from a peak of 1483 in 1972 to 715 in 1998, and increased slightly to 880 in 2001. That is, the proportion of labor relations degrees at the bachelor's level declined from 56 percent of the total in 1972 to 11 percent in 2001. At the master's degree level, the number of labor-relations degrees stood at 300 in 1970 (about equal to the number of HR degrees), increased to a peak of over 1000 in 1981 and thereafter declined to 591 in 2001. The proportion of labor-relations degrees at the master's level, in other words, was between 40 and 50 percent in the 1970s (reaching a peak of 68 percent in 1981) and has more-or-less steadily declined to 10 percent in 2001.

It would be difficult to deny some connection between the decline of the labor movement and the decline in both the absolute and relative number

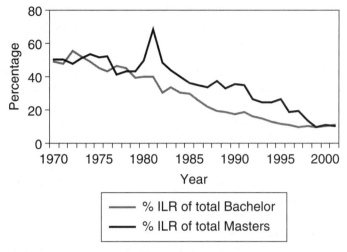

Figure 5.3 *Labor relations degrees as a proportion of degrees granted in labor relations, human resource management and organizational behavior, 1970–2001*

of degrees granted in labor relations by colleges and universities. That connection, however, is not necessarily straightforward. It is common knowledge, for example, that the number of college graduates hired directly out of a degree program by the labor movement has always been quite small. The majority of new degree holders in labor relations obtain jobs with management; it seems apparent that the demand by companies for college graduates has shifted over time from those holding labor-relations degrees to those holding HR and OB degrees. Evidently, the decline in the number of labor-relations degrees has been a consequence of the decline in the labor-relations function in most companies, and the decline in that function is in turn a consequence of the decline of the labor movement.

CONCLUSIONS: THE EROSION OF LABOR'S SOCIAL NETWORK

To reiterate, our central hypothesis is that the relative decline in the US labor movement over recent decades has been associated with the relative decline of organizations and institutions in labor's social network. The weight of the evidence presented in this chapter suggests that our hypothesis is largely but not entirely correct. For many of the organizations we examined, trends in membership, staff, or revenue in absolute terms moved in an upward direction throughout the post-World War II period. However, for most of the organizations we examined, such measures in relative terms reached their maximum levels in the 1970s or 1980s. We have had an easier task confirming our hypothesis for neutral organizations and associations allied with the labor movement, and a more difficult task confirming the hypothesis for organizations allied with business. We are also acutely aware of the methodological limitations on the metrics we have used in our study; we understand that measures of membership, staff and revenue may not fully capture all the central features of social capital, including trust, reciprocity and the strength of connections between organizations and individuals.

Our study is one of the first to examine the generation of social capital in the labor movement's social network, and our methodology follows squarely in the tradition of Putnam and other social capital researchers. We hope future studies will use more sophisticated methodologies to address the social capital effects of the decline of the labor movement. But we are confident that we have captured the essence of an authentic phenomenon that is not likely to be contradicted by additional evidence: the relative decline of the labor movement has been followed by the relative decline of organizations in labor's network and hence in the social capital associated with the labor movement. As we have stressed in this chapter, cause-and-effect is not a straightforward matter. There are intervening or moderating variables that affect the relationship, including globalization, changing public policies, changes in leadership and successorship problems in some of the organizations, among other factors. Nevertheless, we contend that the fate of most of the organizations we examined would have been much different if the labor movement had not entered a period of extended decline.

There are many who hope, and some who fear, that the American labor movement can be revitalized in the future. Can revitalization occur if the social network that has helped to support the labor movement has substantially withered? For example, we have shown that in relative terms the budgets of two important federal agencies, the FMCS and the NLRB, have declined in recent years. A surge of unionism might represent a challenge these two agencies would have difficulty handling with their current resources. We have also shown that a change in strategy has resulted in the AAA shifting resources from labor relations to other dispute areas, and a significant increase in collective bargaining activity would at the very least require the AAA to reconsider its current strategic objectives. A resurgence of the American labor movement might represent a kind of 'winner's curse' for unionists were they to discover that the United States no longer has social institutions strong enough to support a vibrant labor movement.[4]

On the other hand, history seems to demonstrate that the union movement has enjoyed periods of rapid growth (in the 1930s, for example, and in the public sector in the 1960s) in the absence of institutions designed to support and foster labor's growth. The public agencies, neutral organizations and professional associations that to a greater or lesser extent help to maintain the labor movement were generally created in the wake of labor's growth, not before. For example, the dramatic growth of the union movement in the 1930s was followed by the establishment of many of our most prominent academic programs in the late 1940s and by the creation of neutral and professional organizations (for example, LERA and the NAA) in the same period. In our judgment, on balance successful union organizing does not seem to depend on the existence of a large stock of social capital.

We return to the central thesis in Putnam's work. In assessing the prospects for the future growth of the labor movement, a critical factor that virtually all researchers in labor relations have ignored is the declining propensity of Americans to participate in voluntary and civic organizations. There is, of course, considerable debate about the validity of Putnam's thesis. But if he is right, then a significant deterrent to union revitalization – perhaps even surpassing employer opposition – is the lack of interest most Americans seem to have in participating in traditional organizations and associations, even those that seem to serve their own best interests. If the Putnam thesis is correct, then unions – and more broadly, entities representing workers' interests – must continue to develop vehicles suitable to the lifestyle contemporary Americans seem to prefer. For example, it is readily apparent that blogs and Internet communities are overtaking traditional face-to-face interactions in popularity, particularly for younger Americans. Can labor fashion a new toolkit of methods more suitable for reaching the contemporary American worker? That would appear to be a topic for a different study, but the present chapter underscores the importance of such union initiatives.[5]

NOTES

1. See: http://web.worldbank.org/WBSITE/EXTERNAL/TOPICS/EXTSOCIALDEVEL OPMENT/EXTTSOCIALCAPITAL/0,contentMDK:20185164~menuPK:418217~page PK:148956~piPK:216618~theSitePK:401015,00.html. Nahapiet and Ghoshal define social capital as having three components: personal relationships, trusting relationships, and shared goals or mutual interests (Nahapiet and Ghoshal, 1998: 35–9).
2. Several articles do deal with other aspects of the relationship between the labor movement and social capital. See for example Levi (2001); Jarley (2005); Banks and Metzgar (2005); and Clawson (2005).
3. The archives of the WAI are housed in the M. P. Catherwood Library at the School of Industrial and Labor Relations, Cornell University, Ithaca, New York. See http://digitalcommons.ilr.cornell.edu/workinamerica/.
4. Of the many discussions of the 'winner's curse,' see for example, Bazerman and Neale (1992: 49–55).

5. The authors are especially indebted to Ariel Avgar and Kelly Pike for their assistance at every stage of this project. They also want to express their sincerest thanks to Missy Harrington for her help. Finally, they want to acknowledge the able assistance provided by Ben Gruenbaum, Greta James and Marta Novoa.

REFERENCES

Adler, Paul and Kwon, Seok-Woo (2002), 'Social capital: prospects for a new concept', *Academy of Management Review*, **27** (1), 17–40.
Avgar, Ariel (2007), PhD Dissertation, School of Industrial and Labor Relations, Cornell University, forthcoming.
Banks, Andy and Metzgar, Jack (2005), 'Response to "Unions as social capital"', *Labor Studies Journal*, **29** (4), 27–35.
Bazerman, Max H. and Neale, Margaret A. (1992), *Negotiating Rationally*, New York, NY: The Free Press.
Becker, Gary (1993), *Human Capital: A Theoretical and Empirical Analysis with Special Reference to Education*, 3rd edn, Chicago, IL: The University of Chicago Press.
Clawson, Dan (2005), 'Response: organizing, movements, and social capital', *Labor Studies Journal*, **29** (4), 37–44.
Coleman, James S. (1990), *Foundations of Social Theory*, Cambridge, MA: Harvard University Press.
DeFilippis, James (2001), 'The myth of social capital in community development', *Housing Policy Debate*, **12** (4), 781–806.
Dickens, William T. and Leonard, Jonathan S. (1985), 'Accounting for the decline in union membership, 1950–1980', *Industrial and Labor Relations Review*, **38** (3), 323–34.
Durlauf, Steven N. (1999), 'The case "against" social capital', *Focus*, **20** (3).
Durlauf, Steven N. (2002), 'On the empirics of social capital', *The Economic Journal*, **112** (November), F459–F479.
Farber, Henry S. (1985), 'Extent of unionization in the United States', in Thomas A. Kochan (ed.), *Challenges and Choices Facing American Labor*, Cambridge, MA: MIT Press, pp. 15–43.
Freeman, Richard and James Medoff (1984), *What Do Unions Do?*, New York: Basic Books.
Jarley, Paul (2005), 'Unions as social capital: renewal through a return to the logic of mutual aid?', *Labor Studies Journal*, **29** (4), 1–26.
Katz, Harry C. and Kochan, Thomas A. (2004), *An Introduction to Collective Bargaining and Industrial Relations*, 3rd edn, Boston, MA: McGraw-Hill Irwin.
Kaufman, Bruce E. (1992), *The Origins and Evolution of Industrial Relations in the United States*, Ithaca, NY: ILR Press.
Levi, Margaret (2001), 'Capitalizing on labor's capital', in Susan Saegert, J. Philip Thompson and Mark R. Warren (eds), *Social Capital and Poor Communities*, New York, NY: Russell Sage Foundation, pp. 246–66.
Lowi, Theodore (1969), *The End of Liberalism: Ideology, Policy and the Crisis of Public Authority*, New York, NY: Norton.

Madison, James (1788), *The Federalist*, New York, NY: J. and A. McLean, No. 10.
Mincer, Jacob (1958), 'Investment in human capital and personal income distribution', *The Journal of Political Economy*, **66** (4), 281–302.
Nahapiet, Janine and Ghoshal, Sumantra (1998), 'Social capital, intellectual capital, and the organizational advantage', *Academy of Management Review*, **23** (2), 242–66.
Picher, Michel, Seeber, Ronald L. and Lipsky, David B. (2000), *The Arbitration Profession in Transition: A Survey of the National Academy of Arbitrators*, Ithaca, NY: Cornell/PERC Institute on Conflict Resolution.
Portes, Alejandro (1998), 'Social capital: its origins and applications in modern sociology', *Annual Review of Sociology*, **24**, 1–24.
Putnam, Robert D. (1993), *Making Democracy Work: Civic Traditions in Modern Italy*, Princeton, NJ: Princeton University Press.
Putnam, Robert D. (2000), *Bowling Alone: The Collapse and Revival of American Community*, New York: Simon & Schuster Paperbacks.
Quan-Haase, Anabel and Wellman, Barry (2006), 'Hyperconnected network: computer mediated community in a high-tech organization', in Charles Hecksher and Paul Adler (eds), *The Firm as a Collaborative Community: Reconstructing Trust in the Knowledge Economy*, New York: Oxford University Press, pp. 281–333.
Rosen, Sherwin (1977), 'Human capital: a survey of empirical research', in Ronald G. Ehrenberg (ed.), *Research in Labor Economics*, 1, Greenwich, CT: JAI Press.
Ross, Arthur M. and Hartman, Paul T. (1960), *Changing Patterns of Industrial Conflict*, New York: John Wiley & Sons.
Selznick, Philip (1949), *TVA and the Grass Roots: A Study of Politics and Organization*, Berkeley, CA: University of California Press.
Swartout, Kristy A. (2007), *Encyclopedia of Associations: National Organizations of the US (1946–2006)*, (45th edn), Farmington Hills, MI: Gate Cengagè.
Tocqueville, Alexis de (2000), *Democracy in America*, edited and translated by Harvey C. Mansfield and Delba Winthrop, Chicago, IL: University of Chicago Press (originally published in two volumes in 1835 and 1840).
Troy, Leo (1986), 'The rise and fall of American trade unions', in Seymour Martin Lipset (ed.), *Unions in Transition: Entering the Second Century*, San Francisco, CA: ICS Press, pp. 75–109.
US Department of Health, Education and Welfare, Education Division, National Center for Education Statistics (1976–2004), *Digest of Educational Statistics*, Washington, DC: Government Printing Office.
US Department of Health, Education and Welfare, Division of Educational Statistics, Bureau of Educational Research and Development (1962–1974), *Digest of Educational Statistics*, Washington, DC: Government Printing Office.
Whitfield, Keith and Strauss, George (2000), 'Methods matter: changes in industrial relations research and their implications', *British Journal of Industrial Relations*, 38 (1), 141–51.

6. Industrial relations and the law

William B. Gould IV

INTRODUCTION

The American system of labor law has emerged from a period of common law, criminal law, and antitrust regulation that repressed labor organizations or 'combinations' of workers. This was followed by a period of *laissez-faire*, designed to promote freedom of association, and then the bedrock of the American labor law system, the National Labor Relations Act of 1935 (NLRA), which forms the basis for regulation of collective bargaining in the private sector. While the statute has many coverage exclusions, para-doxically, the NLRA has ousted state regulation of labor-management relations in the private sector through the judicially created doctrine of preemption.[1]

The NLRA's exclusions are manifold, the public sector as well as farm workers being foremost among them. The system of collective bargaining in the public sector is regulated by statutes at the federal, state and local level, which are based upon the NLRA, in substantial part, as well as de-cisions issued under that statute. The Railway Labor Act covers employees in the railway and airline industries.

There are still other exclusions. All levels of supervisors are also excluded in the private sector (this is not the case in the public sector generally) and, through statutory interpretation, such individuals as managerial and confidential employees, graduate teaching assistants at private universities as well as university professors are also beyond the reach of the law. Undocumented workers are deprived of effective remedies. At the same time, professional athletes who rely upon both collective bargaining and individual contracts of employment negotiated by professional agents have benefited substantially from the law, particularly the multi-millionaires in baseball and, to a lesser extent, in basketball, football and hockey.

Supplementing and serving as a substitute for collective bargaining are statutes designed to provide a minimum floor. These include the Fair Labor Standards Act of 1938, which provides for minimum wages and maximum hours; the Occupational Health and Safety Act of 1970, which was enacted, as the Supreme Court has said, '[f]or the purpose of ensuring safe and healthful working conditions for every working man and woman in the nation;'[2] anti-discrimination legislation which prohibits discrimination on account of race, sex, religion, national origin, sexual orientation and disabilities; nonstatutory common law protection against so-called wrongful discharges; and the Employee Retirement Income Security Act (ERISA) of 1974, which established the first comprehensive pension labor law. All of these areas of the law have grown simultaneous with the decline of the organized sector of the economy, notwithstanding the fact that the NLRA focuses, for the most part, upon disputes involving recruitment and organizing activity outside of established unionized relationships.

This chapter begins with an overview of the NLRA, followed by a survey of collective bargaining under that law. Subsequent sections discuss public-sector labor law, dispute resolution procedures, employment discrimination law, and the future of labor law in the United States.

THE NLRA

The National Labor Relations Board (NLRB), a quasi-judicial administrative agency that administers and interprets the NLRA, was established along with other so-called alphabet agencies during the Roosevelt New Deal. It remains important, though increasingly less effective.

The NLRB is split into two sides. On the so-called 'judicial' side is a five-member Board with its principal offices in Washington, DC. It issues decisions that can be appealed to the courts. There is also a 'prosecutorial' side of the Board, headed by the General Counsel. The President of the United States, with the advice and consent of the US Senate, appoints all five Board members as well as the General Counsel. Most of the General Counsel's work is divided into two major sections: (a) investigating and litigating before Administrative Law Judges who hear and resolve unfair labor practice allegations; and (b) representing the five-member judicial Board in the courts.

The National Labor Relations Act and the Board perform two basic functions. One is to hold secret ballot-box elections through which a majority of workers determine whether they wish to be represented by union. If the vote is in the affirmative, the union represents all employees within an appropriate bargaining unit as the exclusive bargaining representative over matters relating to wages, hours and conditions of employment. There are frequent disputes in these election cases involving both eligibility to vote in the election, the scope of the unit in which a vote is to be conducted, and conduct engaged in by either employers or unions that might unfairly coerce or influence the voting employees. These disputes create considerable delay in the election cases.

A second major function of the NLRB is hearing unfair labor practice cases which involve disputes about such matters as whether workers have been discriminated against (on account of union membership or activity or because they have protested employment conditions) and whether the employer or the union have bargained with the other side in 'good faith' (that is a good faith intent to consummate a collective bargaining agreement). Certain labor union conduct involving, for instance, the use of secondary boycotts and certain kinds of organizational picketing also constitute unfair labor practices.

Approaches undertaken by various NLRBs have varied considerably over the past half-century depending upon whether the Democrats or Republicans controlled the White House. Congress has deliberately regulated labor–management relations with vague, opaque and ambiguous language giving the NLRB considerable latitude when resolving particular conflicts. The NLRA does not enjoy acceptance amongst a majority of the Republican Party and this position has made the NLRB a lightning rod, translating itself into aggressive hostility to the NLRB in the late 1930s, the early 1950s and the mid- and late 1990s during the present author's Chairmanship.

Inevitably, the President will select Board Members, particularly the Chairman and General Counsel, who reflect his or her overriding political philosophy. (By tradition the Board is divided between three members of the President's party and two from the opposition. The General Counsel also comes from the President's party.) When the Republicans are in office they generally turn to business organizations – like the Chamber of Commerce, the National Association of Manufacturers and newer business groups that have emerged as representatives of high tech companies – to determine how the Board should be composed. The same advice is supplied to Democrats, who turn to organized labor, particularly the AFL-CIO, in reaching their conclusions.

The difficulty with both the unfair labor practice cases and election or representation cases is that the established procedures are convoluted. Moreover, since the 1970s employers have become particularly adept at exploiting loopholes in the Act, which delays the administrative process and often renders NLRB remedies ineffective. The law has been deficient in major respects, and it is one of a number of factors responsible for union decline in the workplace. Again, delays and abuses in the electoral process are a major factor, and workers, who vote for a union but cannot obtain actual representation, let alone a collective bargaining agreement, often become disillusioned and cynical about the NLRA.

This has led Congress to attempt to reform labor law on a number of occasions beginning in the 1970s, the most recent attempt taking place in

2007 when the House of Representatives passed the Employee Free Choice Act of 2007, which would have substituted employee authorization cards (signed by a majority of the workers as a basis for compulsory recognition of unions by employers) for secret-ballot elections. The theory is that employee sentiments are less likely to be frustrated by such a system. However, the US Senate denied a vote on this legislation through use of the filibuster – as it has done with regard to other labor law reform initiatives for the past three decades.

The NLRA purports to protect employees as they organize or protest conditions by prohibiting employers from engaging in retaliation against such workers. This means that union speech and solicitation in the workplace are protected activities as a general matter.[3] But because the US Supreme Court has held that nonemployee union organizers have no access to company property for the purpose of recruitment and since the employer is able to get the company's message across through captive audience speeches (that is, employees can be required to attend the employer's anti-union meetings on company time and property), the protection afforded employees is limited.[4] The Employee Free Choice Act would not have changed any of this, though it is clear that a more comprehensive labor law reform should address this matter.

The right to strike is also protected, but since 1938 the Supreme Court has stated that strikers may be replaced permanently,[5] a step that a large number of major employers have been willing to take during the past quarter of a century. A particularly troublesome ruling by the Supreme Court precludes unions from imposing sanctions in the form of fines and other discipline upon strikebreakers who cross the picket line by allowing such employees to resign membership and to escape disciplinary sanctions by so doing.[6] This approach has undercut the broad policy promoted by a deeply divided Supreme Court in 1967 in *NLRB v Allis-Chalmers*,[7] which held that a union had an interest in imposing sanctions so as to further solidarity amongst the employees that it represents.

The employer may lock out workers in many situations,[8] and, though there is a duty to bargain in good faith imposed upon both sides, the employer may unilaterally institute its own position on terms and conditions of employment subsequent to the time that the parties have bargained to the point of impasse.[9] And even prior to impasse some conditions are viewed as so-called 'management prerogatives,' and involve no employer's obligation to bargain. In a series of decisions, the most prominent of which was rendered in 1981, the Supreme Court held that plant closings are management prerogatives and thus not matters about which the employer is obligated to bargain.[10] Though an employer is required to bargain about the so-called 'effects' of such a decision – and, when the union raises the matter, to bargain about the subject of plant closing when a new collective bargaining agreement is negotiated – the 1981 decision takes the leverage away from unions and explicitly rejects the concept of co-determination or partnership accepted throughout much of northern Europe.

COLLECTIVE BARGAINING UNDER THE NLRA

The NLRA has grown increasingly irrelevant and sometimes hostile to not only the process of union organizing activity, but also to collective bargaining itself. A good illustration of the latter situation relates to bargaining of health care benefits in manufacturing, particularly the automobile industry. Nearly four decades ago, the US Supreme Court held that since retirees are not employees within the meaning of the Act, there is no duty to bargain about health care or benefits for such individuals.[11] But the fact is that this is a principal area of bargaining in a number of established relationships because: (a) so many such benefit packages were negotiated prior to the Supreme Court's ruling; and (b) even those negotiated in its wake nonetheless have been created because of the fact that retiree benefits are a vital aspect of the employment relationship. The absence of universal health care and a national pension system has helped create a collective bargaining crisis in this area with labor and management attempting to step into what is a legislative vacuum.

Cases dealing with both the bargaining process and the economic pressure that labor and management may bring to bear upon one another highlight a fundamental tension in the law. There are a number of important cases that establish an overarching 'freedom of contract' approach towards labor–management relations under federal labor law policy. This approach – its theory being that regulation of tactics inevitably opens the door to regulation of the forbidden fruit of the collective bargaining agreement's substance – has served as a justification for the Supreme Court in upholding the lockout weapon so long as: (a) it is not designed to 'destroy or frustrate the process of collective bargaining' itself; and (b) there is no diminution in the union's capacity to represent employees in the bargaining unit.

This approach relied upon a 1960 Supreme Court ruling, which reversed an NLRB conclusion that work slowdowns could be viewed as unfair labor practices and thus unlawful under the Act.[12] The theory of the Board was that such tactics would tend to preclude discussion, which itself is promoted by the statute. The Supreme Court rejected this argument and took the position that economic pressure that might serve as an irritant, rather than as an immediate promoter of dialogue, was an essential ingredient in the collective bargaining process. Said the Court:

It must be realized that collective bargaining, under a system where the government does not attempt to control the results of negotiations, cannot be equated with an academic collective search for truth – or even with what might be thought to be the ideal of one. The parties – even granting the modification of views that may come from a realization of economic interdependence – still proceed from contrary, and to an extent antagonistic, viewpoints and concepts of self-interest. The system has not reached the ideal of the philosophical notion that perfect understanding among people would lead to perfect agreement among them on values. The presence of economic weapons, in reserve and their actual exercise on occasion by the parties, is part and parcel of the system that the Wagner and Taft-Hartley Acts have recognized. Abstract logical analysis might find inconsistency between the command of the statute to negotiate toward an agreement in good faith and the legitimacy of the use of economic weapons, frequently having the most serious effect upon individual workers and productive enterprises, to induce one party to come to the terms desired by the other. But the truth of the matter is that at the present statutory stage of our national labor relations policy, the two factors – necessity for good-faith bargaining between parties, and the availability of economic pressure devices to each to make the other party incline to agree on one's terms – exist side by side.[13]

Accordingly, within limits, the success and strength of one party ought not to matter in determining whether a statutory violation has been committed. The statute contemplates the coexistence of lambs and lions, even though they may not be compelled to lie down with one another.

This slowdown decision, like the lockout case, relied upon another and even earlier Supreme Court holding from 1952,[14] where the majority found that management could insist on the bargaining of a 'management prerogatives' clause under which the union was ousted from involvement with important conditions of employment and under which matters such as discipline and work schedules were nonarbitrable – that is, management's position with regard to these areas would always prevail. The Court stated that the Board could not 'directly or indirectly compel concessions or otherwise sit in judgment upon the substantive terms of collective bargaining agreements.'[15] The Court rejected the Board's position that an employer was obligated to establish ongoing bargaining on these subjects during the term of the collective agreement.

The 1952 holding in *American National Insurance* dramatizes the fundamental difference between the American and German systems. In Germany, the law explicitly mandates involvement of the *Betriebsrat*, or plant-level works council, in a wide range of employer decisions affecting employment conditions. The German statutory approach does not contemplate the idea that such rights – the right to veto hiring and firing decisions pending Labor Court or conciliation determinations or the right to have worker directors, for example – can be waived under any circumstance. The weakest *Betriebsrat* cannot be induced or required to relinquish any statutory right that it chooses to assert. The American approach contains an antithetical assumption; the weak must fend for themselves in obtaining some little portion of the lion's share. Generally speaking, the American statute guarantees little to the weak.

These decisions are in tension with the overriding policy of the statute to address inequality between capital and labor – and the role of the Board to intervene for the purpose of promoting self-organization – protecting employees' ability to communicate with one another for the purpose of organizing, and shielding workers against employer retaliation in the form of discharge, discipline or other approaches. The Board approach undertaken in both the bargaining and the economic pressure cases that arise in the context of an already established relationship is a *laissez-faire* or 'hands-off' policy, which permits the parties to do things their way unless the collective bargaining process itself is undercut.

THE PUBLIC SECTOR

In recent years, public sector labor law at the state, local and even federal level has grown considerably. Forty-one states have some form of fairly comprehensive legislation protecting the right of public employees to bargain. However, the right to strike is prohibited or limited in 40 states and federal employees who strike can be punished by felony charges and dismissal. An ongoing and seemingly perennial debate about the right to strike in the public sector has taken place and, in recent decades, the difficulty of finding a clear consensus has shifted the focus toward substitutes for the strike, that is mediation, fact finding and arbitration.

At the same time, public employees have a right to union membership independent of any statutory scheme because the right of freedom of association under the First Amendment protects that right.[16] However, the right of membership has not been extended to a constitutional right to collective bargaining.[17]

There has recently been an attempt to cut back on collective bargaining rights for federal employees in the newly created Department of Homeland Security, established in the wake of the terrorist attacks of 11 September 2001. Moreover, there has been a movement toward privatization at the federal, state and local levels, a trend only partially mitigated by the Clinton-era NLRB protection of collective bargaining rights for privatized workers.[18] Nonetheless, public employee unionism has grown by leaps and bounds since the 1960s and, if it were not for union organizing in the public sector, trade union membership nationally would be virtually eliminated (that is, less than a double-digit percentage of the workforce). Part of the reason for this is the ability of public sector unions to use politics to pressure government through support of candidates and ballot initiatives, though sometimes public-sector employers have also been able to use the political arena as a labor-relations tool.[19]

DISPUTE RESOLUTION PROCEDURES

In the organized sector of the economy, dispute resolution procedures address both so-called interest disputes – those affecting the terms of a new collective bargaining agreement (disproportionately existing in the public sector by statute or practice) – and 'rights' disputes, that is, those relating to the interpretation to be given to an existing collective bargaining agreement. Generally the arbitration process – where a third party is chosen to issue an opinion and binding award upon the parties – emerges in the United States as the result of private, voluntary negotiations that are conducted with mutual consent of both parties. Arbitration is encouraged by the NLRA and by Supreme Court decisions handed down since the early 1960s. However, the practice of arbitration developed prior to and in some circumstances in spite of the law, since in some jurisdictions arbitration agreements were considered void as against public policy. Jealous courts did not wish to have their jurisdiction undermined.

Arbitration began in the United States before the turn of the previous century. It appeared in 1903 in the form of the 'umpire' system of the Anthracite Coal Commission, was accepted by the hosiery and clothing industries in the form of the 'impartial chairman' system in the 1920s, and was well on its way prior to the 1935 legislation. It gained greater impetus through the War Labor Board, which, operating under the emergency conditions of World War II, encouraged, nurtured and in some instances imposed no-strike obligations and arbitration machinery. All of this was well in advance of the Taft-Hartley amendments of 1947, which provided the basis for some of the major Supreme Court decisions.

Arbitration has proved to be substantially superior to litigation in the courts and the resort to industrial warfare for a number of reasons: (a) informality; (b) economy of expense; (c) the speed of the process; (d) its ability to diminish resort to the strike and lockout; and (e) the fact that it contains lower steps through which dialogue between labor and management can take place, thus making it unnecessary to resort to the final step (arbitration) in the overwhelming number of instances. In the *Steelworkers Trilogy* in 1960,[20] the Supreme Court deferred to the expertise of arbitrators and confined judicial review of arbitral rulings. A decade later the Court augmented this policy by providing

employers with the ability to enjoin strikes that were in breach of negotiated procedures.[21]

One particularly troublesome area relates to disagreements between individual employees and the union about how an arbitration case should be
processed or whether it should be processed at all. The Supreme Court has
said that there is no absolute right provided the employee to proceed to
arbitration in the absence of a collective bargaining agreement providing
such a right so long as the union acts in good faith without hostility or discrimination toward the employee. This is the so-called duty of fair representation standard, which continues to perplex the courts and the NLRB
and to produce litigation.[22]

There have been two arbitration areas that have raised unique issues and
created difficulties for the courts. One is the role of public law and, in particular, anti-discrimination legislation and the accommodation between
such and arbitration. The Supreme Court in *Alexander v. Gardner-Denver*[23]
has held that a final arbitration award does not preclude an individual from
suing to redress employment discrimination, notwithstanding the importance of voluntary conciliation and arbitration as a means to resolve such
matters. At the same time, the Court stated that 'great weight' was to be
given to the award if the arbitration met certain prerequisites.

In 1991, the Court dealt with a matter of equal importance relating to
the unorganized sector, the treatment of arbitrations where the process is
not provided for by a collective bargaining agreement. In *Gilmer v.
Interstate/Johnson Lane Corp*,[24] the Court held that an individual employee
who was dismissed and sued under the Age Discrimination and
Employment Act of 1967 (prohibiting age discrimination) could be subjected to compulsory arbitration pursuant to an arbitration agreement contained in a securities registration application. In reaching this conclusion,
the Court seemed to express doubt about some of the themes propounded
in *Gardner-Denver* by concluding that there was no 'inherent inconsistency'
between the policies of antidiscrimination law and arbitration of such
claims. The Court rejected arguments that arbitration would be biased in
favor of employers and that discovery would be inadequate, stressing the
fact that arbitrators are not bound by formal rules of evidence – a characteristic applicable to all labor arbitration proceedings. Addressing the question of inequality between the parties in such arbitration agreements, the
Court said: 'Mere inequality in bargaining power, however, is not a
sufficient reason to hold an arbitration agreement is never enforceable in
the employment context.'[25]

Subsequently the Court held in the *Circuit City* case that the Federal
Arbitration Act of 1925, which provides for the enforcement of arbitration
contracts, made pre-employment mandatory arbitration agreements

enforceable in the federal courts[26] – and the California Supreme Court in the *Armendariz*[27] case held that such agreements were enforceable though they had to meet a number of standards in order not to be viewed as 'unconscionable.' Underlying the litigation in the individual contract of employment cases is the fact that employer policies are devised without individual negotiations with individual employees – in contrast to the labor arbitration provisions contained in collective bargaining agreements, where they are the product of arm's length bargaining between labor unions and employers. Many issues arising out of disputes in this area remain to be resolved.[28]

EMPLOYMENT DISCRIMINATION LAW

As arbitration cases like *Gardner-Denver* indicate, employment discrimination law has become particularly important in the United States during the past four decades. Arising from the civil rights struggles and protests of the 1960s, employment discrimination law – particularly Title VII of the Civil Rights Act of 1964, which established the Equal Employment Opportunity Commission (EEOC) – has become as important as modern labor law. Though the initial statute was enacted when collective bargaining was much more vibrant, like health and safety and minimum wage legislation, it has stepped into a vacuum at the workplace arising out of union decline.

Title VII was amended in 1991 as a result of the Anita Hill–Clarence Thomas hearings, during which Justice Thomas was accused of sexual harassment, but nonetheless confirmed by the US Senate in an extremely close vote. Subsequent to this hearing, Congress took the opportunity to reverse a series of Supreme Court decisions that limited remedies in discrimination cases. It provided for punitive and compensatory damages for violations of the statute – remedies not available under the NLRA. The 1964 legislation, as amended in 1991, prohibits discrimination on account of race, sex, religion and national origin; other statutes prohibit discrimination on account of age and disabilities. In some state and local jurisdictions, discrimination on account of sexual orientation is prohibited. During the past 35 years, anti-discrimination law has become the basis for the affirmative action concept in the employment arena.

CONCLUSION: THE FUTURE OF LABOR LAW

The American system of industrial relations law, thought to be a model as recently as the 1960s, now seems archaic and hobbled in its impact upon the workplace. There is little opportunity for workers to obtain information, pro or con, about benefits and limits of collective bargaining. And even if a union is certified as the exclusive bargaining representative for employees in a bargaining unit, the law is limited in assisting the collective bargaining process to function.

The conundrum of the law lies in its inability to reconcile the freedom of contract policy with the need for intervention to support self-organization and collective bargaining. Perhaps the Canadian idea of first contract arbitration, when the parties are unable to negotiate a collective bargaining agreement, is an appropriate accommodation between regulation and autonomy as reflected in the lockout and duty to bargain cases. Interest arbitration should be a last step in the bargaining of initial agreements (when the collective bargaining system is in an embryonic state) and when intervention is necessary to resuscitate a process in need of rescue.

Labor law reform is important, but labor and employment law is not solely responsible for union decline. The reasons are numerous and complex.[29] Thus, labor law reform, an agenda vigorously pursued for more than 30 years, will not reverse the seemingly inexorable decline of unions. Nevertheless, it can play a role – and it can inculcate the idea of respect for the rule of law, something sadly missing in the American system today.

Presently preempted state law is not the answer, as some advocate. Any reform providing for more state autonomy in regulating labor–management relations would reward states like Mississippi, which would repress collective bargaining, notwithstanding any benefit which would flow to states like New York, California and Wisconsin where collective bargaining is already strong. The state law advocates would make the most vulnerable workers more vulnerable and expose them even further to the vicissitudes of the free market.

The Employee Free Choice Act would be a valuable first step, even though it introduces one imperfect mechanism for realizing employee free choice (the use of authorization cards) as a substitute for another (the secret-ballot box, which is subject to abuse and delay). A properly written law would maximize free speech opportunities for unions and employers, provide the real prospect of a collective bargaining agreement when a majority of employees selects a union as their representative, and ensure adequate remedies for statutory violations.

NOTES

1.   A more detailed overview of the American system of labor law is provided in William B. Gould IV, *A Primer on American Labor Law* (MIT Press, 4th edn 2004).

2. Industrial Union Department, *AFL-CIO v. American Petroleum Institute* 448 US 607, 611 (1980).
3. *Caterpillar Inc. 321 NLRB* 1178, 1184 (1996) (Chairman Gould concurring).
4. *Lechmere, Inc. v. NLRB* 502 US 527 (1992). See also *Beverly Enterprises-Hawaii* 326 NLRB 335 (1998) (Chairman Gould dissenting at 361).
5. *NLRB v. MacKay Radio & Telegraph Co.* 304 US 333 (1938).
6. *Pattern Makers' League of North America v. NLRB* 473 US 95 (1985).
7. 388 US 175 (1967). A discussion of these issues is contained in Gould, Solidarity Forever – Or Hardly Ever 66 Cornell L.Rev. 77 (1980).
8. *American Ship Building v. NLRB* 380 US 300 (1965).
9. *NLRB v. Katz* 369 US 736 (1962); *NLRB v. Crompton-Highland Mills* 337 US 217 (1949).
10. *First National Maintenance Corp. v. NLRB* 452 US 66 (1981).
11. *Allied Chemical & Alkali Workers of America, Local Union No. 1 v. Pittsburgh Plate Glass Co.* 404 US 157 (1971).
12. *NLRB v. Insurance Agents' International Union* 361 US 477 (1960).
13. Id. at 488–9.
14. *NLRB v. American National Insurance Co.* 343 US 395 (1952). See generally Case Comment, 85 Harv. L. Rev. 680 (1972).
15. *American National Insurance* supra at 404.
16. *American Federation of State, County and Municipal Employees, AFL-CIO v. Woodward* 406 F.2d 137 (8th Cir. 1969).
17. *Smith v. Arkansas State Highway Employees, Local 1315* 441 US 463 (1979).
18. *Lincoln Park Zoological Society 322 NLRB* 263 (1996) enforcement granted 116 F.3d 216 (7th Cir. 1997). The Board, reversing precedent, has held that it will take jurisdiction over petitions for representation filed under the NLRA, notwithstanding the relationship between the employer and a government contract; *Management Training Corp.* 317 NLRB 1355 (1995).
19. *DiQuisto v. County of Santa Clara* (Superior Court of California, County of Santa Clara, 27 July 2007).
20. *United Steelworkers v. American Manufacturing Co.* 363 US 564 (1960); *United Steelworkers v. Warrior and Gulf Navigation Co.* 363 US 574 (1960); *United Steelworkers v. Enterprise Wheel and Car Corp.* 363 US 593 (1960).
21. *Boys Markets, Inc. v. Retail Clerks* 398 US 235 (1970); discussion is contained in W. Gould, *On Labor Injunctions, Union and the Judges: The Boys Market Case* 1970 S. Ct. Rev. 215.
22. *Vaca v. Sipes* 386 US 171 (1967); *Hines v. Anchor Motor Freight* 424 US 554 (1976).
23. 415 US 36 (1974). See also W. Gould, 'Labor arbitration of grievances involving racial discrimination' 118 U. of Penna. L. Rev. 40 (1969).
24. 500 US 20 (1991).
25. Id. at 33.
26. *Circuit City Stores, Inc. v. Adams* 532 US 105 (2001).
27. *Armendariz v. Foundation Health Psychcare Services, Inc.* 6 P. 3d 669 (Supreme Court of California 2000).
28. For example, one key issue is whether the employer may mandate that the process and its procedures be completely confidential between the individual employee and employer, precluding the publication of the arbitration award itself. For a discussion of this and other contemporary arbitration issues, see William B. Gould IV, 'Kissing Cousins? The Federal Arbitration Act and modern labor arbitration' 55 *Emory Law Journal* 609 (2006).
29. The rise and fall of unions has always been a complex phenomenon triggered by numerous factors. (See, for example, L. Wolman, *Ebb and Flow in Trade Unionism*, New York: National Bureau of Economic Research, 1936.) Today, beyond the law, the sharp union decline is attributable to a number of factors, including: (a) foreign competition, corporate relocation (or the threat thereof) beyond national boundaries; (b) the changing nature of the employment relationship, with the advent of growing numbers of part-time and temporary contingent workers who are particularly vulnerable to employer pressure; (c) undocumented workers who are afraid to protest both poor and illegal working

conditions; (d) a widening union–non-union wage differential, creating another employer incentive to be non-union; (e) deregulation in transportation, which has ravaged the unionized strongholds in trucking and airlines and even affected railroads; (f) the location of non-union foreign transplants in low-wage, rural areas; and (g) union lethargy and a belated willingness to use a sufficient amount of union dues for organizing, which has spawned two AFL-CIO palace revolts in the past decade. (See, generally, W. Gould, *Agenda for Reform: The Future of Employment Relationships and the Law*, Cambridge, MA: The MIT Press, 1993.)

7. How industrial relations is marginalized in business schools: using institutional theory to examine our home base

Daphne Taras

INTRODUCTION

Pandora gingerly lifts the lid of our mysterious business school box and finds, to the surprise of many of her colleagues, that industrial relations (IR) is in decline for reasons that go well beyond the decline in US union density. Otherwise, why is it that in English Canada, in which the lowest union density province falls only slightly short of matching America's highest density state, that the academic field of IR is threatened? Why indeed, in a country with a public sector density rate of almost 72 percent, with almost 20 percent of Canadians employed in the public sector?[1] This briefing will offer insight into factors that currently threaten the already tepid health of IR in many Canadian business schools (as well as such schools outside Canada). These factors often are overlooked, and certainly will seem arcane, but they may be extraordinarily important to the fate of IR.[2] It is odd that a field so comfortable with institutionalist approaches rarely turns this lens onto its own university settings.

The marginalization of IR is insidious and it has been accelerating. Left unchecked, the forces I describe will quietly erode IR's perch in business schools. Please do not for a minute think that business school deans and administrators sit around plotting the demise of IR because of union decline in the US.[3] IR is not even on the Canadian radar screen. That, in a nutshell, is the problem. When a field doesn't matter within its institutional home, it is easy to overlook, to under-resource, and to replace.

On the other hand, business schools matter a lot to IR scholars. Of the almost 100 academic members of the Canadian Industrial Relations Association (CIRA), a substantial number (over 42) identify themselves as belonging to business schools.[4] Outside the business schools there are about 33 members who belong to IR departments in francophone universities in the province of Quebec, where IR remains exceptionally strong compared to the rest of North America. Another 12 academics listed themselves as belonging to IR departments in English Canada, but many of these 12 are cross-appointed with business schools. If one adds all the sessional (non-tenure-track) instructors, and the sheer volume of students we service, business schools likely comprise over half the IR market. Further, many business students eventually emerge as managers – a key actor in the employment setting. Their deference for our field, or their distaste, makes a difference in the world of work. Professors only have a few years of contact with prospective managers as they cluster into trainable cohorts, and their stomping ground is the business school. Like it or not, we deserve to have a strong presence in business schools to provide their students a thorough education.

In this chapter, I will not discuss the differences between IR (a broad, multi-disciplinary field that acknowledges pluralism at the workplace) and human resource management (HRM, which is geared to aligning workers to the corporation). Much has been written by fine scholars, including those in this volume, about the business schools' support for the HRM approach over IR, and about the decline in the field (see especially Kaufman, 2004). I shall not describe the intellectual foundations of IR, and I shall not send accolades to the usual cast of IR luminaries. Instead, my only goal is to expose those taken-for-granted elements that are well known within business schools and hold them up to the light. Through this prism, I will show how IR is on a downward trajectory. It is because of a host of factors that have to do with the actual business strategy of the business school. It is quite sad for IR, but in business schools we do sometimes practice what we preach.

Let me say at the outset that the remarks I am about to make pertain most strongly to the type of business school that is part of the herd rather than the pinnacle schools or those that have pervasive and unusual strategies that set them apart from the others. Some observers have noted that 'the quest for top-tier publications [as well as other proxies used in bench-marking] is especially intense in less prestigious schools' (Leung, 2007, p. 510; Starbuck, 2005).

BUSINESS SCHOOLS RUN LIKE BUSINESSES, FOR BETTER OR FOR WORSE

Here is the way many mainstream business schools operate, particularly in the middle tiers. We compete with each other for students. We believe in demonstrable and measurable inputs and outcomes. We have become rather fanatical about quantifying our products and ourselves. Business schools have found ways of mimicking the private enterprise world of stock market quotes, ISO-900, and market share measures. Our students are counted, their potential is measured in an alphabet soup of GMAT scores and GPAs, and research output often is tallied without scrutiny of its content. Schools' isomorphic adherence to ranking systems creates the need for easily counted proxies for quality, rather than the more difficult assessment of the real thing (Gioia and Corley, 2002). Faculty members are rewarded or shunned based on their ability to help schools achieve 'strategic objectives.' Even our journal citation scores are 'part of the formal accounting process' (Judge *et al.*, 2007: 491), and have been more sinisterly described as 'the number that's devouring science' (Monastersky, 2005). We are astonishingly numerate.

We favor the subjects that reinforce the twin notions that business operations can be quantified and that the right formula will produce success. Fields of finance and accounting are pre-eminent in most top business schools; strategy is well regarded, and marketing has found a good footing. Human resources, organizational behavior and IR have long been considered less central. They weren't all that important to begin with in many schools, and tended to be a little like that old car commercial – every buyer's second choice for an optional or minor course.

Business schools also tend to run in packs (even as they proclaim their niche strengths in order to seek differentiation from their competitors). Business schools seek to be 'accredited' internationally, particularly by the Association to Advance Collegiate Schools of Business (AACSB – www.aacsb.edu). Business schools in Canada have gone through a wave of accreditations. This is a complex, costly, and sometimes off-putting investment of energy. It requires that every system, process, decision, class, major, research paper, resume, and resource of the business school be open to scrutiny by a panel of expert reviewers from previously-accredited schools. It takes years to achieve a first accreditation with AACSB, and many months to be reaccredited.[5]

Added to this desire for accreditation is the hunger for external recognition, which can pay fundraising dividends. Business donors like to support winners. Most schools seek affirmation through international benchmarking. The flagship degree program is usually considered to be the master's degree in business administration (MBA).[6] There are specific international benchmarks that business schools use to compete in this market. Three well-known rankings are produced by the *Financial Times* (London, England), *BusinessWeek* (www.businessweek.com/bschools), the *Wall Street Journal* (www.careerjournal.com/reports/bschool/).[7] The quest for media rankings has been criticized in a widely-circulated paper as 'fostering myopia,' 'short-term thinking' and a 'dysfunctional competition that diverts resources,' and the rankings schemes themselves are described as rife with 'serious error' and statistical 'noise.' (DeAngelo *et al.*, 2005).

Let us dissect the *Financial Times* 'FT 100' ranking system (http://news.ft.com/businesslife/mba) because it is one of the most comprehensive of the benchmarking efforts and it has engendered intense international participation. It proclaims the top 100 schools in the world, according to precise measurement of over 20 indicators. Schools submit detailed information, which may be independently audited. The most important indicators, which together comprise about half of the ranking, are alleged measures of student success. Twenty percent is determined by the weighted average of student salaries (in $US) three years after graduation. Another 20 percent is based on the percentage increase in salary from the entry into the MBA until three years after graduation. An additional 6 percent is a measure of the international mobility of graduating students, and there are a few lesser indicators as well.

The best positive 'bump' tends to come from students in accounting and finance; by contrast, human resource management and labor-relations positions have not contributed the same statistical oomph.

There is, of course, a certain malleability to these indicators.[8] For those schools with a streak of Machiavellianism, it is possible to engineer particular outcomes to great acclaim and rewards. For example, some schools are less inclined to accept students who indicate an interest in pursuing careers that do not provide the exponential gains to entering salaries. Here is an interesting way of manipulating the FT measure: admit former teachers, nurses, unsuccessful entrepreneurs, and low-level managers. In other words, look for occupations with well-known wage structures (so income levels can be easily estimated without asking applicants about their salaries). Among that pool, ensure that students have extremely high scores on the quantitative component of the GMAT test for entry. Look for prospective finance majors. Then quietly admit those students who leave the job market with low salaries and indicate that they will launch careers with hot skills and competitive salaries. Voila!

Do benchmarking and accreditation really matter? Yes, they do (Safón 2007: 217–18). When the *Financial Times* issues its report on January 30 each year, schools' public relations machines go into high gear. A good score is immediately translated into press releases for the local media, and the web pages are changed to reflect the rankings. Schools that rank high celebrate the rankings on the first screen of their web pages. Even Canadian schools that don't break into the top 100 but compete vigorously against other Canadian schools will prominently publicize any of their good benchmarking scores.

Stellar benchmark scores are important particularly in a climate in which business schools are permitted to charge substantially higher tuition than programs in the arts and humanities. Students who can afford to pay the higher tuition also are more attuned to the status and reputation of the programs to which they apply. They are shoppers, and they have developed discerning tastes. Prospective students definitely are attuned to rankings. The survey 'Which MBA?' reported that when its readers were asked to name the portion of its website of most interest, 90 percent said the rankings (Bickerstaffe and Ridgers, 2007: 62). Schools like Western and Queen's are acutely aware of the impact of international rankings on the willingness of their incoming classes to pay top dollar.[9] An accelerated executive MBA at Queen's now costs over $74 000 ($US). No wonder students want reputational bang for their investment buck.

One of the most alarming developments for business schools has been the turbulence in MBA programs worldwide. North American MBA programs were overbuilt, planned for too many students, and especially did not take into account that other countries would develop and deliver their own programs. Putting bodies into seats has become a formidable challenge, especially for the mid- and lower-ranked business schools. While top schools only suffered a post-2000 downturn in applicants of about 10 percent, a 30 to 40 percent drop in enrollments hit lower-ranked schools. My own business school planned for over 110 students, then a class of 62, and it would not be a surprise to see a class of less than 30. This is not unusual these days. Thank goodness for the endless supply of eager undergraduates who absorb the unintentional slack caused by pullbacks in MBA demand.

In the last decade, the fortunes of many business schools were propped up by a surge of foreign applicants, particularly from Asia and, to a lesser degree, from South America and the Middle East. Most schools charge substantially higher tuition for foreign students than for domestic students. For many of these foreign students, the best source of information about where to apply in the otherwise mysterious North American business-school market appears in the AACSB and international ranking systems like the FT list. There are over 3000 business schools from which to become confused; the FT list winnows it down to the 'top' 100. When my business school broke into the top 100, I received substantially greater numbers of admission inquiries to our PhD program from international students; during the years we were on the list, over 70 percent of our PhD program admissions were from international applicants.[10] When we were ranked in the top 100, we also negotiated exchange agreements with dozens of top schools around the world. Our undergraduates had more opportunities for international exchanges, and they took advantage of exchanges in great numbers. Suddenly, our MBA program received a welter of applications from Chinese and Middle Eastern students (whose 'axis of evil' origins caused tremendous visa processing delays in the US). When the US market became difficult after 11 September 2001, applicants diverted their attention to Canada, and sought information from ranking studies. We had cachet!

When most costs are fixed, as they are in universities, incremental additions to revenue are very desirable. Upping a class from 20 to 45, or from 80 to 150 (while putting strain on professors who receive little or no extra remuneration), is exceptionally lucrative. IR professors have little market 'pull' and even if they do, they are 'pulling in' the wrong students for benchmarking purposes. It is better to have a world expert in finance in the faculty than a distinguished IR professor.

RESEARCH DILEMMAS: HOW DID IR GET LOST?

Where to publish? What type of work gets rewarded? How to think about IR in a business school? Perhaps the two most important developments are the use of 'approved' journal lists as a proxy for the prestige of an article and the exponential importance of article citations as a performance metric (Judge *et al.*, 2007).[11]

Let us revisit the FT ranking system for clues about business school research culture regarding journal lists. Ten percent of the FT ranking comes from research, and this is important because research productivity is in the hands of the engineered research culture of each school. Through deliberate hiring practices, and a program of rewards and incentives, business schools can create a particular research culture. While a school cannot always control the job market for its graduates, it can certainly refuse to hire or promote faculty members who do not contribute to research measures. However, research scores are precisely calibrated in a manner that excludes IR scholarship.

The *Financial Times* counts only those faculty members' publications appearing in 40 journals, the 'FT 40'. Some schools (like mine) even provide financial incentives to faculty members in exchange for on-list publications. Not a single journal is from the IR field. While there are many opportunities to publish on the list for IR scholars in HR journals, strategy journals, and business ethics and selected US-based practitioner journals, such top IR vehicles as *Industrial and Labor Relations Review* (Cornell), *Industrial Relations* (Berkeley), and the *British Journal of Industrial Relations* are missing from the list.[12] Yet, as can be seen in this chapter's appendix, some of the strong IR journals are certainly playing in the same citations-league as journals in the bottom to middle range of the FT list. Canadian journals are invisible for ranking purposes (not just IR journals, but all Canadian journals), and law journals do not appear on the FT list regardless of their impact in labor-relations scholarship or any other field. It is a shame, for much of IR and law are national and local; discussions of Canada's multiple jurisdictions' experimentation are of vital interest to Canadians, but international and American journals fail to see the relevance even as they stress the value of comparative studies.

The FT 40 list was carefully engineered. All major business schools were asked to submit three journal titles in each of 10 subject areas relevant to business research. A list of 30 top journals was eventually compiled based on the collective recommendations received. In addition, five practitioner journals were selected using the same method. Eventually, the list expanded to include a total of 40 journals. These 40 academic and practitioner journals are generally considered the most prestigious and respected in their fields. (Of course, some are much better than others, but a discussion of the quality of this list is beyond the scope of the present chapter.) All are provided in Table 7.1, listed by subject.

Books, book chapters, conference papers, and conference organizing activities make no contribution to the FT research ranking. My colleague Allen Ponak's wildly successful labor arbitration and policy conference, now in its 25th year, nets him virtually no recognition or rewards from our university (www.ucalgary.ca/cted/labourarb). When I was a junior scholar, I decided to run a boutique conference on nonunion employee representation in Banff, and was strongly counseled by major academics to drop the idea – it was 'too risky,' 'would make little contribution to tenure,' and 'would divert time away from journal articles.' In short, bridging the town–gown divide and making contributions to practitioner-based concerns are not normally rewarded in business schools. (The exception in my setting was a conference on Mergers and Acquisitions, held once, with about 150 participants. It received more accolades than the cumulative total of 25 years of labor arbitration and policy conferences, with over 400 participants annually.)

Let me compare now the conference scene between management and labor relations. The Academy of Management (AOM) conference is where our rewards and recognition come from. The AOM has a number of journals that appear on the FT list – the *Academy of Management Journal*, which publishes empirical pieces, and the *Academy of Management Review*, which publishes literature reviews and builds hypotheses for future research, and the *Academy of Management Executive*, a practitioner-oriented journal that translates research into layman's language. The editorship of these journals is a coup for faculty members, and the editors and editorial board regularly turn over to renew and refresh the journals.

Table 7.1   The Financial Times *40 Top Journals, 2007*

1. *Journal of Accounting and Economics* (Elsevier)
2. *The Accounting Review* (American Accounting Association)
3. *Journal of Accounting Research* (University of Chicago)
4. *The American Economic Review* (American Economic Association, Nashville)
5. *Journal of Political Economy* (University of Chicago)
6. *Econometrica* (Econometric Society, University of Chicago)
7. *Journal of Business Venturing* (Elsevier)
8. *Entrepreneurship Theory and Practice* (Baylor University, Texas)
9. *Journal of Small Business Management* (Blackwell)
10. *Journal of Finance* (Blackwell)
11. *Journal of Financial Economics* (Elsevier)
12. *Review of Financial Studies* (Oxford University Press)
13. *Strategic Management Journal* (John Wiley and Sons)
14. *Academy of Management Journal* (Academy of Management, Ohio)
15. *Academy of Management Review* (Academy of Management)
16. *Administrative Science Quarterly* (Cornell University)
17. *Human Resource Management* (John Wiley and Sons)
18. *International Journal of Human Resource Management* (Routledge)
19. *Organizational Behaviour and Human Decision Processes* (Academic Press)
20. *Journal of Applied Psychology* (American Psychological Association)
21. *Journal of International Business Studies* (Academy of International Business)
22. *Management International Review* (Gabler)
23. *Journal of Marketing Research* (American Marketing Association)
24. *Journal of Consumer Research* (University of Chicago)
25. *Journal of Marketing* (American Marketing Association)
26. *Management Science* (Informs)
27. *Operations Research* (Informs)
28. *Journal of Operations Management* (Elsevier)
29. *Information Systems Research* (Informs)
30. *MIS Quarterly* (University of Minnesota)
31. *Harvard Business Review* (Harvard Business School Publishing)
32. *California Management Review* (UC Berkeley)
33. *Sloan Management Review* (MIT)
34. *Long Range Planning* (Elsevier)
35. *Academy of Management Executive* (Academy of Management/OUP)
36. *Accounting, Organizations and Society* (Elsevier)
37. *The Rand Journal* (The Rand Corporation)
38. *The Journal of Business Ethics* (Kluwer Academic)
39. *Organization Science* (Informs)
40. *Journal of the American Statistical Association* (American Statistical Association)

More pertinent, perhaps, is that publications are routinely marketed to the thousands of members of the AOM (now numbering 17962 and growing), by direct e-mail, so that not only is work regularly disseminated, it also is very likely to be cited by those who receive it. Aggressive marketing by journals is just one type of 'potential unintended consequences of [the use of citation scores], particularly through institutional level actions designed to influence citation counts' (Ilgen, 2007: 507).

To appear in the AOM's annual conference requires the submission of a full-length paper, which is then blind-reviewed by at least three colleagues. Well under one in two papers is accepted, keeping the prestige of the conference list high. Only 10 to 15 percent of symposia submissions are approved, ensuring that winning the chance to run a symposium is a feather in the cap of the organizer. The submission process is a tightly controlled industry, and the website methods for submission are state-of-the-art, with tracking numbers and measures of efficiency and quality. There were over 7000 registrants to the AOM conference in 2007, and 5602 submissions with 1677 sessions. AOM membership has been growing annually by about 1000 new members a year for the past decade.

By contrast, the same concern for quality and peer-review appears only in the small, refereed track of the Industrial Relations Research Association (now called Labor and Employment Research Association), and the processes for review are not nearly as efficient and mechanized as those of the AOM. The rest of the LERA papers are accepted based on one-page abstracts or by-invitation-only symposia. That is not to say that the creativity and energy of the conference is lacking – only the perception among business school colleagues that there is status associated with acceptance of a paper. LERA meets with the Allied Social Sciences Association (ASSA), which is dominated by the fields of economics and finance. LERA is a minuscule portion of the ASSA meetings. The International Industrial Relations Association, though strong, has not reached nearly the stature of the AOM.

Here is something I've been noticing over the years. Some top IR scholars who once appeared at LERA now are sending their work to the Human Resource track of the AOM, minimizing the labor-relations significance of their topics and recasting their work to fit the HRM paradigm. Even I delivered a paper to the AOM in 2006, after a decade of resisting the urge; for me, this signals more about IR and the business school setting than most readers can possibly imagine.

The CIRA, meanwhile, accepts presentations with almost no peer review, based on one-page abstracts. It is a superb venue to give graduate students their first friendly exposure to academic conferences, and it is a tight-knit group with little of the unpleasant, competitive edge of the AOM. But it is not an august forum in which to present research. Similarly, the bilingual

Canadian journal *Relations industrielles*, has been published out of Laval since 1945, and within business schools it is considered a peer-reviewed 'B' quality journal. Articles receive few citations (partly because of the language barrier), and the readership is fairly limited.

FORDISM AND THE PRODUCTION OF THE NEXT GENERATION OF BUSINESS SCHOOL SCHOLARS

Many of the most well regarded academic settings are, in actuality, research mills that grind out new PhDs at a regular rate. These schools are located mostly in the US. A group of distinguished senior professors, buffered by a cadre of ambitious juniors, form teams and produce new PhDs who are their spitting image. Knowledge of the 'journal formula' – how to structure and write research that is likely to survive the 'double-blind peer-review process' and be accepted into pinnacle journals is the standard fare of these schools. Their graduates crack into the top tier of scholarship and are offered the best jobs. These people eventually become the gatekeepers of the journals and the scholars that ambitious academics tend to emulate.

How are resources amassed in this system? Scholars who have a demonstrated track record for breaking into the top journals actually score higher in points in major grant competitions than scholars who have not yet (or never will) play in that league. Even in Canada, the Social Sciences and Humanities Research Council of Canada (SSHRC, the principal granting council) awards 60 percent of the total score of a grant application on the basis of published research record, and only 40 percent on the quality of the grant itself, the ingenuity and potential contribution of the topic being assessed. For junior scholars, the percentages are reversed, but still, 40 percent based on the quality of published research is more than enough to make or break an application before any management committee. (In the most recent round of SSHRC, a perfect aggregate score was 12 points, and applications below 8 points were not funded. Without the spring launch of publications, it is difficult to scrape over the bar of an 8-point hurdle.)[13]

It is the strength of IR, and also its greatest current weakness, that it has not positioned itself well to play this particular game. We gain strength from the multiplicity of contributions we make that fit well with our multidisciplinary field – books, conferences, public policy submissions, arbitration awards and mediations, and so on. But because of this openness, our value to business schools has declined every bit as precipitously as has union density in the US. We operate with the flexibility and desires of social scientists (many of whom value books over articles), but within the confines of the more-restrictive business faculties.

TRAINING STUDENTS

Because I become especially depressed over the topic of textbooks, I shall make this brief. Most students in business schools are trained using textbooks that either come from the US, or are Canadianized versions of US textbooks. Where they are written entirely by Canadian authors, they tend to mimic the topics and structure of the US texts. Because unions have lost so much density in the US, they receive scant mention in US texts. HRM texts usually devote only a chapter to unions and collective rights. Sadly, even though Canadian union density is two-to-three times greater than that of the US, this is not proportionately reflected in the content of books used to train our Canadian students. That is why it is especially important to pay attention to the factors that enhance or inhibit the dissemination of IR scholarship in business school materials.

At business schools (and also law schools), sessional instructors are employed quite often to teach labor and employment matters. Sessionals, no matter how distinguished, do not usually contribute to the research culture, rarely work on research teams or secure funding from SSHRC and other bodies for research, and seldom encourage their students to embark on academic careers. Waves of retirements of distinguished faculty members have not resulted in a strong new generation of replenishments, and schools that were longstanding IR powerhouses have been gutted. The lure of the low-paid, but highly skilled, sessional instructor is a particular problem. Schools can show that they have no hole in their curriculum; yet they are developing a yawning emptiness at their intellectual heart. There is no current shortage of people with technocratic skills, but there is a dearth of thinkers who produce the books and articles that sessionals rely upon for their instructional materials. It has been my experience that sessional instructors can bring tremendous joviality and practical knowledge to a department, but not much scholarly vitality. They are colleagues but not really equals in the production of scholarship that disseminates beyond their wonderfully incisive classes. The most successful of them occasionally produce textbooks that compile and distill other scholarly work.

ABANDON SHIP OR INFILTRATE?

The situation I have outlined is not one that would give rise to optimism. It might be gratifying – temporarily – to consider simply abandoning the business schools and moving the field to more fertile grounds, such as labor studies programs in faculties of arts. This would be a major mistake, in my view. IR does not take place in academic life; it takes place in the world of employment. Managers are a powerful force there; if we abandon business schools, their lack of knowledge of (and respect for) IR will play out badly.

Ultimately, here is the problem. Many of us are in business schools. Institutional forces that have resulted in the marginalization of our field drive these schools. These forces are the competitive drive for rankings according to externally driven benchmarking systems that exclude our journals, notwithstanding respectable citation rates and distinguished histories. Scoring systems give virtually no recognition for books or book chapters, even ones that represent important contributions, and offer little respect for the town–gown interactions that are at the heart of our nuts-and-bolts, problem-solving field. In other words, many of the ways we define ourselves and our field are excluded from the business school narrative. The result is that IR faculty and courses are at the periphery and lose out in the competition for resources, course development, and those all-important faculty slots. It is not that anyone within business schools is making a conscious or deliberate decision driven by animus against our field (although examples certainly may exist), but rather, in the race for reputation, our energies are not viewed as significant contributions and hence we have become irrelevant. Most of us are benignly tolerated, and a perhaps a disproportionate number of us IR types even become senior administrators (in the very enterprises that ignore our field) because our pluralistic tradition makes us good managers and gives us skills in resolving disputes. Unfortunately, our academic field is not celebrated, cultivated, or nurtured.

In conclusion, we ought to be nervous indeed. While we might be jittery at the Zeitgeist of business schools, the reality is that the forces described in this chapter are accelerating. Easy information technology certainly supports the 'glory and tyranny' of citation impact counting (Leung, 2007). The embedding of institutional assaults of the magnitude described in this chapter requires concerted countermeasures. If we are to place IR scholars into business schools – and this is itself merits it own freestanding debate (e.g. Pfeffer and Fong, 2002; Mintzberg, 1996; Leavitt, 1989) – then surely we ought to be addressing the challenges head-on.

Rather than individually navel-gazing about our past and current victories, we ought to be taking collective action of our own to promote long-term and stable new funding for chairs, professorships, and junior scholar hiring in business schools. Without faculty positions, we cannot have much of an academic field. At one time, it was Rockefeller money that kick-started and sustained many important industrial relations initiatives in universities. The field of IR ought not to turn its back on such funding. Business schools routinely make solicitations for massive donations; there is no shame in 'the ask'. Today the Alfred P. Sloan Foundation is making its mark through its Standard of Living and Economic Performance initiative, which has funded a number of lively industry study programs. There is much to be admired about the provision of long-term, stable funding directed at rescuing IR and ensuring it is integrated into business school offerings. Specific initiatives aimed at soliciting funds earmarked for this entrenchment of IR ought to be investigated, developed and applauded.

We also ought to pay a lot of attention to the perhaps distasteful though pragmatic task of repositioning our journals so they gain greater prominence in the numbers game that business schools play these days. We also should be training our future scholars to celebrate the toolkit of our field and its deep intellectual roots by developing rigorous research that cracks the difficult review process of top management journals. Given that half the colleagues in our field live in the business school setting, it would be foolhardy to ignore the norms and practices that have developed inside this venue.

NOTES

1. Canadian figures from 'Fact Sheet on Unionization,' *Perspectives on Labour and Income*, Statistics Canada. August 2005. US figures from Bureau of Labor Statistics. The US figures are from the 2005 information provided by the Bureau of Labor Statistics. Alberta is Canada's lowest density province, with 21.8 percent membership and 23.7 percent coverage. New York is the highest density state, at 26.1 percent membership.

2. My experience as associate dean of the Haskayne School of Business from 2001 to 2004 helped me gain many of these insights. I also discussed the pressures on IR with senior administrators in other business schools during these years, so I am not simply describing my own School. However, I probably am not representing Canada's community colleges or lesser-ranked business schools, and I am certainly not portraying the situation of IR in Quebec (although Quebec business school professors may face similar pressures to their English–Canadian colleagues).

3. Union decline is an important element that explains US IR academia's current wasting disease. In a roundabout way, it spills over onto Canadian soil, but the relationship is not as direct as in the US. Canada's density is 30 percent and, though there has been a decline over the past two decades, it is much slower than in the US.

4. This counting is based on a rough tally using the CIRA website listing of members. The allocation into business schools versus other venues was based on how the members identified themselves or their e-mail address location.

5. Accredited schools in Canada, in order from the earliest to be accredited to the most recent, are: University of Alberta, University of Calgary, University of British Columbia, Simon Fraser University, University of Manitoba, Memorial, Dalhousie, Saint Mary's, Brock, McMaster, Ottawa, Queen's, University of Toronto, Wilfred Laurier, Concordia, HEC Montreal and Laval.

6. There has been a more recent development in using the ranking methodologies to assess Executive MBA programs as well as the full-time MBA programs.

7. Note that Canada has wholeheartedly embraced the ranking game through deference to the *Maclean's University Rankings* (http://www.macleans.ca/universities/). *Maclean's* assesses universities as a whole rather than simply business schools within them. The *Maclean's* rankings definitely thrill top-scored schools (which celebrate high scores) and

chill those at the bottom of the list (whose presidents predictably scramble to provide criticisms of the ranking methodology). Another benchmarking effort is the Economist Intelligence Unit's 'Which MBA?' which concentrates more on student expectations and experiences and omits the business schools' research output.

8. This malleability is also possible in AACSB accreditation, and in every measurement system I've ever encountered. There is a lot of research on how we have to be careful about what we measure because organizations will take extraordinary steps to achieve successes by subverting the measurement system. Benchmarking has unintended consequences; the weakening of IR is only one of many of these perversities.

9. Most Canadian schools have pegged their tuition rates to levels most comparable to the in-state tuition of US state schools. Even the top-ranked University of Toronto and the well-known McGill University have tuition that is about the same as other major Canadian schools. Even medical degrees are considered a bargain at top Canadian schools. Business schools have broken away from this tuition uniformity by charging high rates for executive programs and by boosting tuition differentials for regular degree programs as well.

10. I was director of the PhD program from 2001 to 2003, and interviewed somewhere between 30 and 50 international students to determine how they came to select our business school.

11. Of course this pressure can create conformity among top journal article submissions, and prevent novel approaches from being published. As Starbuck put it in his analysis (2005, p. 180), 'there is much overlap in articles in different prestige strata. Indeed, theory implies that about half of the articles published are not among the best ones submitted to those journals, and some of the manuscripts that belong in the highest-value 20% have the misfortune to elicit rejections from as many as five journals.'

12. *ILR Review*, *Industrial Relations*, and a few other IR journals, have a long and distinguished track record. Historically, their impact and citation scores (on the ISI-web of science, used to measure journal strength) exceeded many of the newer and weaker journals on the FT list. By any measure of excellence, a case could have been made for at least one IR journal's inclusion on the list. However, the domination of US business schools, with their declining attention to union–management matters, meant that there were few champions of IR journals and they likely received insufficient nominations. From within the FT list, IR scholars would be most comfortable submitting their work to journals numbered 13 to 20, plus a few more depending on the topic. Diverting IR articles to the FT list results in a bit of a tradeoff: the visibility within the IR field is reduced, but the rewards within business schools are enhanced.

13. Thankfully, IR still is represented on the management committee that reviews most SSHRC applications coming out of business schools. I was one of two IR scholars on the committee in its 2006 round. I can write, with confidence, that publishing a single paper in a top-ranked journal does result in an appreciably higher research track record score than publishing a number of articles in 'obscure' journals.

REFERENCES

Bickerstaffe, George and Ridgers, Bill (2007), 'Ranking of business schools,' *Journal of Management Development*, **25** (1), 61–6.

DeAngelo, Harry, DeAngelo, Linda and Zimmerman, Jerold L. (2005), 'What's really wrong with US business schools?' working paper, SSRN, available at http://ssrn.com/abstract=766404.

Gioia, D and Corley, K. (2002), 'Being good versus looking good: Business school rankings and the circean transformation from substance to image,' *Academy of Management Learning and Education*, **1** (1), 107–20.

Ilgen, Daniel R. (2007), 'Citations to management articles: Cautions for the science about advice for the scientist,' *Academy of Management Journal*, **50** (3), 507–9.

Judge, Timothy A., Cable, Daniel M., Colbert, Amy E. and Rynes, Sara L. (2007), 'What causes a management article to be cited – article, author, or journal?' *Academy of Management Journal*, **50** (3), 491–506.

Kaufman, Bruce (2004), *The Global Evolution of Industrial Relations*, Geneva: ILO.

Leavitt, Harold J. (1989), 'Educating our MBAs: On teaching what we haven't taught,' *California Management Review*, **31** (3), 38–50.

Leung, Kwok (2007), 'The glory and tyranny of citation impact: an East Asian perspective,' *Academy of Management Journal*, **50** (3), 510–13.

Mintzberg, Henry (1996), 'Ten ideas designed to rile everyone who cares about management,' *Harvard Business Review*, July–August, 61–8.

Monastersky, Richard (2005), 'The number that's devouring science,' *Chronicle of Higher Education*, **52** (8), A12.

Pfeffer, Jeffrey and Fong, Christina T. (2002), 'The end of business schools? Less success than meets the eye,' *Academy of Management Learning and Education* **1** (1), 78–95.

Safón, Vincente (2007), 'Factors that influence recruiters' choice of B-schools and their MBA graduates: Evidence and implications for B-schools,' *Academy of Management Learning & Education*, **6** (2), 217–33.

Starbuck, William H. (2005), 'How much better are the most-prestigious journals? The statistics of academic publication,' *Organizational Science*, **16** (2), 180–200.

APPENDIX: SELECTED JOURNAL CITATION
IMPACT SCORES, ISI WEB OF SCIENCE 2002–6

ISI (which stands for Institute for Scientific Information, now a part of Thomson Scientific) produces Journal Citation Reports, an accumulation and tabulation of citation and article counts for over 7600 journals. According to the ISI, the impact factor 'identifies the frequency with which an average article from a journal is cited in a particular year.' There are other measures that could be used, including the cited half-life and the total cites, but the impact factor tends to standardize the citation scores on a per-article basis and so is likely the best measure within the ISI menu.

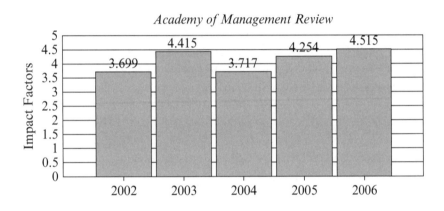

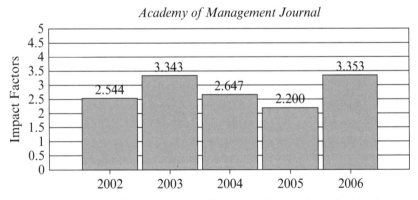

Figure 7A.1   Journal citation scores for selected journals ranked by the
Financial Times

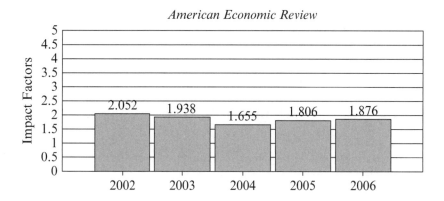

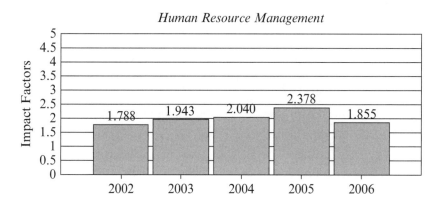

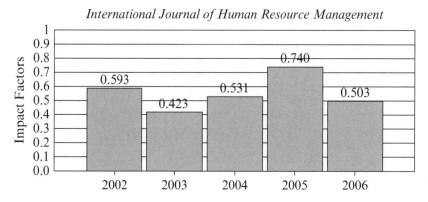

Figure 7A.1   (continued)

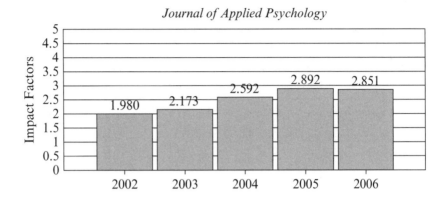

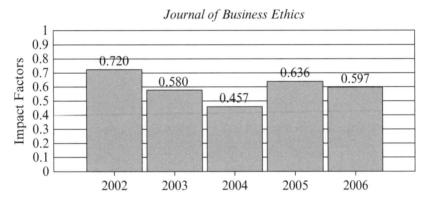

Figure 7A.1   (continued)

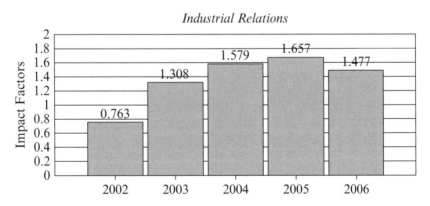

Figure 7A.2   Journal citation scores for selected industrial relations journals

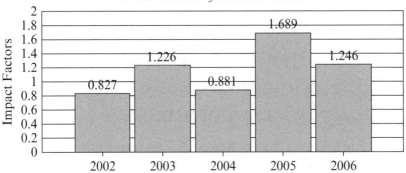

British Journal of Industrial Relations

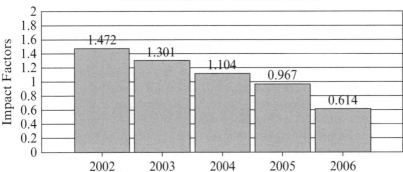

Industrial and Labor Relations Review

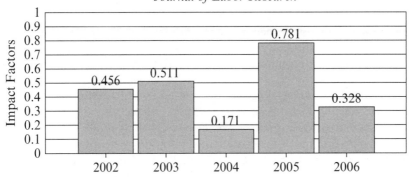

Journal of Labor Research

Figure 7A.2 (continued)

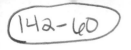

8. Let a thousand journals bloom: the precarious landscape of labor and employment publishing

Immanuel Ness, Bruce Nissen and Charles J. Whalen

INTRODUCTION

On the surface, recent trends in the publication of labor and employment journals aimed at academics, practitioners and activists seem to belie the widespread concern that the industrial relations field – regardless of whether one defines it narrowly to include only union-management relations or more broadly to include all aspects of work and employment – is in crisis. Online access to journals and consolidation in the publishing industry mean that today's labor publications are, overall, reaching more readers, resting on a more secure financial footing, and producing higher-quality products than in the past few decades. Moreover, the evolution of the study of labor and employment over the past few decades has resulted in a proliferation of journals.

A closer look, however, reveals a more precarious landscape. The study of work and employment is becoming less its own interdisciplinary area and more a specialty field within traditional academic disciplines. There may be more journals, but there is a downside to this fragmentation, especially for those interested in the resolution of society's labor problems. Corporate publishing also brings risks along with rewards. It can put financial pressure on libraries and editorial boards, and is susceptible to political influence.

This chapter surveys and assesses the labor and employment journal terrain. The authors are US-based editors and the chapter, divided into three sections, focuses primarily on labor publishing in the United States. The first section traces the evolution of publishing in the labor field since the late 1800s. The second section, which identifies specific journals as 'case studies,' focuses on the recent trends of corporate consolidation and electronic publishing. The final section looks ahead and considers what would be ideal as well as what is more readily attainable, a distinction that strikes us as essential to shaping the journal realm in a way that helps revitalize the study of labor and employment as an academic enterprise.[1]

DISCIPLINARY FRAGMENTATION: AN HISTORICAL PERSPECTIVE

In the past decade, labor journal publishing has seen the emergence and vast expansion of corporate and electronic publishing. To succeed in the world of electronic publishing, it is often necessary for labor journals to depend on the clout of large publishers to produce, print, market and distribute their product, especially to academic libraries and other institutional subscribers. Corporations are rapidly acquiring these publications, and even financially sound journals are attracted to such publishers by the chance to expand their circulation and reach a larger audience.

While corporate consolidation and electronic publishing may be the most prominent developments in labor and employment journals in the last decade, they are not the only changes or publishing issues of concern to these journal editors and readers. The labor literature is also in the midst of a major shift in emphasis – it is increasingly the product of a subfield within traditional disciplines – as a result of the evolution of labor and employment studies. This section examines that evolution and its implications for journals and for work-oriented scholarship as an academic enterprise.

From Labor Problems to Management Dominance

After the Civil War, the study of 'labor problems' in the United States was an element of the broader study of social problems and within purview of scholars teaching moral philosophy and social science. In the late 1800s, however, Richard T. Ely and other reform-minded economists moved the study of labor into economics departments. At first, this research was published in collections such as *Studies in Historical and Political Science*, a series produced by Johns Hopkins University. Soon thereafter, though, professional journals such as the *Quarterly Journal of Economics*, the *Journal of Political Economy*, and the *American Economic Review* became the preferred place to publish on labor and other practical socioeconomic problems (McNulty, 1984: 131–6).

Over time, however, the central thrust of US economics drifted away from practical problems and toward construction of theories rooted in the assumption that market-based economic systems are self-regulating. As a result, economists interested in labor problems met at the annual meetings of the American Economic Association in the mid-1940s and formed the Industrial Relations Research Association (IRRA). 'We first met as rebels,' recalls Clark Kerr of the University of California, Berkeley, one of the group's founders (Labor and Employment Relations Association, undated). The postwar enthusiasm of these dissenters from economic orthodoxy led not only to creation of the IRRA, but also to the establishment of numerous academic units of industrial relations (at Cornell University, the University of Minnesota, and the University of Illinois, for example) and to the publication of journals such as the *Industrial and Labor Relations Review* (*ILR Review*) and *Industrial Relations: A Journal of Economy and Society* (*IR:JES*).

For the first 25 years after World War II, the labor issues that received the most academic and media attention involved collective bargaining and other aspects of union–management relations. This trend was reflected in the literature's widespread use of the term 'industrial relations' and the near disappearance of the 'labor problems' moniker. The *ILR Review*, *IR:JES* and other academic journals reflected the focus of this era by devoting the bulk of their space to the study of issues such as strikes, the negotiation of wages, labor law, and the resolution of labor–management disputes. Industrial relations programs and journals may have been created and staffed by dissenters from economic orthodoxy, but these entities were solidly neutral on labor–management matters.

In addition to industrial relations programs, campus-based 'labor studies' programs began to appear on the scene in a regular way shortly after World War II (isolated programs existed even earlier at the University of Wisconsin, Bryn Mawr College, and elsewhere). Unlike industrial relations as defined in the early postwar era, the field of labor studies does not aim for neutrality between employers and employees. Just as departments of management in business schools research and teach how to manage employees, labor studies centers and programs research and teach workers and their representatives how to deal (usually collectively) with management. Thus, labor studies as a field aims to pragmatically train union leaders and activists in the skills needed to bargain and administer a contract and to conduct a labor organization's administrative and political affairs. It also educates workers and union leaders to think strategically and critically about how to empower workers and their organizations (primarily unions) in the broader society. While labor studies and postwar industrial relations obviously share much common ground, their orientations are distinctive.

Labor studies programs blossomed in the 1970s in the wake of the Civil Rights movement and other social movements of the 1960s and early 1970s. At that time, labor studies reflected university trends toward interdisciplinary studies and community outreach, and often involved leadership development programs, certificate programs and courses designed for workers, union leaders and community activists. The result was creation of new academic units, including the Center for Labor Studies at Empire State College (established in 1971), which serves adult learners across New York, the Center for Labor Education and Research at the University of Alabama at Birmingham (1972), and the City University Centers for Worker Education (first established in 1981). Labor extension programs offered by Cornell and other universities with industrial relations units also expanded in this period.

Academic and practitioner interest in the area of labor studies, and the social movements that nurtured its expansion, led to establishment of a number of journals covering labor and the working class, such as *Labor Studies Journal (LSJ)*. Important labor debates were also often published in journals such as *New Left Review* and *Politics and Society*. While, many of the publications created in that era were discontinued when the movements declined, *LSJ* and *Working USA: The Journal of Labor and Society* continue to embody that period's emphasis on promoting labor-oriented discussions across many disciplines and among scholars, union leaders, and activists.

In the past few decades, two interrelated trends have dramatically reshaped the field of labor and employment studies and threatened the existence of both 'industrial relations' (narrowly defined) and 'labor studies.' One is that the number and size of these interdisciplinary centers have dwindled. Industrial relations programs were closed, for example, at Columbia University, the University of Chicago, and the University of Wisconsin, the latter of which was long a major center of labor and employment teaching and scholarship. Still others have been renamed to include the words 'human resources' or 'employment relations' in their title, and have been transformed into programs with a management focus.

Labor studies programs have also experienced funding cutbacks and the threat of being shuttered, including, most recently, those at Indiana University, the University of Missouri at Kansas City, and the University of California. A 2003 study found that the labor studies field held its own in the 1990s, but only because of enormous growth in one state (California); overall, the number and size of programs was stagnant or declining (Byrd and Nissen, 2003). Since that time, there has been a worsening of this trend, both in terms of program closures and cutbacks in existing ones. To some extent, labor studies programs have been under even more pressure than industrial relations units because the former are so closely associated with the labor movement and a pro-worker perspective.

The other trend reshaping the labor field is the emergence of business schools as the primary home of work and employment studies. These schools have often attracted students and faculty away from other university programs and into departments such as human-resource management, organizational behavior and occupational (or industrial) psychology (Kaufman, 1993: 143–8). Many of these students and professors have in recent years become members of the Academy of Management (AOM) and its large Human Resources Division, which functions as a specialty society. That division alone – one of over two-dozen AOM segments – contains more members than the Labor and Employment Relations Association (LERA, the successor to IRRA) and vastly more members than the United Association for Labor Education (UALE).[2]

Journals have been greatly affected by the migration of employment-related studies to business schools. This migration has fueled the explosion of academic and practitioner journals dealing with employment issues, including many with an international flavor (these include the *Journal of Occupational and Organizational Psychology*, *The International Journal of Human Resource Management* and *Human Resource Management*). It has also introduced a change in perspective: human-resource journals are overwhelmingly published from the perspective of management and are generally perceived as biased against unions and the labor movement. The migration – and the erosion of union membership in the United States – has even affected long-established industrial-relations journals such as the *ILR Review*, which do not exhibit such a bias and usually treat unions as being on an equal playing field with management; in the past decade or so, these journals have given increasing attention to human-resource management as well as to the study of non-union employment relations.

The Hollowing Out of Industrial Relations

The rise of the study of employment within business schools and the decline of academic units of industrial relations and labor studies point to a fundamental shift in the academic enterprise surrounding work and labor issues. The study of labor and employment has, in recent decades, increasingly come to be viewed as a subfield or specialty area within standard academic disciplines. It is no longer widely seen as its own interdisciplinary realm (and it has rarely been treated as an integral part of economics, political science, sociology or other disciplines).

The result is an inconsistency between surface appearances and underlying reality. On the surface, one sees a proliferation of journals, most of which are less than 40 years old. In addition to those mentioned above, current specialized journals on labor and employment include, for instance, the *Journal of Labor Economics*, *Labor History* and *Work and Occupations*, each tied to a specialty field within a major academic discipline (economics, history, and occupational sociology, respectively).

Beneath the surface, however, is both what Bruce E. Kaufman (2004: 335) calls the 'hollowing out' of industrial relations and the severe marginalization of labor studies within the academy. To the extent that the most prestigious industrial relations journals are different from management journals, it is largely because they have become convenient outlets for articles by neoclassical labor economists and others who do not consider themselves part of the academic industrial relations community.[3] Combine that with the decline in the study of collective bargaining and union–management disputes – largely a result of the diminished and weakened role of organized labor in the United States – and the departure of much human resource management scholarship from industrial relations centers (and LERA) to business schools (and organizations such as AOM), and one must begin to doubt whether industrial relations can survive as a distinct scholarly community.[4] The survival of the labor studies field is even more doubtful, since it is almost entirely defined by union-oriented scholarship and education.

In other words, while one can look across a wide range of disciplines and see many specialty journals devoted to particular aspects of work and employment, this fragmentation is in large measure a symptom of the weakness of industrial relations and decline of labor studies, not a sign of strength. The fragmentation makes having a coherent community of labor scholars almost impossible. Moreover, as one of many possible specialty fields within a broader discipline (economics, sociology and the like), labor scholarship has become marginalized within standard academic areas of instruction.[5]

Indeed, within conventional disciplines the marginalization of labor and employment scholarship has become so serious that many academics see little reward for publishing in even the most respected journals in this specialty. That is because within many academic departments there is little prestige associated with publishing in even the best labor journals. For instance, the *Financial Times*' international list of the top 40 business journals contains no labor and employment journals.[6] Thus, scholars conducting labor and employment research – even those working in a conventional business area such as human-resource management – may not contribute much to business-school benchmarking, which means they risk not being recruited or rewarded by business schools unless they can publish beyond labor journals.

Science Building versus Problem Solving

The fragmentation of labor and employment-relations scholarship (and the associated decline of industrial relations and labor studies academic programs) is especially troubling to those interested in contributing to the resolution of contemporary labor problems. Since real-world problems do not confine themselves neatly to the boundaries of academic disciplines, an academic enterprise interested in problem solving as well as science building requires interdisciplinary terrain. The fragmentation of labor scholarship has moved us in the other direction.

Early scholars in the labor area may have often focused a bit too much on problem solving at the expense of science building, but, rather than find a better way to pursue both ends simultaneously, the dominant trend since the 1970s has been to pursue science building at the expense of problem solving (Kaufman, 2004: 609). The most secure path to tenure and promotion for most of today's academics involves restricting analyses to one dimension of a social phenomenon. There is considerably more professional risk associated with striving to understand a problem across disciplines and seeking to offer recommendations for institutional change and public policy reform.

Despite the many journals that currently exist as publishing outlets for labor and employment scholarship, most are tightly focused in a way that reinforces the current emphasis on science building and the neglect of problem solving. Publishing options for problem-oriented labor scholars are further constrained because the top-ranked labor journals are widely perceived to privilege articles that emphasize quantitative methods over historical and institutional analyses and that steer clear of radical perspectives. Some journals, including *WorkingUSA: The Journal of Labor and Society* and the Canadian *Labour/Le Travail* have recently aimed to produce a well-ranked publication and remain receptive to a wide range of methods and perspectives on labor and the working class. These are exceptions, however, and their ability to succeed is not yet certain.[7]

RECENT TRENDS IN LABOR JOURNAL PUBLISHING

Until recently, four types of labor and employment journals shared the market: association journals, independent journals, publications of academic institutions and other small publishers, and the journals of large publishing companies that own the rights to numerous periodicals. The growth of electronic media and consolidation in the publishing industry, however, is tilting the terrain in favor of large corporations.

Today, journals are increasingly read in electronic form and are rarely published without a corporate or large university intermediary, which can offer many journals as a package and can raise electronic subscription fees when adding to its catalog of related publications. In the United States, for example, Wiley-Blackwell and SAGE seem to be taking hold of a large number of labor journals.[8] The publications that corporations distribute electronically have the potential to reach a much larger – and more international – audience than ever before.[9]

Association Journals and Independent Publications

Professional societies and associations have long created journals to keep members up to date in specific areas of study. For example, the University and College Labor Education Association (UCLEA) and its successor, the UALE, have published *LSJ* for over 32 years. In 1974, UCLEA was formed as an association of postsecondary professors and labor-studies instructors. In the year 2000, the organization merged with a non-academic labor education association (Workers Education Local 189) and changed its name to UALE to reflect it broadened membership. The majority of today's UALE members are university-based labor educators and labor studies faculty, but the organization includes union- and community-based worker educators and a few labor-oriented faculty members in traditional academic departments such as sociology and political science.

LSJ is a multidisciplinary quarterly journal publishing double blind peer-reviewed articles on work, workers, unions and worker organizations, labor studies, and worker education. In the mid-1990s, a shift in leadership within the AFL-CIO sparked new interest in the *LSJ* and UALE among labor activists as well as educators. Most articles published in *LSJ* concern unions and labor movements, primarily within the United States although increasingly in other countries as well. Other issues concerning work and working class life also appear in the journal, but the labor movement is a clear focus. The general orientation of most articles is pro-union and favorable to the role that a labor movement plays in society, although within that general perspective numerous criticisms of unions and the overall labor movement are given.

UALE provides a copy of *LSJ* to each of its approximately 400 members. The journal also relies on library subscriptions. In a reflection of the dynamic nature of contemporary publishing and the increasing role and influence of big companies, three different organizations have published the journal since 1999: Transaction Periodicals Consortium (Rutgers University), West Virginia University Press, and (beginning in 2007) SAGE, a large corporate journal publisher. While *LSJ* has had a wide distribution through the Internet via Project Muse (a subscription-based online database of nonprofit journals, established by the Johns Hopkins University Press), SAGE will likely expand the journal's readership.[10]

Another association journal is *Perspectives on Work* (*POW*), produced and published by the LERA. Founded in 1947 as the IRRA and dedicated to promoting research and dialogue on all aspects of employment, LERA acquired its current name in 2005. The organization claims approximately 3000 members, including academics and practitioners. In addition to educators, LERA welcomes all stakeholders in the employment relationship – including union officials, management and human-resource professionals, third-party neutrals, government policymakers, and worker advocates.

POW was inaugurated in 1997 as part of IRRA's commemoration of its fiftieth anniversary. Over the last decade, *POW* has become a leading barometer on the state of labor–management relations and the crucial issues faced by workers and human-resource managers. Recent issues have addressed topics such as workplace bullying, the emerging skills shortage in the aerospace industry, whistle-blower job protections, and the erosion of retiree health benefits. *POW* regularly devotes attention to global concerns and to employment relations outside the United States. It also presents a range of views on policy issues such as trade, labor law and immigration.

While *POW* accepts unsolicited manuscripts, an editorial board of scholars and practitioners commissions most articles featured in its semi-annual print editions. Until recently, members of the editorial board evaluated all manuscripts. Since early 2006, however, the journal has experimented with a double-blind review process involving a wider group of academic and practitioner readers.

POW is unusual in the current era in that it is distributed by LERA without the aid of a corporate publisher. The clear trend is for association journals to be transferred to large corporations as a way to benefit from economies of scale, skilled library marketing arms, and electronic distribution networks. In contrast, LERA's small office staff coordinates *POW* distribution and the journal's editorship has been handled as a service commitment by a number of LERA members (production and printing is done as contract work by the University of Illinois Press). Still, the financial strain of falling LERA membership is causing the association to reevaluate *POW* along with the rest of the association's products and services. For example, there has been some discussion about the possibility of producing only one *POW* issue per year and/or moving to an all-electronic format (in addition to the print journal, two small Internet editions have been published each year since 2005).

Even with the challenges facing LERA and other association publishers, the situation is often more difficult for labor journals unaffiliated with professional societies. Most independent labor journals that reach their audience via print editions are declining in readership and face a significant risk of corporate takeover or closure. Even the most prodigious independents must continuously seek new subscribers every year as about 30 percent of individual subscriptions are not renewed. Moreover, these journals are at a significant disadvantage relative to corporate publishers because they have very limited ability to reach out to libraries and find new market niches. In 1996, for example, the highly regarded journal *Labor Research Review* (*LRR*) discontinued publication due to a lack of resources.[11]

LRR, established in 1982 by the nonprofit Midwest Center for Labor Research (now the Center for Labor and Community Research), provided thematic issues on topics ranging from union organizing to regional strategies for dealing with deindustrialization. It had a knack for focusing on the latest labor movement developments and was widely read by union leaders and labor scholars. However, despite its influence in the labor movement and the labor-studies community, *LRR* had few institutional subscribers and was constantly under pressure to raise money to cover editorial, production and distribution expenses. Designed as a semi-annual journal, *LRR* published only 23 issues in 15 years, most edited by Jack Metzgar of Roosevelt University.

From Small Publishers to Large Corporate Publishing

The *LRR* was discontinued in the middle of a volume year just as organized labor seemed primed for an upsurge after the 1995 election of John Sweeney as president of the AFL-CIO. In 1997, two new labor journals began publishing and offered to honor *LRR* subscriptions; *New Labor Forum* (*NLF*) and *Working USA* (*WUSA*) were both aimed at an audience of worker-oriented and progressive readers. The publishers and editors of *NLF* and *WUSA* considered the planned revitalization of the AFL-CIO to be a sign that organized labor in the United States was recovering from the doldrums of the previous two decades.

During their first three years, the similarities of the two publications outweighed their differences. Articles written by leading authors in the labor field (who often drew on the latest labor literature and their own book projects) were organized into regular departments and addressed popular issues. Indeed, one of the most significant differences from 1997 to 2000 was that *WUSA* published six issues per volume annually, while each semi-annual issue of *NLF* was considered a volume in itself. Another difference is that the for-profit M.E. Sharpe Inc. published *WUSA*, while *NLF* was published by the Queens College Labor Resource Center in New York City.

In the year 2000, Sharpe, which publishes several journals, decided to transform *WUSA* from a glossy, magazine-style publication into a traditional, peer-reviewed journal. To cut costs and appeal to university libraries, the publisher initiated a shift in editorial direction and moved toward a plain appearance mirroring *Challenge*, the company's leading economic journal. *WUSA* became a quarterly with a large and active editorial board, and the journal's name was expanded to *WorkingUSA: The Journal of Labor and Society*.

In 2004, *WUSA* migrated from Sharpe to Blackwell Publishing, now Wiley-Blackwell, one of the world's largest journal publishers. *WUSA* maintains a double-blind review process and relies entirely on unsolicited articles. The Wiley-Blackwell company steadfastly grants the journal's board editorial autonomy and has agreed to the editorial board's request that *WUSA* be made available at a low cost (and in some cases no cost) in the global South. As a result, the journal reaches a wider audience than in the past. Moreover, a crucial factor in the journal's shift to Blackwell is the publisher's vast reach through Synergy, its online library consortium program. The merger of Blackwell with Wiley will further expand the journal's readership.

The scope of *WUSA* is also broader than ever. It still addresses issues involving the US labor movement, but the journal also examines – from a multidisciplinary perspective – the working class more broadly. *WUSA* also now covers international labor issues to a far greater extent than in the past. Not reliant on labor-movement funding, it can and does publish articles with positions that are openly critical of labor organizations.

In contrast, *NLF* maintains an appealing cover that changes with each issue. (It is now published three times per year, but has plans to publish four times a year in the near future.) *NLF* has regularly included special sections on labor arts and poetry and has featured photographs and other types of artwork. Many of its articles are opinion pieces that do not have to conform to the 'scholarly research' orientation demanded by most strictly scholarly journals. By means of appearance and content, it seeks to appeal to worker and community activists as well as to academics and labor leaders.

NLF does not have a peer-review process. Instead, it edits articles and submissions through its in-house editorial staff. While unsolicited submissions are permitted, the journal typically seeks out leading practitioners and academics write essays on topics that the editors identify as relevant to workers and organized labor. In 2005, *NLF* shifted production and distribution to Taylor & Francis, a large corporate publisher of periodicals. Another change is the relocation of *NLF* from Queens College of the City University of New York (CUNY) to the newly created Joseph S. Murphy Institute for Labor, Community, and Policy Studies, a partnership between organized labor and the CUNY School of Professional Studies.

Electronic publishing and corporate consolidation have even affected the two leading, university-sponsored journals of labor–management relations in the United States, *ILR Review* and *IR:JES*. Both of these journals are quarterly, refereed and interdisciplinary publications geared to the academic community. In January 2007, the editor of the *ILR Review*, which has been produced by the Cornell University School of Industrial and Labor Relations since 1947, reported that although print subscriptions had fallen by 40 percent in the previous eight years, the journal's readership has risen significantly and its overall revenue has remained stable due to royalties received from its inclusion in the electronic databases of EBSCO (www.epnet.com) and JSTOR (www.jstor.com) (Hammer, 2007). Meanwhile, *IR:JES* – published since 1961 by the Institute of Industrial Relations at the University of California, Berkeley – is printed and distributed by Wiley-Blackwell, which makes it available online through the Synergy system.[12]

Financial Stability and Academic Excellence

No journal can avoid the financial facts of life. Money is required to produce, distribute and even market a journal. Independent and association journals have often had to rely on donations from editorial board members or subscribers to provide funding during periods of economic difficulty. Indeed, appeals for such donations have sometimes become necessary on a regular basis. For example, LERA, the publisher of *POW*, depends on funds raised by offering premium-level memberships that enable donors to take a tax deduction for their contributions.

The expansion of corporate publishing has lessened the need for private donors and contributed to greater financial stability in the journal world. Even if a corporate journal loses individual subscribers during a pronounced recessionary period, it can usually expect to maintain its electronic presence through libraries and consortia agreements. The opportunity to partner with a large corporate publisher has enabled many labor and employment journals to continue operating. Thus, corporate publishing frees editorial boards from the possibility that large donors will seek to influence journal content.

Corporate control has also often enhanced journal quality. This is because publishers expect consistency and often press for rigor in scholarship. Large publishers want their publications to appear on a regular basis and on time. They view a failure to make deadlines as potentially damaging to their reputation.

Scholarly rigor is important because it helps attract library subscriptions and because professors must publish in peer-refereed academic journals to maintain an academic career. (Indeed, this is a reason why LERA's *POW* has been experimenting with a referee process.) To this end, corporate publishers usually press for an editorial policy including a blind manuscript review process. They also often seek ranking by the Thomson Scientific Journal Citation Reports – the leading service rating journals on the basis of scholarship, importance and quality. A journal's high ranking, widely regarded as a mark of academic excellence, can be more important to libraries and academics than its circulation.[13]

The Risks of Corporate Publishing

Despite the aforementioned benefits of large, corporate publishing, it should be noted that such publishing is not a cure-all for academic journals on labor and employment. For example, the system puts new pressures on libraries. Rather than choose specific labor journals across a range of publishers, the high cost of corporations' electronic subscription packages means that budget-constrained labor librarians are under pressure to select publishers with the largest number of journals. Journal editors might also feel economic pressure from publishers, such as the pressure to produce more issues per year so a publisher can increase subscription rates.[14]

Corporate journal publishing also reinforces the marginalization of the study of labor and employment. Rather than view labor as integral to the study of society and the political economy, the current treatment of labor as a subfield within broader academic disciplines means that workers are viewed as one of countless interest groups and many factors in the production process (in the latter case, for example, labor is just one factor alongside – and often seen as subordinate to – management, physical inputs, technology, finance and the institutional features of business enterprises). Corporate academic publishing contributes to this marginalization by bundling journals according to broad disciplinary categories and by encouraging journals to have a distinct focus in harmony with conventional categories.

One must also recognize the possibility that political pressure can be brought to bear on editorial boards by corporate publishers. There have been times in American history when publishers have come under attack for publications with their imprint (cases have even cropped up in the past few years); there is the risk that it can happen again. Labor journals with a left-leaning political stance could be particularly vulnerable. Their editorial boards would then be forced to find new ways to engage in independent publishing or disband.[15]

While a confluence of economic and political considerations has not yet put great strain on labor and employment journals overall, the risks are real just the same; indeed, it is clear that corporate considerations have for decades been contributing to a transformation of both the field that these journals serve and society at large, especially in the United States.[16] To the managers of US companies and many public agencies (especially at the federal level, where steps have been taken to increase managerial discretion and flexibility), 'the labor question' has become a relatively minor issue of concern. Unions have declined precipitously in terms of numbers and influence, and few other types of labor activism have emerged to replace them. Indeed, from the point of view of managers, dealing with human resources in general – beyond the narrower matter of dealing with unions – is often considered just another item associated with running a business (along with purchasing, marketing, and so on), and a relatively unimportant one at that. Thus, labor relations specialists no longer warrant an independent organizational focus and have been marginalized or eliminated, while the 'bean counters' of accounting and finance have acquired central enterprise roles.

Universities are no exception to the influence that corporate values and imperatives have exerted on American society. Their missions and goals are increasingly defined by corporate goals, and the role of their presidents has become analogous to that of a corporate chief executive. As labor becomes evermore marginal to corporate concerns, teaching and scholarship devoted to work and employment undergo a simultaneous devaluation within higher education.

The result of this trend toward the corporate-oriented and 'corporatized' university is, for now and the foreseeable future, low prestige for 'employment relations' and 'human resource management,' marginal status for 'industrial relations,' and the almost total elimination of 'labor studies,' which not only can represent a challenge to the mission of a modern university, but also is rarely capable of generating a solid revenue stream.[17] Indeed, this situation will probably persist until the conventional labor movement begins to be revitalized or a new type of labor movement becomes prominent (or disruptive). In other words, attention to work and employment issues – by professionals within and outside the academy – will likely continue to be minimal in the United States as long as the labor force remains easily managed and the population continues to tolerate the greater workforce insecurity and social inequality that are the consequences of diminishing worker influence and union decline.

LOOKING AHEAD

This chapter has examined labor and employment journals in the United States and found that they are, overall, growing and more secure today than in recent decades. In large part, this is due to the expansion of corporate publishing and development of electronic media services. While most publications without ties to corporate publishing and electronic networks are finding it difficult to stay afloat, those partnering with corporations and using the Internet are reaching more readers and are generally on a more solid financial footing than ever. At the same time, the labor journal terrain is fragmented and corporate publishing entails risks as well as rewards.

Since academic and public discourse benefit most from a publishing landscape that lets 'a thousand journals bloom,' it would be best for a diverse array of labor and employment journals to be published by a variety of professional associations, independent organizations, small academic centers, large universities and corporate publishers. Given the financial and professional constraints facing today's authors, editors, publishers, and libraries, however, it might be more realistic – at least initially – to hope for this literature to offer a range of hybrids that, as a group, achieve a better balance with respect to highly specialized and more inclusive content.

Further corporate expansion in the journal realm could come in two ways. It could involve more consolidation of journal ownership, as societies and non-profit publishers transfer their publications to the industry's large corporations. In late 2002, for example, the nonprofit Tamiment Institute sold *Labor History* to Taylor & Francis. The further expansion could also come in the form of more corporate production, distribution, and marketing partnerships with nonprofits, as in the case of *IR:JES*, produced by the University of California and distributed by Wiley-Blackwell. In today's publishing environment, hybrids forged by such partnerships make sense. It is not likely that a market in which corporations have full control would best serve the scholarly community.

With regard to content, meanwhile, today's labor and employment scholars must devote more attention to producing successful, interdisciplinary journals. The path to solid achievement for interdisciplinary labor journals – and the road to revitalization of industrial relations (in either its narrow or broad sense) as an academic enterprise – cannot be founded upon serving as a second-tier outlet for specialized scholarship. Rather, these journals must be broad in scope, committed to methodological pluralism, open to trans-disciplinary investigations, and accepting of unconventional viewpoints. Most important is that they must be uncompromising in their dedication to problem solving, but still committed to science building. There is certainly no scarcity of real-world labor problems warranting our attention; as Kaufman writes, 'The world of work is more important than ever for peoples and nations across the globe' (Kaufman, 2004: 621). Providing support for the development of refereed, problem-oriented hybrids must be integral to efforts aimed at revitalizing the study of labor and employment.

There is also a longer-term project underway in the world of academic publishing. It seeks to incubate alternatives to the rapidly emerging corporate publishing model. Scholarly Publishing and Academic Resources Coalition (SPARC), an alliance of university and research libraries, is at the forefront of this movement. SPARC is dedicated to reducing journal costs and to enhancing competition in scientific publishing by using electronic technologies to create new forms of scholarly communication. *Labor: Studies in Working-Class History of the Americas*, the first labor journal formed in collaboration with SPARC, had a successful launch that garnered the Council of Editors of Learned Journals' Best New Journal award in 2005.

Another innovative publication worthy of note is *Ephemera: Theory and Politics in Organization*, which has been published by an editorial collective of academics and practitioners since 2001. *Ephemera* is an all-electronic, refereed and interdisciplinary journal devoted to 'developing and extending discussions of critical perspectives on organization' ('What is Ephemera?' undated). It operates on the principle of 'open access,' which means there are no price or permission barriers to reading and distributing the journal's content. While this approach runs counter to conventional notions of copyright ownership and journal funding, pioneers in the open access movement maintain that their alternative is both advantageous to those involved and economically feasible.[18]

It is not yet possible to suggest that a countertrend in labor journal publishing has emerged in reaction to corporate consolidation. Given the current state of labor studies and industrial relations, however, its scholars have little to lose and might have much to gain from experimenting with new publishing models. A world in which a thousand labor journals bloom – and in which the study of labor and employment are revitalized – may not be all that far away after all.[19]

NOTES

1. This chapter offers a thematic survey, not a comprehensive look at all labor and employment journals, which would be impossible in the space available. The authors are editors of *WorkingUSA: The Journal of Labor and Society* (Ness), *Labor Studies Journal* (Nissen) and *Perspectives on Work* (Whalen).
2. See Academy of Management (undated). Another large management-oriented organization in the employment field is the Society for Human Resource Management (SHRM), which is oriented primarily toward practitioners, but includes academics. In fact, in 1996 SHRM established an affiliated research, publications and education foundation that is overseen by a board composed primarily of scholars.
3. In his sweeping history of the labor field, *The Global Evolution of Industrial Relations*, Bruce E. Kaufman states that industrial relations scholarly journals have lost so much of their distinctiveness that today they resemble 'a modestly eclectic second-tier journal in applied labor economics' (Kaufman, 2004: 609).

4. For a similar view based on a study of authorship in industrial relations journals, see Jarley *et al.* (2001).
5. For instance, like the AOM, the American Economic Association recognizes labor as one of around two-dozen specialty fields within economics.
6. See 'FT Top 40 Journals – 2006' (undated). For more on this subject, see Chapter 7 by Daphne Taras in the present volume.
7. Recent labor journal rankings provide some reason for optimism regarding the possibility that broader journals can be successful as measured by citations and professional influence. The *British Journal of Industrial Relations*, which has surpassed American industrial relations and labor journals by some measures, regularly publishes articles with a 'pro-labor' orientation that would most likely be too 'radical' for US journals like *ILRR* or *IR:JES*. Similar articles can be found within the Canadian journal *Relations Industrielles/Industrial Relations* (which appears in the most widely cited rankings) and the well-regarded Australian *Journal of Industrial Relations*.
8. Another large corporate publisher is Elsevier, which publishes the research series *Advances in Industrial and Labor Relations* in addition to journals on labor topics.
9. Journals with individual and library subscribers have long been lucrative operations for publishers. A base of 200 institutional subscribers (paying a premium so that copies are available to students and academics) has traditionally been enough to earn the publisher a healthy return. In the past five years, however, the growth of electronic media and consolidation of the publishing industry has changed this system. The contemporary academic journal industry – not just in the United States, but across the globe – has become much like the cable television industry, in which subscription packages are sold that require viewers to purchase channels they would ordinarily not (or never) watch just to get those they view on a regular basis. An academic library that has maintained a specific journal for many years is now likely to find that the publisher requires it to acquire the electronic rights to a number of journals in a specific subject area or lose access to that journal.
10. Society journals are attractive to corporate publishers because their products usually have a well-defined aim and scope and because society members represent a solid subscriber base.
11. More recently, the global publisher Springer acquired the well-regarded *Journal of Labor Research*, which had been published by the Economics Department of George Mason University and the Locke Institute. (The journal is now produced in association with the John M. Olin Institute at George Mason University.)
12. In April 2007, the Berkeley-based Institute of Industrial Relations changed its name to the Institute for Research on Labor and Employment.
13. Thomson Scientific was, until recently, known as the Institute for Scientific Information (ISI). Journals ranked by ISI have traditionally been considered a cut above most non-ISI journals. (In 2006, ISI ranked 15 labor and industrial relations publications.) Regardless of their content, journals seeking stature in academic circles must abide by the standards set by the indexing services. According to Thomson Scientific, for example, the five critical standards for maintaining academic excellence among labor and employment journals are as follows:

    1. There must be a blind peer review process that unmistakably distinguishes referee articles from commentary or other features.
    2. There must be compelling and scholarly essays that address the most pertinent questions under scholarly scrutiny. Journals cannot just publish one or two labor essays now and then, but must continuously cover the subject of industrial relations and labor as it unfolds.
    3. There must be an active editorial board comprised of leading scholars in the field. It is vital that journals list only scholars who actively participate in the journal.
    4. There must be an international editorial board drawn from both the global North and the global South. It is unacceptable to contend that scholars from the global South are nonexistent. Today, scholars from every continent can be identified in labor and industrial relations.

5. The journal must include full biographical and contact information for all contributors of articles, reviews, or commentaries (including postal address, telephone, and e-mail).

14. Alleging that its new corporate publisher engaged in 'business interference' and wanted more issues per year (in order to raise subscription rates), the entire editorial staff of *Labor History* resigned in 2003 and created a new journal, *Labor: Studies in Working-Class History of the Americas*. (*Labor History* was previously owned by an independent foundation.) The new publication is now the official journal of the Labor and Working-Class History Association (established in 2000) and is published by the nonprofit Duke University Press (see Smallwood and Glenn, 2003 and McLemee and Byrne, 2003).

15. For a discussion of how political pressure has exerted itself on pro-worker, non-academic publications in the United States, see Martin (2004: 57–63). There is no reason to believe today's trend toward corporate publishing of academic journals comes in a form that will keep these publications free from similar pressure at all times.

16. For a discussion of the post-World War II spread of corporate influence in US society that is still relevant despite having been written nearly two decades ago, see Dugger (1989).

17. As Kent Wong and Janna Shadduck-Hernández state in Chapter 12 of this volume, there may currently be a nationwide emphasis on the establishment of university–community partnerships and the development of opportunities for service learning, but educational programs that pursue those ends by means of social-justice and critical pedagogical perspectives often meet stiff resistance.

18. For details on open access publishing, see Suber (2007).

19. The authors thank David Jacobs, Daphne Taras, and David Zalewski for refereeing this chapter. They also acknowledge comments and suggestions provided by Linda Whalen.

REFERENCES

Academy of Management (Undated), 'Divisions and Interest Groups,' http://www.aomonline.org/aom.asp?ID=18, accessed 17 July 2007.

Byrd, Barbara and Nissen, Bruce (2003), *Report on the State of Labor Education in the United States*, Berkeley, CA: Center for Research and Education, Institute of Industrial Relations, University of California.

Dugger, William M. (1989), *Corporate Hegemony*, Westport, CT: Greenwood Press.

'FT Top 40 Journals – 2006' (Undated), http://business.queensu.ca/faculty_and_research/research_news/FTBEjournals.pdf, accessed 17 July 2007.

Hammer, Tove (2007), Remarks delivered at a roundtable discussion of 'The Future of Industrial Relations and Labor Market Journals,' Labor and Employment Relations Association Annual Meeting, 5 January, Chicago, IL.

Jarley, Paul, Chandler, Timothy D. and Faulk, Larry (2001), 'Maintaining a scholarly community: casual authorship and the state of IR research,' *Industrial Relations*, **40**(2), 338–43.

Kaufman, Bruce E. (2004), *The Global Evolution of Industrial Relations*, Geneva: International Labor Office.

Kaufman, Bruce E. (1993), *The Origins and Evolution of the Field of Industrial Relations in the United States*, Ithaca, NY: ILR Press.

Labor and Employment Relations Association (Undated), 'History and purpose of the LERA,' available at: http://www.lera.uiuc.edu/chapters/handbook/CHBHistory&Purpose.htm, accessed 17 July 2007.

Martin, Christopher R. (2004), *Framed: Labor and the Corporate Media*, Ithaca, NY: ILR Press.

McLemee, Scott and Byrne, Richard (2003), 'Labor Journals Exchange Words,' *The Chronicle of Higher Education*, 17 October, accessed via http://chronicle.com.

McNulty, Paul J. (1980), *The Origins and Development of Labor Economics*, Cambridge, MA: The MIT Press.

Smallwood, Scott and Glenn, David (2003), 'Editor of *Labor History* quits, and dozens join him,' *The Chronicle of Higher Education*, 4 July, accessed via http://chronicle.com.

Suber, Peter (2007), 'Open Access Overview.' http://www.earlham.edu/~peters/fos/overview.htm, accessed 29 July 2007.

'What is Ephemera?' (Undated), http://www.ephemeraweb.org/about/index.htm, accessed 29 July 2007.

PART 3

Reenergizing practice

9. Revitalizing industrial relations

Michael J. Piore

INTRODUCTION

Industrial relations (IR), broadly defined as the study of work and employment, has existed as a field of study for over a century. But when we think of the crisis of the field, particularly in the context of the professional association now called the Labor and Employment Relations Association (LERA, formerly the Industrial Relations Research Association), we are really talking about a period, beginning in the 1930s and extending roughly up to 1970 or 1975, when IR was intellectually most active and exciting, attracting the brightest and most dedicated students, enormous public interest and support (especially among policymakers and politicians), and, most importantly, considerable institutional support and dedicated research funding. It is nostalgia for those years that prompts the kind of hand wringing about the future of the field in which we are engaged today. I share many of these concerns, but I have reservations as well. Since this will not be an altogether welcome message in this forum, I want to begin by asserting my credentials as a member of the discipline – this is meant to be an insider's critique.

Although I was trained as an economist and my primary academic appointment has always been in an economics department, I think of myself as an IR scholar. My thesis advisor was John T. Dunlop, whose own contribution to the field of IR was at least as great as his contribution to economics. I have always been affiliated with the Industrial Relations Section at the Massachusetts Institute of Technology (MIT), which, while housed throughout my career in the business school, had only just moved there from the economics department when I came on board. Perhaps more to the point, I have always felt that my view of economics – and the somewhat aberrant role I have played there – has been more influenced by IR than that my position among IR scholars has been influenced by my training in economics. In a certain sense, I feel more at home among my colleagues trained in the schools of IR at the University of Wisconsin and Cornell University than I have ever felt among my economics colleagues. Thus, I share the sense of loss and displacement at the place where IR now finds itself, the sense that it has atrophied in recent years, and a longing for its revitalization.

However, I am also skeptical about the revival of the IR field, certainly about the possibility and to some extent about its desirability as well. I do not, moreover, have the feelings I expected to have following the demise of the intellectual and institutional context in which I have functioned over these years: I do not feel any loss of intellectual vitality in my own life or in that of the people around me. Indeed, I find that the intellectual environment in which I work remains exciting and creative. My students, many of whom are actually studying in the IR program, are working on interesting problems and are at least as vital intellectually as any I have had in what is now getting to be a long career. So, for me anyway, there is something of a paradox: The field does seem to be in need of revitalization, but I do not feel a pressing need for that to happen. It is that paradox which I propose to explore here.

INDUSTRIAL RELATIONS AND TRADE UNIONS

To understand the current situation, one has to look at what IR was when scholars widely viewed it as a vital field. I know that everybody will have a personal view on this, and it is impossible to do justice to the subject in a chapter of this length. Still, for me, what made the field vital were the trade unions.

Trade unions were key. First, this is because they posed a problem that society – and any social science that spoke to the needs of society – had to address, that is the problem of industrial peace, or, to put it differently, the continual threat of anarchy, which worker organizations posed in an industrial society. The danger of anarchy threatened the very existence of people in an economy that had come to be composed of parts so specialized, and as a result so interdependent, that when one of them ceased to play its role, the ability of the rest to function was lost. Second, trade unions involved the willingness of people to act as parts of a cohesive social group, in a way that defied that 'free rider' problem, and thus could not be understood in terms of the individualistic social science through which we otherwise understood and sought to address problems in the economy. Third, the major alternative to conventional economics, which addressed both the issue of cohesive social groups and the problem of anarchy that trade union action posed, was Marxism, a body of thought that led to a series of political conclusions that many found troublesome and entailed a series of questionable intellectual premises. Fourth, trade unions and the values they expressed seemed to address the central moral problems posed by capitalism (or, to use the alterative vocabulary that IR scholars adopted to evade Marxism, the problems posed by 'industrial society').

Finally, because it evaded the theory both of conventional economics and of Marxism, and because it was motivated more than anything else by the pressing needs of society to solve the problem of industrial peace, IR took an approach to understanding the world that involved going out, talking to and working with the economy's actors (the practitioners as we learned to call them) and then building models, or at least understandings and interpretations, that incorporated the actors' perspectives and in which they could recognize themselves. Indeed, IR scholars tended to become practitioners themselves and/or to regularly exchange places with them. The hallmark of LERA is that it seeks to combine both scholars and practitioners in a single organization. This is one of the strengths of the field, but it has also turned out, I will argue, to be its greatest weakness.

Understood in this way, it is obvious why IR is no longer a field of compelling scholarly interest. First and foremost is the decline of trade unions. The decline, at least in the United States, has been of startling magnitude. Even more important in terms of the factors that generated the field in the first place, however, is the fact that the threat to industrial peace, which unions once posed, has entirely disappeared. Working time lost through strikes has become virtually zero. Industrial peace is no longer a preoccupation of public policy. Finally, Marxism as a competing intellectual framework had been discredited, in part by the collapse of the Soviet Union and its satellite states, but perhaps even more so by the fact that the organization of work in capitalist societies has taken forms very different from those that Marxism led us to expect and gave us the tools to analyze. Finally, trade unions no longer seem to address the central moral dilemmas of capitalism. Indeed, they seem as often to be part of the problem as part of the solution.

IR as a field, and the LERA as its institutional arm, is not, however, a wholly innocent victim of these developments; it has in certain ways contributed to them. Here the great strength of the field – that it combined in a single organization not only scholars and practitioners but also people from both sides of the bargaining table, labor and management, along with the mediators, arbitrators and government officials whose roles were to facilitate the bargaining process – is also its major weakness. In bringing all of the legitimate actors together in a single organization, and one, more-over, which essentially monopolized academic research on their activities, it created and maintained a tight consensus about what was legitimate in terms of action and scholarship. It was that consensus and the limits it placed upon behavior (limits embodied in law such as the prohibition of strikes while a collective-bargaining agreement is in effect, the arbitration of grievances, and the restriction of secondary boycotts) that made it possible for society to tolerate the strikes and other forms of direct action involved in labor disputes. No longer was there the fear that such disputes would degenerate into industrial anarchy.

Dunlop argued that in any IR system there was a shared ideology, and the Industrial Relations Research Association (IRRA) was in many ways the guardian of that ideology in the United States. Playing that role had its costs, however, both in terms of the range of practice and of scholarship. One of the greatest of these in my mind was the way the field celebrated 'business unionism' and led its members to believe that this was responsible for union survival in the United States.

LERA members including Jack Barbash in Madison, Charles Myers and John Dunlop in Cambridge, and Clark Kerr and Lloyd Ullman in Berkeley – who on some questions were quite far apart – scorned and ridiculed students who questioned business unionism. These scholars encouraged labor leaders to act, and more important to present themselves to the general public as acting, in the narrow self-interest of their members. In so doing, the labor movement failed to recognize that organized labor operated within a protective shell of labor legislation during the early post-World War II period. That shell was justified in the eyes of the public at large by an identification of labor with the broad national interest, a view that grew out of the Great Depression and was reinforced in the postwar period by the role of the labor movement as the leader of a broad, progressive movement (supporting not only the protection of union organization, but also wider measures such as the minimum wage, social security, unemployment insurance, civil rights, and medical insurance).

After 1968, however, labor broke with this coalition – first over the war in Vietnam and then over equal employment opportunity and environmental protection. Organized labor painted itself increasingly as a narrow interest group. The break with the broader progressive movement represented a retreat toward business unionism, and it is hard to believe that this is not in some way responsible for the erosion of support and legal protection that unions received from the courts, the National Labor Relations Board, the Congress, and ultimately the public at large.

The IR community had a similar impact upon scholarship. I remember a conference session at an IRRA meeting in 1978 in Chicago. Although it was convened to discuss research, a suggestion to investigate the origins of seniority in promotion and layoff in the United States was suppressed by the senior scholars in the room who responded in unison, 'The answer (to the question of the system's origins) is obvious.' The chorus then degenerated into an incomprehensible babble as each went on to provide a different answer. The question was never researched. Seniority, like business unionism, was simply the way IR was conducted in America.

REDEFINING THE FIELD

To the extent that the institutions that surrounded IR have attempted to address the problems posed by the decline of trade unions, they have done so largely by redefining the field as one concerned with work and employment. At MIT, we changed the name of our Industrial Relations Section to the Institute for Work and Employment Research (IWER). At the University of California at Berkeley, the name was recently changed from the Institute of Industrial Relations to the Institute for Research on Labor and Employment. The Industrial Relations Research Association is now called the Labor and Employment Relations Association.

Work, labor, and employment do indeed pose a set of problems for society, but those problems are very diffuse, nowhere near as sharp, pointed and pressing as the problems posed by trade unions. The problems, moreover, are arguably as susceptible to understanding through the individualistic assumptions of conventional economics as through the assumptions about social cohesion that seemed absolutely essential to an understanding of trade union behavior. The broader labor issues also do not imply any particular hypotheses about the direction of the evolution of industrial society. And they have no particular moral implications; indeed the fact that these issues are now pursued primarily in business schools, often under the rubric of 'human resource management,' has made the field often seem about manipulation and control.

An alternative way to think of IR as a field is in terms of the intellectual approach that grew out of the efforts to understand trade unions, but is presumably applicable to other social problems. This would imply a focus on a subset of work and labor problems, but would also include the study of other problems associated with technological change, the family, all that goes under the rubric of social capital, and so on. Here, however, it is important to recognize that the scholarly community has changed greatly since IR staked out its claim as a distinct field of study. As a result, approaches to understanding the social world that once distinguished IR are now much more widely shared; other social science fields are now better able to address the kinds of problems that were once the exclusive domain of IR.

The most important development in this regard is undoubtedly the emergence of a 'new institutionalism' in virtually all of the social science disciplines. The new institutionalism represents a reaction to the behaviorism of the immediate postwar period in which institutions were viewed as a veil on much more fundamental social forces. In the earlier period, it was widely held that science should focus on these forces, rather than on the institutions themselves. The forces, of course, varied across social science disciplines and across intellectual traditions within disciplines; they ranged from individual optimizing behavior in conventional economics to power and class in Marxism. Nevertheless, outside of IR, the dominant feature of that era was the treatment of the trade union an epiphenomenon that did not deserve serious scholarly attention.

Behaviorism was, moreover, a deliberate and quite explicit rejection of the institutional and historical approach of the 'Wisconsin School' of labor and IR, especially in economics. The magnitude of the change that has occurred in recent years is symbolized by the fact that in economics the new institutionalism has adopted the terminology of John R. Commons. Other social science disciplines have drawn less upon the vocabulary of the Wisconsin School but arguably are more in tune with its spirit. The new institutionalist revolution (or counterrevolution if you will) has by and large focused on institutions other than trade unions, no doubt because trade unions themselves are no longer so central to the operation of the economy. But many of the insights that IR developed specifically to under-stand trade union behavior have become particular cases of what are now understood as general phenomena.

Consider the following examples. The notions of orbits of coercive comparison and of wage contours, which Arthur Ross and Dunlop devel-oped to understand wage determination under trade unions in the postwar period, can be understood as examples of institutional isomorphism, a concept now central to organizational behavior and economic sociology.[1] The problems of union governance and the effect of different governance structures on union behavior have been subsumed into the broader field of political economy; what were once verbal models or even the oral tradition of IR on this score are now easily subsumed under the formal models devel-oped in both political science (especially the field of American politics) and economics to explain the behavior of political parties and the differences in the outcomes under various legislative and parliamentary arrangements. The insights about collective bargaining in a classic IR text like Walton and McKersie's (1965) *A Behavioral Theory of Labor Negotiations* are now cap-tured by formal bargaining models in economics and psychology, and a specialized interdisciplinary field of negotiations has emerged encompass-ing economics, psychology, sociology and law, in many ways competing with IR for the allegiance not only of scholars who study labor negotiations but also of practitioners of the art of labor mediation and arbitration.

Economic sociology has also emerged as a separate field within the broader discipline of sociology, one that is a very active domain of research, encompassing not only the new institutionalism but also other aspects of economic behavior that were once largely the province of IR. Thus, for example, Marc Granovetter's article on the strength of weak ties in careers is the fountainhead of a wide-ranging literature not only on labor market outcomes, but also on the success of various groups in the labor market (Granovetter, 1983; Etzkowitz *et al.*, 2000). And Frank Dobbin and a series of co-authors have pioneered a whole literature on the interaction of public policy and the management of labor within the firm (Dobbin and Sutton, 1998; Kelly and Dobbin, 1999). The field of labor organization has become a part of another subfield of sociology focused on social movements (for example, Skocpol *et al.*, 2006; Public Sphere Project (n.d); Ganz, 2008).

In recent years, an increasing number of economists have grounded their work in real world 'practice' in a way that brings them in contact with (and gives them an appreciation of) the environment in which economic actors operate. As a result, such work has much of the flavor of IR. This is especially true in the areas of labor economics and, more recently, development, which have both cultivated an approach to field research whereby students go out and immerse themselves in the work of the actors in a way that used to be the exclusive province of IR.

Most economists have backed into this approach, so to speak, in the process of trying to collect data themselves (as opposed to relying on government surveys) and seeking to understand the data-generating world well enough to anticipate, and test for, biases produced by their data collection approach. It is true they remain attached to a theory rooted in what many IR scholars consider a radical and naive individualism. In the hands of these economists, however, the theory generates an unexpectedly rich and original set of hypotheses, which one suspects must come out of their field experience.[2] Although economics invariably seems to disappoint, such scholarship could eventually lead to changes in the theory itself.

In short, a number of disciplines have broken the IR field's monopoly over institutions and practice. When I was a graduate student – and indeed for a long time after I became a professor – a standard trope of IR types in arguments with mainstream economists was to overwhelm them with practical knowledge, details about the technology or the institutions, especially those that were theoretically anomalous. My thesis advisor, John Dunlop, was particularly adept at this art, but all of us practiced it in one way or another. It has become much more difficult to do this today. And that is not because scholars in other disciplines are so much more grounded in practice, but because they are no longer so afraid of it. They have come to see institutional details less as distractions to be ignored than as phenomena worthy of explanation and understanding. All of this leads me to believe that even if trade unions were a more prominent feature of contemporary life, IR would have had much more competition in the academy from other disciplines seeking explanations and understandings of union behavior.

IR is also not alone in its interest in society's moral challenges. Much of labor economics may have moved away from the moral commitments that underlay the field of IR; its prospective students are more often motivated by the opportunity to model social behavior the way the hard sciences model the physical world (in areas such as marriage and vocational commitment) than by social change. However, the field of development – development economics in particular, but also development studies more broadly – has come to be associated with the kind of moral commitment that originally adhered to IR. In fact, this is surely one reason development attracts students, including many that in an earlier time would have wanted to study unions.

In summary, IR can be redefined to encompass more than the study of trade unions, but developments in the social sciences suggest that the problems faced by IR in the academy are no longer attributable simply to the demise of unions and the threat they posed to industrial peace. Much of the intellectual agenda of the field has been taken up and absorbed into the more conventional social sciences. IR no longer has a monopoly on a theoretical stance that takes institutions as independent forces worthy of study, an empirical stance that focuses on practice, or attention to capitalism's moral issues.

ROOM FOR AN INTERDISCIPLINARY INDUSTRIAL RELATIONS

The way that mainstream disciplines have approached the world characteristic of IR, however, has not been wholly satisfactory. Their approach has been to break up the key methodological and empirical issues into a series of separate components and parcel them out to different social sciences – disciplines that speak to each other in very limited and stylized ways or not at all. Thus, economics has come to recognize institutions, but it tries to understand their behavior in terms of a methodological individualism that does not recognize cohesive social groups; economic sociology tends to focus on social and collective behavior, but distances itself from normative and policy concerns; and so on. This leaves space in the intellectual landscape for a more integrated, interdisciplinary approach. As far as I can tell from talking with MIT's IWER students, the search for such an approach is what attracts them to the field and distinguishes them from students in other programs.

But an interdisciplinary graduate education of the kind our students appear to be seeking poses another set of problems. The way the component problems of the old IR have been taken up by mainstream social science means that it is difficult to obtain professional recognition and an audience within the scholarly community without an understanding of a disciplinary perspective and context for the particular issues one chooses to address. This implies the need for a much more profound disciplinary background and training than an education in IR has in the past entailed.

We have tried to address this problem at MIT by requiring our students to commit themselves to one of the major social science disciplines and to, in effect, take the core curriculum that is required of graduate students in that discipline. At the same time, we recognize that IR is distinguished from other interdisciplinary programs by the fact that it has had a distinctive approach to the study of society – one that grows out of its focus on trade unions, but, as I have tried to suggest above, is actually separate and distinct and can presumably be applied to other problems. We try to demonstrate that approach by a focus on the history of IR and the core theory generated by that history; at its best, the new focus on work and employment becomes a way of illustrating how ideas that originally emerged in the study of trade unions can be applied to other social problems.

I am not sure that this qualifies as a revitalization of IR. It has certainly made the field more dependent upon, and perhaps derivative of, other social sciences. But it has also freed the field from the responsibility of sustaining an ideological environment that is conducive to industrial peace, and it has fostered a broader and more open research agenda. It does seem to attract an interesting and creative set of students and gives rise to a stimulating intellectual environment.

NOTES

1. Institutional isomorphism is the process that leads one organization (or set of organizational working rules) to resemble another organization under similar environmental conditions.
2. One study in development economics, for example, finds significant differences in the political agenda and the public policy outcomes between male-managed villages and female-managed villages – and leads one to wonder why there is no comparable study (indeed no comparable literature) on the difference between male and female leadership in trade union policy (Chattopadhyay and Duflo, 2004). A very different study, but equally important for IR, looks at why temporary help services provide training and the role of that training in screening candidates (Autor, 2001).

REFERENCES

Autor, David (2001), 'Why do temporary help firms provide free general skills training?' *Quarterly Journal of Economics*, **116** (4), 1409–48.

Chattopadhyay, Raghabendra and Duflo, Esther (2004), 'Women as policy makers: evidence from a randomized policy experiment in India,' *Econometrica*, **72** (5), 1409–43.

Dobbin, Frank and Sutton, John R. (1998), 'The strength of a weak state: the rights revolution and the rise of human resources management divisions,' *The American Journal of Sociology*, **104** (2), 441–76.

Etzkowitz, Henry, Kemelgor, Carol and Uzzi, Brian (2000), *Athena Unbound: The Advancement of Women in Science and Technology*, Cambridge, New York: Cambridge University Press.

Ganz, Marshall (2008), *Why David Sometimes Wins: Leadership, Organization and Strategy in the Unionization of California Agriculture*, (forthcoming).

Granovetter, Mark (1983), 'The strength of weak ties: a network theory revisited,' *Sociological Theory*, **1** (1983), 201–33.

Kelly, Erin and Dobbin, Frank (1999), 'Civil rights law at work: sex discrimination and the rise of maternity leave policies,' *The American Journal of Sociology*, **105** (2), 455–92.

Public Sphere Project: A CPSR (Computer Professionals for Social Responsibility) Initiative (n.d), www.cpsr.org/program/sphere/.

Skocpol, Theda, Liazos, Ariane and Ganz, Marshall (2006), *What a Mighty Power We Can Be: African American Fraternal Groups and the Struggle for Racial Equality,* Princeton, NJ: Princeton University Press.

Walton, Richard E. and McKersie, Robert B. (1965), *A Behavioral Theory of Labor Negotiations: An Analysis of Social Interaction Systems*, New York: McGraw Hill.

Australia, Germany,
USA,
Sweden, China, S. Korea
Japan, S. Korea

JS³
L6² f23
P16 p23
     p26

10. Varieties of capitalism and employment relations under globalization: evidence from the auto industry

Nick Wailes, Russell D. Lansbury and Jim Kitay

INTRODUCTION

In recent times, it has been broadly accepted that changes in the international economy, normally referred to as globalization, have significant consequences for national patterns of employment relations. There are, however, competing views about globalization's significance and the types of changes it is likely to produce. Some analysts have argued that globalization produces convergence in labor standards across countries and regions, while others have suggested that the pressures associated with globalization are refracted through national level institutional arrangements, resulting in continued diversity (see Wailes *et al.*, 2003 for a review of these arguments). Empirical studies of comparative changes in employment relations provide little support for either of these views, revealing a complex pattern of both continuity and change across countries. In our earlier work, we have argued that rather than focusing exclusively on the role of institutional arrangements, there may be benefits associated with focusing on the interplay between interests and institutions in shaping national patterns of employment relations in the context of globalization and have applied this framework to a study of changes in employment relations in autos and banking in Australia and Korea (see Lansbury *et al.*, 2003 and 2006).

This chapter reports on a research project that seeks to continue our constructive engagement with the new institutionalism. Recent institutionalist scholarship has gone beyond the focus on single institutions and begun to examine the relationship between institutions. These theories of capitalist diversity attempt to distinguish different varieties of capitalism according to the institutional matrix which shapes the operation of a market society. We argue that by shifting the focus away from single institutions and examining the connections between institutional arrangements, these theories of capitalist diversity overcome some of the limitations of the earlier new institutionalism. In doing so, they offer a promising basis for the study of globalization and national patterns of employment relations. There are, however, a number of criticisms of the varieties of capitalism approach, which suggests the need to take into account a broader range of factors.

The chapter is structured as follows. The first section provides an overview of the most influential theory of capitalist diversity, Hall and Soskice's varieties of capitalism approach. The second section reviews some of the criticisms of that approach, many of which are relevant to the study of employment relations. The third section outlines some aspects of the approach we have taken in our recent study of employment relations in the auto industry in seven countries, which is designed to overcome some of the problems identified above.

THE VARIETIES OF CAPITALISM APPROACH: A BRIEF SURVEY

Crouch (2005: 2) argues that the emerging body of literature on capitalist diversity reflects the culmination of a quarter of a century of the application of neo-institutionalist analysis to the comparative study of capitalism and has 're-established the role of political science and sociology in the study of economic phenomenon.' This section focuses on the varieties of capitalism (VoC) approach outlined by Hall and Soskice (2001), and the links it draws between corporate governance and labor management. As Howell (2003: 103) notes 'the varieties of capitalism approach [has] achieved a level of theoretical sophistication, explanatory scope and predictive ambition that has rapidly made it close to hegemonic in the field [of comparative political and economic systems].'

The VoC approach rejects the notion that there is one best way to organize capitalism and points to the role that institutional arrangements play in shaping how market societies function. It is this emphasis on the interrelations between institutional arrangements which differentiates the VoC approach from earlier new institutionalist analysis. Hall and Soskice draw on what they describe as 'the new economics of organization' to develop a firm-centric theory of comparative institutional advantage. They argue that in market economies firms are faced with a series of coordination problems, both internally and externally. They focus on five spheres of coordination that firms must address: industrial relations; vocational training and education; corporate governance; inter-firm relations and relations with their own employees (Hall and Soskice, 2001: 6–9).

It is claimed by Hall and Soskice that it is possible to identify two institutional equilibria associated with these coordination problems. The first they call Liberal Market Economies (LMEs), in which firms rely on markets and hierarchies to resolve coordination problems. LMEs are, thus, likely to be characterized by, among other things, well developed capital markets and outsider forms of corporate governance, market-based forms of industrial relations with few long-term commitments by employers to workers, and the use of market mechanisms and contracts to coordinate their relations with supplier and buyer firms. The United States is the prime exemplar of an LME but the literature also often includes the United Kingdom, Australia, New Zealand, Canada and Ireland in this category. The second variety of capitalism identified by Hall and Soskice, Coordinated Market Economies (CMEs), includes countries in which firms make greater use of non-market mechanisms to resolve coordination problems internally and externally. In comparison to LMEs, CMEs are more likely to be characterized by insider forms of corporate governance and 'patient' forms of capital, industrial-relations systems based on bargaining and which reflect a longer-term commitment to employees, and the use of non-market mechanisms (such as industry associations) to coordinate relations between firms within and across industries and sectors. Germany is the prime exemplar of a CME but the literature also often includes other northern European countries, Japan and South Korea within this category.

Central to Hall and Soskice's argument, and the identification of distinct varieties of capitalism, is the concept of institutional complementarities. In the VoC model institutional complementary refers to two related but separate effects. First, institutions are said to be complementary to the extent that the existence of one enhances the effectiveness of another. Thus, for example, the existence of a cohesive industry association may enhance the economic efficiency of industry-wide collective bargaining. In this sense institutional complementarity helps explain why two contrasting institutional configurations, LMEs and CMEs, are able to produce superior economic outcomes.

Second, the VoC model also suggests that over time institutional arrangements are likely to converge on one or other institutional equilibria. Hall and Soskice (2001: 18), thus, argue that 'nations with a particular type of coordination in one sphere in the economy should tend to develop complementary practices in other spheres as well' (see also Amable, 2003: 54–66). For example, the VoC model suggests that in countries which are characterized by well developed capital markets and outsider forms of corporate governance it is difficult to sustain industrial-relations practices that imply long-term commitment to employees. Over time, there are likely to be pressures for the adoption of more market-based forms of industrial relations. In this sense the VoC model predicts what has been described as 'dual convergence' (Hay, 2004).

While contributions to the VoC model examine the complementarities across a range of institutional spheres (see Jackson and Deeg, 2006 for a review), recent work in this tradition has highlighted the centrality of the relationship between corporate governance and industrial relations. Hall and Gingerich (2005), for example, seek to provide empirical support for the core contentions of the VoC model. They do so by 'estimating the impact of complementarities in labor relations and corporate governance on economic growth' drawing on measures of shareholder power, dispersion of control, size of the stock market, level and degree of wage coordination and labor turnover (Hall and Gingerich, 2005: 3). Their results suggest not only that there is a strong degree of institutional congruence across countries (the higher the level of coordination in corporate governance factors, the higher the level of coordination in labor-relations factors), but also provide strong empirical support for the assertion that these practices are complementary (each raises the returns to the other) (for a more detailed discussion and further empirical testing see Hopner, 2005).

A number of VoC explanations draw on transaction cost theory to explain why two significantly different institutional configurations produce superior economic outcomes, and again the link between corporate governance and labor-management practices figures prominently in these arguments. Drawing on Aoki's (2000) work, it has been argued that firms in CMEs are likely to compete through quality-based differentiation of relatively mature products. The existence of significant blockholders of capital, and corporate governance mechanisms that support insider forms of monitoring, create the conditions for managers and employers to invest in the development of the firm-specific assets required to generate (technological and motivational) 'X efficiencies.' This supports the development of diversified, quality-oriented production systems where the main focus is on incremental improvements to existing products and technologies (Streeck, 1991).

Lacking certainty in the long-term financial commitment of investors, and unwilling to provide employees with the commitment necessary to encourage investment in firm-specific human capital, the competitiveness of firms in LMEs are less likely to be based on the development of firm-specific assets and more likely to be derived from innovation and experimentation (Jurgens, 2003). The predominance of market-based coordination mechanisms in LMEs, including relatively short-term commitments to employees, implies that firms that operate in this institutional matrix find it easier to restructure their activities in response to shifts in technology and product innovations and that capital markets can quickly reallocate capital from declining to emerging industries. While both strategies, differentiation and innovation, may produce competitive advantages, a number of VoC accounts have suggested that these differences in institutional matrix help explain why the US economy appears to have out-performed those of Japan and Germany during the 1990s (see, for example, Amable, 2000). This argument is consistent with studies in the strategic management literature that show that different types of resources and capabilities may be more or less valuable depending of the relative stability of underlying technologies and markets (see, for example, Miller and Shamsie, 1996).

As this brief review suggests, the VoC approach appears to offer a number of potential benefits both for scholars interested in assessing the impact of globalization and employment relations and those with an interest in the relationship between corporate governance and labor management. First, we would argue that the VoC approach overcomes some of the limitations of the new institutionalism that we identified in our earlier work (Wailes *et al.*, 2003). By focusing on the interconnections between institutional arrangements it overcomes the tendency of the new institutionalism to treat industrial-relations institutions in isolation. Second, the firm-centric nature of the VoC approach overcomes the tendency of the new institutionalism to treat institutions as separate from the social actors who engage with them. In particular, the firm-centric nature of the VoC approach makes it possible to bring employers back into the analysis of change in industrial relations (Swenson, 1991). Third, by providing mechanisms for identifying varieties of capitalism, the VoC approach may explain the empirical pattern of continuity and change in employment relations that has been observed in recent years. For example, the VoC framework may help explain why globalization appears to be associated with significant falls in union density and collective-bargaining coverage in some countries (mainly the LMEs), but has not produced the same outcomes in other countries (the CMEs) (for further discussion on the application of the VoC to industrial relations see Godard, 2005).

For those interested in the relationship between corporate governance and labor management, the VoC approach also appears to offer some benefits. First, this approach affirms the importance of examining national patterns of corporate governance when examining changes in industrial relations. As Hall (in Crouch *et al.*, 2005: 373) wrote recently:

> If the economic impact of a specific set of institutions in the sphere of labor markets (or industrial relations) depends on the type of institutions for corporate governance present in the economy, then most efforts to assess the impact of labor-market arrangements that do not also consider the nature of corporate governance will produce misleading conclusions.

Second, while the growing body of literature of corporate governance and labor management has established a strong relationship between particular forms of governance and certain labor-market outcomes (see, for example, Jacoby, 2005 and Gospel and Pendleton, 2005), as a number of authors note it is difficult to identify a clear causal relationship between the two. The VoC approach, and especially its notion of institutional complementarity, suggests a number of causal pathways for governance and labor management scholars to explore; it also highlights the need to situate the analysis of governance and labor in a broader institutional context.

LIMITATIONS OF THE VARIETIES OF CAPITALISM APPROACH

Despite these potential benefits, it is important to acknowledge that the VoC approach has been the subject of considerable criticism. Rather than provide an exhaustive overview of these criticisms, our intention here is to briefly highlight some of the issues with direct relevance for those studying the links between corporate governance and labor management. In doing so, we attempt to draw links between criticisms of the VoC approach and debates taking place within the comparative corporate governance literature.

Since the publication of the Hall and Soskice edited volume, the VoC approach has been the subject of criticism from a range of different sources including those sympathetic to the aims of the project. A number of the criticisms focus on the limited number of varieties of capitalism that Hall and Soskice identify and the limited number of countries to which the model can be said to apply. One line of criticism suggests that the VoC approach confuses the distinction between ideal types and real world examples, and that the two varieties of capitalism reflect an attempt to generalize key features of the political economies of two countries (the United States and Germany) (see Crouch 2005: 27–30). It is interesting to note that Hall and Soskice's (2001: 21) own analysis reveals that six European countries – France, Italy, Spain, Portugal, Greece and Turkey – are difficult to accommodate within either the LME or CME category and they raise the prospect of a Mediterranean variety of capitalism, but leave this variety relatively underdeveloped. At the very least, it can be argued that the VoC model, as Hall and Soskice present it, is excessively parsimonious. There are a number of alternative frameworks that identify a broader range of types and which may make it possible to capture a broader range of countries (see, for example, Amable, 2003; Whitley, 1999).

A second set of criticisms of the VoC approach relates to the extent to which the LME and CME categories capture differences between countries within the same category. The main focus of much of this line of criticism has been on the classification of Japan and Germany as CMEs. As the contributions to two collections by Streeck and Yamamura (2001, 2003) demonstrate, while Japan and Germany can both be seen as examples of non-liberal capitalism, there are important differences between these two countries which the VoC approach overlooks. Jackson (2001), for example, notes that even though German and Japanese corporate governance arrangements produce similar outcomes, they differ both in terms of the institutional foundations on which they are based and the historical forces which shaped them. Thus, for example, while employees in both Japan and Germany have a greater role in corporate governance, in the German case workers' corporate governance rights are contained in legislation, which is not the case in Japan. Interestingly, Jackson argues that in both cases the role of the state played a significant part in the decision of both countries to reject a more liberal approach to corporate governance. A number of criticisms of the VoC approach focus on the relative absence of the state, and politics more generally, from the framework.

While many of the criticisms of the VoC approach stress the inability of the framework to account for variations amongst CMEs, it can also be argued that the framework does not adequately capture differences between LMEs. Thus, for example, while it may be the case that Australia shares a number of the institutional arrangements associated with the LME category, it differs from the United States in a number of important respects. For example, as Cheffins (2002) notes, while Australia has many of the corporate governance arrangements of other common law countries, its traditional pattern of shareholding is much less dispersed than might be expected.

Perhaps more significant than the differences between LMEs at any particular point in time is the relative inability of the VoC model to explain changes in LMEs over time. A number of authors highlight the example of changes in the UK pre- and post-Thatcher eras to illustrate this point (for example, Howell, 2003; Pontusson, 2005). It might also be argued that, despite long having many of the institutional arrangements associated with an LME, there has been considerable change in the Australian political economy over the last two decades, which mean that similar institutional arrangements have produced significantly different outcomes.

These criticisms point to one of the fundamental weaknesses of the VoC approach, and something that it shares with the earlier new institutionalism: a relative inability to account for change. It has been suggested that this is in part a reflection of the fact that the model is built around comparative statics. However, a number of authors have suggested that the problems with accounting for change are more deeply rooted in the VoC approach. Howell (2003), for example, notes the relative absence of politics, and the particular neglect of the role of the state, in the VoC approach. Pontusson (2005) highlights the failure of the model to take into account the role of class and class conflict in shaping economic and political outcomes in the VoC model; in his view, by concentrating on the role of institutional arrangements, the framework loses sight of the fact that these are capitalist economies. Writing from a more sympathetic perspective, Crouch (2005) argues that that the VoC approach ends up producing a highly deterministic view of social action. As he puts it (2005: 1):

> The main emphasis of the [VoC approach] . . . was that there was no single form of capitalism . . . But I was increasingly struck by the paradoxical determinism behind this ostensibly liberating message: There were two but only two viable forms of capitalism. Nation states possessed one of the other of these two, the institutions appropriate to which extended in a coherent way across a wide range of economic, political and social areas, determining their economic capacities over most products and types of production. And once a country had a particular set of such institutions, there was very little it could do to change it.

The inability to account for change can be said to reflect a key feature of the VoC approach and the intellectual tradition from which it is drawn. Consistent with the earlier new institutionalism, the VoC approach tends to treat the preferences of social actors as endogenous (Allen, 2004). That is, in emphasizing the importance of institutional context, institutionalist accounts tend to argue that institutional arrangements are the primarily determinant of what social actors see to be in their best interests. In doing so, this approach downplays the possibility that non-institutional factors may play a role in shaping preferences (Pontusson, 1995). This implies that once an institutional order is established, social action is path dependent. Formulated in this way, exogenous shocks, which fundamentally alter taken for granted patterns of behavior and preference formation, are the only potential sources of change in these institutionalist models (Wailes, 2003: 46–9).

Recent institutionalist scholarship has acknowledged the difficulties associated with accounting for change. Streeck and Thelen (2005), for example, argue that there is a need to move away from assuming path dependency and to examine the influence non-institutional factors and politics play in producing both continuity and change in institutional arrangements. Crouch (2005) suggests that if institutionalist theory is to account for change and to become less deterministic, it must develop a theory of agency. Building on our earlier work, we would argue that this theory of agency needs to take into account the role that the material interests of social actors play in shaping their institutional preferences. In our view, these interests will in part be shaped by issues related to product and capital market conditions and are likely to differ across industries and sectors (Lansbury *et al.*, 2003). For example, it has been shown that the willingness of employers to operate within the existing institutions of industrial relations is shaped by the extent of international competition in their industry and their views of the extent to which they can compete successfully within existing arrangements (see Pontusson and Swenson, 1996).

A final set of criticisms levelled at the VoC approach relates to the concept of institutional complementarities. While a full discussion of concept of complementarity is beyond the scope of this chapter (see Hopner, 2005; Crouch *et al.*, 2005), for the purposes of the present discussion it is worth noting several issues. First, the coherence of institutions does not necessarily imply complementarity (Crouch in Crouch *et al.*, 2005). Thus, for example, it is conceivable that a country will have coherent institutions (like outsider forms of corporate governance and a decentralized bargaining regime), but that these institutions will not necessarily enhance the performance of each other. The relatively poor economic performance of New Zealand economy under the Employment Contracts Acts serves as a clear illustration of this pattern (Dalziel, 2002).

Second, it may also be the case that institutions that are not necessarily coherent may produce complementary outcomes. The experiences of Ireland under incomes policies during the 1990s and of Australia under the (union-government) Accord are examples of this pattern. Complementarity is thus not a characteristic of institutional patterns, but rather is an outcome (Streeck in Crouch *et al.*, 2005). Indeed as the studies contained in Streeck and Yamamura's edited volumes illustrate, the development of institutional arrangements associated with CMEs was not driven by concerns about complementarity; instead, complementarity was achieved once the institutional arrangements themselves were in place. This view of complementarity as an outcome again implies the need for attention to be placed on the role that agency and politics play in shaping the development of market economies.

GLOBALIZATION AND EMPLOYMENT RELATIONS IN THE AUTO INDUSTRY

The previous section reviewed some of the criticisms of the VoC approach and drew links between these criticisms and recent debates in the comparative corporate governance literature. This section outlines of some of the main features of the approach we have taken in our recent study of the impact of globalization and employment relations in the auto assembly

Table 10.1   The GERAB framework

Liberal Market Economies (LMEs)	Coordinated Market Economies (CMEs)	Asian Market Economies (AMEs)
Australia	Germany	China (People's Republic)
USA	Sweden	Japan
		South Korea

industry, one of two industries we have been studying simultaneously (the other is retail banking) (see Kitay and Wailes, 2007). This research project, which began in 2006, examined whether the impact of globalization on employment relations differs from country to country, and, in particular, whether there is systematic variation in the impact of globalization on employment relations across varieties of capitalism. It has done so by comparing changes in employment relations practices in the automobile assembly and retail banking industries in seven countries – Australia, the United States, Germany, Sweden, Japan, Korea and the People's Republic of China.

Broadening the Varieties of Capitalism Approach

There are strong reasons to suspect that differences in national institutional arrangements mean that globalization is likely to produce differential outcomes across varieties of capitalism. However, it should be acknowledged that in its original form, the VoC model is excessively parsimonious, downplays the potential for differences within varieties of capitalism and does not provide a framework for understanding change. We would also argue that some of these features reflect the failure of the VoC framework, and the institutionalist tradition from which it is drawn, to accommodate a role for agency or to take into account the role of interests in shaping the preferences of social actors. Our study is designed to overcome some of these difficulties.

In response to the view that the VoC approach is too limited, our research project has introduced a third variety of capitalism, which we call Asian Market Economies (AMEs) and includes case studies from Japan, South Korea and China as examples of AMEs (see Table 10.1). The identification of an AME is derived from our reading of Whitley's (1999) national business systems approach. Whitley argues that there are a number of significant differences between Western and Asian business systems, across a broad range of variables including forms of property law, capital market structures, and cultural patterns and beliefs. Yeung (2000: 408), who coined the term Asian Market Economies, uses Whitley's framework to argue that these economies are characterized by strong business networks, a heightened role for personal relationships, and close involvement of the state in economic activity. While Asian countries are unquestionably heterogeneous, Whitley, Yeung and others within the national business systems approach demonstrate that they are sufficiently different to Western business systems to warrant separate attention. In our globalization of employment relations in automobiles and banking (GERAB) study, we sought to test Yeung's hypothesis that AMEs are more susceptible to the pressures of globalization than the coordinated economies of Western Europe and are therefore more likely to adopt employment relations practices that resemble developments in LMEs.

A second feature of our study has been the focus on variation within varieties of capitalism. In addition to expanding the number of varieties of capitalism, our study drew on more than one example of each of the three varieties of capitalism. Moreover, within each variety we chose examples of both small and large countries. This allowed us to examine whether size effects were more important than institutional effects in explaining differences between cases. In relation to the AME variety, we chose three cases – Japan, Korea and China – because there are relatively fewer studies of the impact of globalization on employment relations in Asian countries than there are in LMEs and European CMEs and also because the literature suggests that there is a greater degree of heterogeneity within Asian business systems than is the case for Western varieties.

A third feature of our study has been its focus on two industries – auto assembly and retail banking – across all seven cases. These industries were chosen because they are both significantly affected by globalization, although in different ways. The research design allowed us to examine whether industry effects were more important than variety effects in shaping the relationship between globalization and employment relations. The focus on these industries also made it possible to compare whether there were differences in the impact of globalization on employment relations in manufacturing and service industries. Finally, the focus on two different industries with different competitive market dynamics made it possible for us to examine how non-institutional preferences impact on employment relations outcomes, thus addressing one of the important weaknesses of the VoC approach. (Space limitations restrict the discussion below to an examination of the auto industry. For a discussion of banking, see Kitay *et al.*, 2007.)

A final feature of the GERAB study has been its use of detailed case studies. The research focused on two companies in each industry across each of the seven countries, and in each case the research was conducted (between —— and ——) by national research teams working from an established protocol. There were a number of benefits from this case study approach. First, it allowed comparison within industries and made it possible to identify evidence of diversity in national changes in employment relations patterns. Second, it provided the opportunity to contextualize contemporary changes and thus ensured the analysis was attentive to both issues of change and the role of agents in bringing about that change. Finally, because the research drew on an established research protocol from an earlier study, it was possible to include longitudinal elements in this project for some countries.

The GERAB research protocol drew on an earlier project devised by international researchers, coordinated by Thomas Kochan and other scholars at MIT, who examined changes in employment relations during the 1980s and 1990s in a selected number of industries (including autos and banking) in a variety of countries (see Kochan *et al.*, 1997; Locke *et al.*, 1996; Regini *et al.*, 1999). Like the MIT study, the GERAB research focused on five key issues in employment relations at the enterprise level: work organization, skill formation, compensation systems, staffing arrangements and employment security, and enterprise governance and employee-management relations (for more about these issues and the GERAB project, see Lansbury *et al.*, 2003, 2006).

The Automotive Assembly Industry

The automotive industry is a prime example of globalization in which multinational enterprises have developed networks, alliances and cross-shareholdings across regions and nations. From the end of World War II until the mid-1960s, US producers, especially the 'Big Three,' General Motors, Ford and Chrysler, dominated the auto industry, with their vast domestic market and expansion into Europe and elsewhere. By the 1970s, as trade barriers fell, European and especially Japanese auto companies, led by the Toyota Motor Company, were capturing new markets around the world and beginning to penetrate the United States. The 1980s marked the ascendancy of the Japanese automakers and a period of crisis for the 'Big Three.' By the mid-1990s, Japanese auto firms accounted for one-third of all sales in the United States. European auto manufacturers, particularly from Germany, extended their manufacturing facilities to Asia and US dominance began to decline. During the 1997–98 Asian economic crisis, Japanese and Korean auto companies experienced difficulties while American and European companies embarked upon recovery. Since the late 1990s there has been a new phase of global expansion, a number of mergers and acquisitions and the development of strategic alliances and joint ventures. Demand in the existing 'triad' markets of Europe, North America and Japan is stagnant due to saturation, while expansion is expected in emerging markets, especially in Asia and South America. This leads to highly competitive pressures among automakers to capture emerging markets (Lansbury *et al.*, 2007).

The standardized mass production of cars based on narrowly defined tasks and centralized control was achieved in its most exemplary form in the Ford production plants in the early twentieth century ('Fordism'). It was seen as the most efficient and advantageous production system until the Japanese and in particular Toyota captured the American market in the 1970s and 1980s using a production system that produced high quality vehicles at lower costs. Toyota's 'post-Fordist' production system was termed 'lean production' in the influential book, *The Machine that Changed the World*, by James Womack and others (1990). Toyota demonstrated that it was possible to continuously improve production processes while building relatively cheap, standardized vehicles of high quality. In contrast to mass production, which was inflexible and based on standardized products on production lines, the key characteristics of Toyota's lean production system were continuous process improvement (Kaizen) of quality and production, zero defects, just-in-time production, the elimination of waste, close integration of all parts of the production process from suppliers to customers, rapid product and process development, and efficient small-lot production. It was described as more flexible, with products 'pulled' by customer demands rather than 'pushed' by the production process. Womack *et al.* (1990) described lean production as 'an interrelated set of technological, organizational and human resource policies that, when implemented together, constitute a new flexible system of work.' While there are critics who argue that lean production is simply an old-fashioned 'speed up' production device portrayed as a new idea in order to more subtly control the workforce, elements of lean production have been widely adopted by auto manufacturers around the world. However, it has been observed that there are many variations of 'hybrid systems' that combine elements of both lean and mass production (Kochan *et al.*, 1997).

In the auto assembly case studies, work organization was found to be strongly influenced by the system of production in each plant, but also tempered by the national context in which plants were located. The Japanese plants followed the lean production system most closely, but their application of the concept varied between different firms. The Korean and Chinese plants were predominantly focused on mass production, although the Korean plants used higher levels of automation than their Chinese counterparts. The German and Swedish plants adopted hybrid approaches to production with a strong emphasis on modularization and 'diversified quality production,' which emphasized the importance of work groups and teamwork. The American-owned plants in the United States tended to follow mass production with repetitive assembly-line work, while the

Japanese transplants in the United States were more oriented to lean production and team organization. In Australia, plants tended towards a
hybrid approach but, with the exception of one Japanese-owned plant, did
not generally adopt a team-based work organization.

Skill formation and development was more formally structured in the
German and Swedish plants, where apprenticeship systems and vocational
training are still strongly emphasized. By contrast, the American-owned
plants in the United States and the Australian plants placed less emphasis
on skill development, although the former Labor government in Australia
in the 1980s and 1990s encouraged skill development to make the industry
more internationally competitive. The Japanese plants practiced extensive
on-the-job training and transferred employees between departments in
order to enhance their cross-functional skills. The Korean plants emphasized job-related skills, but limited job rotation, while the Chinese plants
trained workers for immediate tasks.

A major issue in most auto companies is the degree to which pay is contingent upon performance, rather than based on age or length of service. The
Japanese plants have introduced significant changes in their pay systems in
recent years as they have sought to link pay more directly to performance
measures. However, pay is still related to job grades and annual bonuses are
paid to the workforce as a whole, based on each enterprise's overall
profitability. Korean firms have retained more traditional payment systems,
which link pay closely to seniority and length of service. However, the
Korean plants also use a complex array of allowances and bonuses. The
Chinese plants are influenced by tradition and focus on job position rather
than performance. However, increased competition for skilled workers in
China has led to increased use of bonuses to attract and retain autoworkers.

In Germany and Sweden, the auto companies are covered by collective
agreements with the unions, but there are a range of incentive pay systems
and bonuses negotiated at the plant level in Germany. The Swedish plants
provide supplementary pay for skills and qualifications. In the US-owned
plants in America, unions still play an important role in negotiating pay,
but most of the Japanese transplants are union-free. In Australia, unions
have largely retained their bargaining power and pay is relatively uniform
across plants, but there is growing disparity between the pay at the least
profitable plants compared with the more profitable plants.

In most countries, there have been significant changes in staffing and job
security within the auto industry. There has been considerable growth in the
contingent workforce, which is employed in assembly work on a contract
and/or temporary basis. These workers earn lower pay and fewer entitlements (such as access to health insurance and severance pay) relative to the
workers who have continuing employment in the industry.

In Japan, both the number and proportion of regular, full-time workers has declined in comparison with subcontracted and 'dispatched' workers. The latter workers do not enjoy the same pay and entitlements as the regular workforce and are the first to be laid off when there is a downturn in demand. In Korea, the number of contract and temporary workers increased substantially during the economic crisis of the 1990s. While many of these temporary workers later became regular workers when the industry began to recover from the economic downturn, there remain a significant proportion of contract workers who are employed in assembly plants with lower wages and entitlements. In Chinese plants there has also been the growth of contract workers and some labor hire firms provide most of the workforce for the assembly plants. During the economic downturn of the late 1980s, which also affected China, there were large-scale layoffs in some plants in China.

In Germany and Sweden, there have been some significant lay-offs due to a downturn in demand for autos, but unions have been strong enough to negotiate generous redundancy and severance payments for workers who have been laid off. Some companies, such as Volkswagen, have been shifting production to lower cost locations in Eastern Europe and Asia, and this is a growing cause of tension between unions and employers. In the United States, many production facilities in the more highly unionized northern states have been closed and new facilities opened in less-unionized regions. There has also been considerable expansion of production facilities in lower-cost countries such as China. The proportion of workers employed in assembly plants, compared with component manufacturing, has also declined as a result of modularization. In Australia, declining sales of locally manufactured vehicles has resulted in an overall decline in employment within the industry. One firm is using a labor hire firm to recruit and manage all new employees (known as variable temporary labor) who are paid at a lower rate and have less job security. However, other Australian auto assemblers have not yet followed this example.

The involvement of employees and unions in enterprise governance varies considerably between countries. In Germany and Sweden, unions continue to exercise strong influence at the plant and enterprise levels. In Sweden, there is an emphasis on consultation with unions and their plant level representatives on issues related to work environment and production systems. In Germany, works councils extend the influence of employees in workplace decision making while co-determination laws give unions a role at the board level. However, in both Sweden and Germany, unions have been willing to make concessions on pay and various working conditions in order to maintain the economic prosperity of the auto industry and thereby preserve employment levels in the industry as much as possible.

In Japan, severe industrial conflict between unions and auto companies in the first decade following World War II led to reforms which emphasized consultation between employers and workers at the plant level. This has resulted in a considerable variety of consultative activities and involvement of workers in decision-making in the workplace, even though the influence and bargaining power of trade unions has declined. In Korea, severe industrial conflict within the auto sector in the late 1980s, and again in the late 1990s, led to a number of reforms aimed at improving workplace consultation. The government has introduced labor–management councils at the plant level, but unions have been suspicious that these measures are designed to reduce their influence and have been generally cautious in their attitude to these councils. The tradition of authoritarian management systems in Korea has also impeded reforms in consultation and involvement of workers and their unions in enterprise governance, although this appears to be changing. In China, unions have played a limited role in fostering employee involvement in enterprise governance because the unions still operate as an agency of the state. However, as the number of informal and illegal industrial disputes has continued to increase, the Chinese government is searching for ways to reform workplace relations without fostering independent trade unions.

In the United States, unions have steadily lost influence at the plant and industry levels as their membership has continued to decline. Old plants, where the unions had members, have been closing and new plants in the South (many of which are owned by Japanese and other foreign companies) have successfully resisted the union's membership drives. There have been some examples of greater employee involvement (such as in health and safety committees) at the plant level, and some success with more participative workplace systems (such as at the GM-Toyota joint venture, NUMMI). However, the boldest experiment in co-management between the employer and the union at the GM Saturn plant was not sustained (see Rubenstein and Kochan, 2001). In Australia, there have been some examples of employee involvement in plant level decision-making and participation in team development, but these have generally been short-lived experiments and have not been integrated into mainstream management systems.

CONCLUSIONS: CHANGE, CONTINUITY AND HYBRIDIZATION

The automobile industry case studies reveal complex patterns of change and continuity as the impact of globalization has been experienced in auto assembly plants around the world. While there has been global convergence towards lean production in many plants in different countries, these tend to have resulted in hybrid forms of production which reflect local conditions in each country. Hence, there continues to be divergence in employment practices that arise, in part, from national differences in labor-market institutions and legal requirements at the national and industry levels. The case studies lend support to the findings reported by Katz (in Lansbury *et al.*, 2007: 118) that there appears to be 'a process of hybridization and adaptation (to lean production) with considerable variety in the terms and extent of hybridization across plants, companies and countries.' Katz also observed that, rather than multinational corporations creating one single approach to production systems and employment relations, 'there has been the emergence of more regional and global structures, within the MNCs, in the face of more global markets, global supply chains and efforts to integrate production systems within the corporation' (Katz, in Lansbury *et al.*, 2007: 119).

While the case studies of plants in the LMEs of the United States and Australia differed from those in CMEs of Germany and Sweden, and broadly followed the predictions of the VoC approach, the Asian countries appeared to be more diverse. Japan has followed fairly closely the employment practices of the CMEs, whereas Korea and China have become increasingly aligned with the practices of the LMEs. Hence, while the VoC approach provided some useful indicators of how western market economies differ in relation to employment practices, the Asian economies require a more nuanced interpretation. There needs to be a greater appreciation of the diverse characteristics of the political environment, the nature of the business systems and variations in the levels of economic development within Asia. The results of our project provided confirmation of the hypothesis by Yeung (2000) that AMEs are more susceptible to the pressures of globalization than the coordinated economies of Western Europe. They are, therefore, more likely to adopt employment relations practices that resemble developments in LMEs.

As our case study of the Japanese auto industry has revealed, the characteristics of the Japanese economy differ sufficiently from the CMEs for it to be regarded as a special case. The continuing, long-lasting success of the 'Toyota model' suggests that it is not only the type of capitalist system, at the macro-level, which influences outcomes but also the characteristics of the firm and how it adopts its employment relations to the global environment. Japan appears to be in transition from a coordinated market economy, in which Japanese enterprises had strong 'communal' characteristics, to a more liberal market economy. Some of the traditional characteristics of the Japanese employment system, such as seniority-based payment systems and long-term employment, have changed as companies have responded to the pressures of global competition and the aging workforce. Japanese auto assembly plants, like other sectors of the economy, have been making greater use of non-permanent contract workers in order to reduce wage costs and reduce their dependence on the aging permanent workforce within companies. Hence, Japanese firms are relying less on 'communality' and more on 'market relations' by restructuring the rules of both employment relations and inter-company relations (see Ishida *et al.*, 2007).

It is often suggested that although these types of case studies provide a mass of empirical detail, they reveal few generalizable theoretical propositions. However, a close reading of the literature indicates that what has been needed is not different research methods, but more sophisticated theoretical models capable of capturing and explaining the complex, contingent and multi-causal relationship between employers and employees in a changing world economy. The GERAB project builds on the VoC approach to develop and apply a model that moves in this direction.

The GERAB project provides evidence of the usefulness of a VoC approach to employment relations, but also indicates that a broader range of factors must be considered when examining globalization and employment. It is hoped that the results of this project will provide the basis for development of a more sophisticated theoretical framework that can help explain the ongoing changes in the relationship between globalization and employment relations.

REFERENCES

Allen, M. (2004), 'The varieties of capitalism paradigm: not enough variety?' *Socio-Economic Review*, **2**: 87–107.

Amable, B. (2000), 'Institutional complementarity and the diversity of social systems of innovation and production,' *Review of International Political Economy*, **7**(4): 645–87.

Amable, B. (2003), *The Diversity of Modern Capitalism*, New York: Oxford University Press.

Aoki, M. (2000), *Information, Corporate Governance and Institutional Diversity: Competitiveness in Japan, the USA and the Transitional Economies*, Oxford: Oxford University Press.

Cheffins, B. (2002), 'Comparative corporate governance and the Australian experience,' in I. Ramsay (ed.), *Key Developments in Corporate Law and Trusts Law*, Sydney: Butterworths, pp. 13–38.

Crouch, C. (2005), *Capitalist Diversity and Change: Recombinant governance and institutional entrepreneurs*, Oxford: Oxford University Press.

Crouch, C., Streeck, W., Boyer, R., Amable, B., Hall, P. and Jackson, G. (2005), 'Dialogue on "institutional complementarity and political economy,"' *Socio-Economic Review*, **3**: 359–82.

Dalziel, P. (2002), 'New Zealand's economic reform: an assessment,' *Review of Political Economy*, **14**(1): 31–46.

Godard, J. (2005), 'The new institutionalism, capitalist diversity and industrial relations,' in B.E. Kaufman (ed.), *Theoretical Perspectives on Work and the Employment Relationship*, Champaign, IL: Industrial Relations Research Association.

Gospel, H. and Pendleton, A. (2005), 'Corporate governance and labour management: an international comparison,' in H. Gospel and A. Pendleton (eds), *Corporate Governance and Labour management: An International Comparison*, Oxford: Oxford University Press, pp. 1–32.

Hall, P. and Gingerich, D. (2004), 'Varieties of capitalism and institutional complementarities in the macroeconomy: an empirical analysis,' MPIfG Discussion Paper 04/5.

Hall, P. and Soskice, D. (2001), 'An introduction to varieties of capitalism,' in P. Hall and D. Soskice (eds), *Varieties of Capitalism: The Institutional Foundations of Comparative Advantage*, New York: Oxford University Press, pp. 1–69.

Hay, C. (2004), 'Common trajectories, variable paces, divergent outcomes? Models of European capitalism under conditions of complex economic interdependence,' *Review of International Political Economy*, **11**(2): 231–62.

Hopner, M. (2005), 'What connects industrial relations and corporate governance? Explaining institutional complementarity,' *Socio-Economic Review*, **3**: 331–58.

Howell, C. (2003), 'Varieties of capitalism: and then there was one?' *Comparative Politics*, **36**(1).

Ishida, M., Ono, A., Mitani, N., Tomita, Y. and Kirsch, A. (2007), 'The automotive industry in Japan,' in R.D. Lansbury, N. Wailes and J. Kitay (eds), *Globalisation and Employment Relations in the Auto Assembly Industry: A Study of Seven Countries*, The Hague: Kluwer Law International.

Jackson, G. (2001), 'The origins of non-liberal corporate governance in Germany and Japan,' in W. Streek and K. Yamamura (eds), *The Origins of Nonliberal Capitalism: Germany and Japan in Comparison*, Ithaca, NY: Cornell University Press, 121–170.

Jackson, G. and Deeg, R. (2006), 'How many varieties of capitalism? Comparing the comparative institutional analyses of capitalist diversity,' MPIfG Discussion Paper 06/2.

Jacoby, S. (2005), *The Embedded Corporation: Corporate Governance and Employment Relations in Japan and the United States*, Princeton, NJ: Princeton University Press.

Jurgens, U. (2003), 'Transformation and interaction: Japanese, US and German production models in the 1990s,' in W. Streeck and K. Yamamura (eds), *The End of Diversity? Prospects for German and Japanese Capitalism,* Ithaca, NY: Cornell University Press, 212–39.

Katz, H. (2007), 'Afterword,' in R.D. Lansbury, C.S. Suh and S.H. Kwon (eds), *The Global Korean Motor Industry: The Hyundai Motor Company's Global Strategy*, London: Routledge, pp. 119–120.

Kitay, J. and Wailes, N. (eds) (2007), 'Globalization, varieties of capitalism and employment relations in retail banking,' *Bulletin of Comparative Labour Relations*, No. 63, The Hague: Kluwer Law International.

Kochan, T.A., Lansbury, R.D. and MacDuffie, J.P. (eds) (1997), *After Lean Production: Evolving Employment Practices in the World Auto Industry*, Ithaca, NY: Cornell University Press.

Lansbury, R., Kitay, J. and Wailes, N. (2003), 'The impact of globalisation on employment relations: some research propositions,' *Asia-Pacific Journal of Human Resources*, **41**(1): 62–74.

Lansbury, R., Kitay, J. and Wailes, N. (2006), 'Globalization and working life: a comparative analysis of the automobile and banking sectors in Australia and Korea,' in G. Wood and P. James (eds), *Institutions, Production and Working Life*, Oxford: Oxford University Press, pp. 83–103.

Lansbury, R.D., Suh, C.-S. and Kwon, S.-H. (2007), *The Global Korean Motor Industry: The Hyundai Motor Company's Global Strategy*, London, New York: Routledge.

Locke, R., Piore, M. and Kochan, T. (1995), 'Introduction: employment relations in a changing world economy,' in R. Locke, T. Kochan and M. Piore (eds), *Employment Relations in a Changing World Economy*, Boston, MA: MIT Press, pp. xiii–xxix.

Miller, D. and Shamsie, J. (1996), 'The resource-based view of the firm in two environments: the Hollywood film studios from 1936 to 1965,' *Academy of Management Journal*, **39**(3): 519–25.

Pontusson, J. (1995), 'From comparative public policy to political economy: putting political institutions in their place and taking interests seriously,' *Comparative Political Studies*, **28**(1): 117–48.

Pontusson, J. (2005), 'Varieties and commonalities of capitalism,' in D. Coates (ed.), *Varieties of Capitalism, Varieties of Approaches*, London: Palgrave Macmillan, 163–88.

Pontusson, J. and Swenson, P. (1996), 'Labor markets, production strategies and wage bargaining institutions: the Swedish employer offensive in comparative perspective,' *Comparative Political Studies*, **29**(2): 223–51.

Regini, M., Kitay, J. and Baethge, M. (eds) (1999), *From Tellers to Sellers: Changing Employment Relations in Banks*, Cambridge, MA: MIT Press.

Rubenstein, S. and Kochan, T.A. (2001), *Learning from Saturn: Possibilities for Corporate Governance and Employee Relations*, Ithaca, NY: Cornell University Press.

Streeck, W. (1991), 'On the institutional conditions for diversified quality production,' in E. Matzner and W. Streeck (eds), *Beyond Keynesianism: The Socio-Economics of Production and Full Employment*, Aldershot, UK and Brookfield, US: Elgar, pp. 21–61.

Streeck, W. and Thelen, K. (2005), 'Introduction: institutional change in advanced political economies,' in W. Streeck and K. Thelen (eds), *Beyond Continuity: Institutional Change in Advanced Political Economies*, Oxford: Oxford University Press, pp. 1–39.

Streeck, W. and Yamamura, K. (eds) (2001), *The Origins of Nonliberal Capitalism: Germany and Japan in Comparison*, Ithaca, NY: Cornell University Press.

Streeck, W. and Yamamura, K. (eds) (2003), *The End of Diversity? Prospects for German and Japanese Capitalism*, Ithaca, NY: Cornell University Press.

Swenson, P. (1991), 'Bringing capital back in, or social democracy reconsidered: employer power, cross-class alliances, and centralization of industrial relations in Denmark and Sweden,' *World Politics* **43**(4): 513–45.

Wailes, N. (2003), 'The importance of small differences: globalization and employment relations in Australia and New Zealand,' Unpublished PhD Thesis, University of Sydney.

Wailes, N., Lansbury, R.D. and Ramia, G. (2003), 'Interests, institutions and industrial relations,' *British Journal of Industrial Relations*, **41**(4): 617–37.

Whitley, R. (1999), *Divergent Capitalisms: The Social Structuring and Change of Business Systems*, Oxford: Oxford University Press.

Womack, J.P., Jones, D.T. and Ross, D. (1990), *The Machine that Changed the World*, New York: Rawson Associates.

Yeung, H. (2000), 'The dynamics of Asian business systems in a globalising era,' *Review of International Political Economy* 7(3): 399–433.

USA
JS^3
$J16$
$L67$ $JS2$
$JS1$
JS

11. Evolving labor relations in the women's apparel industry

Katie Quan

INTRODUCTION

Labor relations are in essence the power relationships between labor and capital. Various labor market institutions serve that power relationship, and in the twentieth century labor unions arose as the most important institution for workers to organize and bargain collectively for power. Among these unions, the International Ladies' Garment Workers' Union (ILGWU) was an early champion of issues such as the eight-hour workday, the abolition of child labor, health and safety regulations, and women's suffrage. For tens of thousands of immigrant women and men, the union became the ticket to the American dream – raising penniless sweatshop workers to proud middle-class citizens. The key to the ILGWU's success was its ability to parlay public outrage over nineteenth-century-sweatshop conditions into a unique, triangular collective bargaining relationship between jobbers, contractors, and the union. As a result, by the 1950s garment workers were the second-highest-paid production workers in the country.

In spite of these achievements, in the 1960s we began to hear the ILGWU protest outsourcing of apparel jobs to foreign countries where workers toiled under conditions similar to the sweatshops that the union had helped eradicate. In 1995 we even heard of Los Angeles garment workers who had been enslaved – smuggled in from Thailand under false pretenses, held under armed guard behind razor-wire fences, and paid less than 50 cents per hour. What happened to the power that led to such impressive union victories only a few decades earlier? What happened to the unique bargaining relationship that won those gains? Given current conditions, what steps can be taken to construct a new paradigm for labor relations in the women's apparel industry?

In this chapter, I argue that relations between labor and capital are dynamic, and that the labor unions, collective bargaining relationships, labor laws and organizing strategies must adapt to this changing reality or union power will suffer. By tracing the history of the women's apparel industry, I will show that while triangular bargaining once won significant increases in wages for workers, now global markets have changed the effectiveness of that system, and unions have been slow to respond and adapt. I will review the anti-sweatshop movement that began in the 1990s, as well as current organizing among garment workers internationally, and will suggest that these strengths will become the basis of a new paradigm for labor relations in the global apparel industry. Finally, I will consider what role industrial relations experts may play in assisting garment workers to forge that new paradigm.

The research for this chapter was obtained from numerous secondary sources, as well as interviews with primary participants. The author is also a primary participant, having previously been a rank and file garment worker and ILGWU organizer in New York City, district council manager in San Francisco, as well as an international vice-president of the successor union to the ILGWU, the Union of Needletrades, Industrial and Textile Employees (UNITE). I am also currently a member of the boards of directors of Sweatshop Watch, the Workers Rights Consortium, and the International Labor Rights Fund.

TRIANGULAR BARGAINING

Mass production of clothing became possible after the invention of the sewing machine in 1846. Thereafter New York became the center of the US apparel industry, where most garment workers worked for small contractors assembling the clothing according to the specifications of the manufacturers or 'jobbers.' Manufacturers were firms that designed the fashions, produced some clothing in-house, and then sold the clothing. Jobbers only designed and sold clothing, but did not produce in-house. Since there were many more jobbers than manufacturers, industry insiders often referred to jobbers as a category that included both manufacturers and jobbers, as will I in this chapter.

The jobber–contractor system fueled a fiercely competitive, chaotic, cutthroat business. Jobbers not only competed with each other for fashion distinction and placement in retail stores, but they also attempted to squeeze profits from labor by lowering the prices that they paid the contractors. They did this by playing contractors against each other, and giving work to the contractor who offered the lowest bid. This forced the contractors into fierce competition, and they in turn attempted to make their profits by lowering the piece-rate wages of the workers. Workers were told that they could either take the wage reduction or leave; and since they had no one they could squeeze to make up the wage reduction, and they had nowhere to go, they had no choice but to accept their employers' demands.

As a result, sweatshop conditions arose – long hours of workers toiling over piecework, child labor, industrial home sewing by whole families, and horrendous health and safety violations like those that led to the Triangle Shirtwaist fire in 1911, where 146 women were killed because the employer locked factory doors to keep union organizers out (Tyler, 1995: 86–97). These horrific sweatshop conditions were documented by many social activists, writers, artists, and government officials. The resulting public outrage set the stage for the union to successfully lead a series of strikes in 1909, 1910 and 1913, each involving tens of thousands of workers that finally led to the unionization of the industry (Levine, 1924: 292–341). With widespread public support, a strong and militant membership, and newly-acquired collective bargaining rights, union leaders and their supporters now had an opportunity to devise creative labor relations structures that would empower workers and their union.

Beginning in 1923, the ILGWU moved to rationalize the chaos in the industry and create conditions for its own expansion. It began by defining jobbers and contractors as 'joint employers' in an 'integrated process of production.' Most garment workers received their wages from contractors, but the union argued that contractors had no independent ability to alter the design of the product or to market products, and therefore contractors were completely dependent upon the jobbers for their existence. Therefore, jobbers should also be considered as employers of the workers, and should share joint liability for workers' wages, benefits and working conditions. Later this legal definition was enshrined in the National Labor Relations Act's Garment Industry Proviso, an amendment to the secondary boycott prohibitions of the Act that exempts the garment industry (Zimny and Garren, 1994: 4–9).[1]

Joint employership led the union to establish a triangular bargaining re-lationship: (a) first the union negotiated a collective bargaining agreement with the jobbers; (b) then the union negotiated an agreement with the con-tractors; and (c) finally the jobbers and the contractors negotiated an agree-ment with each other. Key in this process was the 'pass through' provision, where jobbers agreed to pass through increases in wages and benefits to workers by increasing their prices to the contractors. When the union negoti-ated with the contractors, it negotiated for the contractors to pass through the increases provided by the jobbers to the workers. Finally, when the contrac-tors negotiated with the jobbers, they negotiated for the jobbers to give them the same percentage increase that had been agreed in union negotiations. In this way, the jobbers paid wages, health and welfare benefits, retirement benefits, vacation pay and in later years even child-care benefits to workers in contracting shops. This was a brilliant method of distributing value from the jobbers through contractors to the workers, and it became the predominant labor-relations model throughout the women's apparel industry.[2]

One potential danger in the system was the possibility of jobbers evading their 'pass through' responsibilities by sourcing to new contractors at lower prices instead of raising prices to existing contractors. To address this problem, the triangular contracts provided that each jobber designate a list of contractors it regularly used, and required that the jobbers not terminate the use of these contractors except for just cause. This ensured that from one year to the next the same contractors would be used and that negotiated increases in wages and benefits would in fact be passed down from jobber to contractor to worker. This arrangement also greatly reduced competition among contractors, which stabilized the industry.

An important component of the triangular bargaining was the process of negotiating with employers in associations. Just as hundreds of thousands of workers cannot effectively negotiate unless they are represented collectively by unions, the same is true for the thousands of contractors and jobbers in the apparel industry. The union supported the formation of these employer associations and signed collective bargaining agreements with them. Thus union contracts were not negotiated factory by factory, but with employer associations in various segments of the industry such as cloak and suit, sportswear, underwear, children's wear and accessories. They were negotiated in separate segments because these apparel industry segments had different fashion trends, production systems, and profit margins. However, each segment had the same contract terms for various geographic locations, so, for example, the cloak and suit wage levels were the same in New York, Chicago, Los Angeles and San Francisco. The main objective was to equalize labor costs among firms in the same segment of the industry, effectively removing wage gouging and other exploitative labor practices as competitive factors.

To ensure that the jobbers, contractors and union became locked in an interdependent relationship, the triangular bargaining contracts provided that union jobbers source only from union contractors and union contractors get work only from union jobbers. Furthermore, if a union jobber used a non-union contractor, then the union could strike the non-union contractor, and if a non-union jobber used a union contractor, then the union could strike the non-union jobber. In this way, striking non-union firms became the main organizing strategy for persuading non-union firms to join employer associations that were signatories to union contracts. And since unionized firms dominated the women's apparel market from the 1940s through the 1960s, non-union firms often joined these employer associations with little resistance.

Because the union shop clause in union contracts required workers to join the union within 30 days or be terminated, union membership grew. Thus, a high density of union jobbers led to a high density of union contractors, which led to high density of union members. In the mid-1950s, when the average unionization density in the United States was 35 percent, the ILGWU's membership numbered 450 000 (Esbenshade 2004: 19), or 70 percent of all garment workers at the time.

Thus, the triangular bargaining relationship featured a labor relations system that: (a) provided for distribution of value from the jobbers through the contractors to the workers; (b) leveled competition among jobbers and contractors by equalizing labor costs; and (c) locked labor-market actors in an interdependent relationship by requiring union labor. This system was tremendously successful and led to garment workers enjoying a steady rise in working conditions from the 1930s through the 1960s. When employers began to move from New York into Pennsylvania and then to the South, the union followed the labor markets and organized. Even when the employers moved to Puerto Rico in the late 1950s, the union moved there to organize. The problem for the union came afterwards, when the apparel industry moved beyond US territorial borders.

INDUSTRY GLOBALIZATION AND THE NEW ANTI-SWEATSHOP MOVEMENT

Labor relations began to take a new turn in the 1960s when American jobbers began to source apparel manufacturing to Latin America and Asia. Lured by the prospect of making tremendous profits from low labor costs, and buoyed by US government policy that encouraged apparel manufacturers to set up factories in politically friendly developing countries, overseas outsourcing became the wave of the future. Unlike the previous period, during which union organizers 'followed the work' and maintained a high level of union density in new labor markets, now the union stopped at southern borders. The union's main strategy to address overseas outsourcing was to advocate for trade policies that would limit imports. One such policy was the 1974 Multi-Fibre Arrangement, a worldwide trade agreement that exempted the garment industry from free trade provisions of the General Agreement on Tariffs and Trade and instead placed quotas on apparel imported into the United States and Europe from developing countries for the next 30 years (Dickerson, 1991: 335–65).

Trade restrictions did not stop American and European apparel manufacturers from sourcing overseas in factories with horrific working conditions, however. Paltry wages, 16-hour workdays, child labor and unsafe working conditions became the norm first in the 1960s and 1970s in Japan, Hong Kong, South Korea and Taiwan, and later in Thailand, Indonesia, the Philippines, Mexico, El Salvador, Honduras and the Dominican Republic (Bonacich *et al.*, 1994). Often the workers were young women from the countryside who left extreme poverty to earn cash for whole families back in the village. Many courageous workers did organize unions at their factories, often in the face of severe employer opposition and in some cases with danger to their lives. In a few countries, like the Philippines, Thailand and Indonesia, workers established garment unions that covered the whole sector rather than just one factory; because they bargained only with contractors and not the foreign jobbers, however, their ability to make significant gains was limited.

Meanwhile in the United States, jobbers pitted overseas contractors against American ones in an attempt to drive down the prices of American contractors. Contractors in turn demanded deep concessions from the union. Jobbers stopped passing through prices to contractors, and contractors stopped passing on wage increases to workers. The density of union employers in the associations plummeted to single digits, as did union membership. By the time I became the head of the garment workers union in San Francisco during the 1990s, the industry's labor relations were in crisis. Jobbers like the Gap refused to join the union because all of its production was done by overseas contractors. Without union jobbers, union contractors closed almost daily. Those who stayed wanted deep wage and benefit concessions because they were competing with factories that paid $8 a day on the Mexican border and $1 a day in China. The triangular bargaining agreements that had served me well as a rank and file member in the 1970s now were useless, and my members were left powerless to defend the labor standards they had struggled so hard to establish.

In the 1990s, amid repeated news of sweatshop conditions in factories producing for Nike, the Gap, Kathie Lee Gifford and others, labor rights activists began to demand that jobbers and retailers adopt 'codes of conduct' for their contractors that would ensure labor standards and labor rights. This new anti-sweatshop movement was led primarily by non-governmental organizations that supported labor, such as consumer groups, human rights activists, religious groups and student organizations. Over the next ten years they succeeded in bringing labor abuse to light and helped to define labor rights as human rights. Their tireless picketing, boycotting, and campaigning forced the majority of American and European apparel jobbers to adopt codes of conduct and to accept corporate social responsibility for implementing labor standards among their contractors.

However, in spite of the many achievements of the modern anti-sweatshop movement, sweatshops continue to abound,[3] and the power gap between labor and capital is growing wider. Moreover, while the anti-sweatshop movement changed some business practices, it had not resulted in garment workers and their unions gaining organizational strength, except in a very few cases.

Thus the challenge at this historical juncture is the same as it was in the 1920s: how can garment workers and their unions and organizations parlay their own organizing successes, as well as the successes of the anti-sweatshop social movement, into a new labor relations system that will allow workers to organize for improved standards and labor rights?

TOWARD A NEW PARADIGM

As discussed above, the key to garment workers' historical successes was a labor relations systems that featured: (a) distribution of value from the jobbers through the contractors to the workers; (b) leveling competition among jobbers and contractors by equalizing labor costs; and (c) locking labor-market actors into an interdependent relationship through requiring union labor. Given current conditions, how might we achieve the same effects in a new labor relations system? The answer to this question is far beyond the scope of this chapter, however we can begin the discussion by analyzing what conditions have changed in the apparel industry in the past 20–30 years and suggesting ways to use this information to build a new paradigm of labor relations in the industry. These new conditions can be grouped as power relations, ways of distributing value and leveling competition, and forms of worker representation.

Power Relationships

In the past 20 years, retail stores have replaced jobbers as the apex of the supply chain. Whether they are high-end stores like Macy's and Nordstrom's, or everyday low price stores like Target and Wal-Mart, around 60 percent of their merchandise is apparel, and they now dictate to jobbers exactly what fashions they will sell and what price they will pay by forcing jobbers to bid against each other. This shift in power relationships has been identified by Gary Gereffi as the shift from the 'producer-driven' supply chain to the 'buyer-driven' supply chain (Gereffi, 1994). This new link in the supply chain adds yet another level of 'squeezing' of profits that intensifies an already chaotic and cut-throat industry. It also potentially puts workers across the bargaining table not just from contractors and jobbers, but retailers as well.

Another important change in the structure of the supply chain is the rise of quite a few multinational contractors. Headquartered in Hong Kong, Taiwan, South Korea and China, these corporations own dozens of factories spread across the globe, from Latin America to Southeast Asia, Africa, and even the United States (Asia Monitor Resource Center, 2005). These firms perform many of the functions formerly done by jobbers, such as making samples, ordering fabric, and cutting fabric, and are known as 'full package' manufacturers. The largest shoe producer in the world, Yue Yuen Industrial Holdings of Taiwan, posted $3.6 billion in sales in 2006, and owns a factory in Shenzhen, China that employs 60 000 workers who produce shoes for Nike, Reebok, and other well-known international brands.[4] Because of their size, they have more negotiating power over prices with brands than small apparel contractors employing 50–300 workers, and their profit margin is much higher. It also means that they have the independent means to improve workers' conditions without needing increases to be passed down from the jobbers.

Logistics and distribution systems connect various entities in the supply chain to each other, and their power has risen greatly in the past couple of decades. In the New York apparel industry during the twentieth century, truckers who transported goods from contractors to jobbers and from jobbers to retailers were critical to production, so the ILGWU organized these truckers into the same union as seamstresses. In the 1970s through the 1990s, some of these truckers became manufacturing brokers, setting up factories and leasing sewing machines to new contractors – all for a price. However, during the last 15 years logistics and distribution firms have become even more powerful, having undergone a 'revolution' and greatly expanded their operations vertically along the supply chain and horizontally across the globe by land, sea, and air (Bonacich, 2003).

Whereas power in the apparel industry used to be defined in terms of hierarchy on the production chain, in the past 20 years capitalism has grown more complex, and those who service the production chain, such as financiers and agents, have become important power players. For example, Macy's is owned by the Federated department store chain, which might hypothetically be financed by other entities such as bond funds, pension funds, and a range of other investors. To organize building service workers, the Service Employees International Union (SEIU) and a few other unions have made important use of corporate research to follow the 'money chain' from building owners to real estate investors, land use developers, and financial investors (Shaffer, 2005). Others who service the supply chain and play a critical role (especially given the global scope of the market) are agents, who help retailers find investors, retailers find jobbers, jobbers find contractors, and contractors find workers.

Two other related kinds of non-production, supply-chain power are brand power and consumer power. Today consumers buy branded products because they want to identify with an advertised look or feel, and they are willing to spend far more than the normal mark-up from production to retail for this brand identification (Klein, 1999). While successful brand names bring tremendous marketing power, this success can also be a liability. As has been shown in numerous anti-sweatshop campaigns, when consumers are organized to put pressure on brands, the brands are forced to listen.

Finally, although most garment industry experts have focused on identifying power within the production chain, additional consideration might be given to 'upstream' industry links to producers of raw materials for apparel, such as cotton growers, wool producers and synthetic manufacturers. The South African Clothing and Textile Workers Union (SACTWU) has long integrated cotton producers into their union with the express intent to organize workers at all levels of the supply chain into one union.[5] The active organizing of cotton and wool producers by environmentalists and human-rights groups might also provide an opportunity for workers further downstream in the production chain to find more allies.

Redistributing Value and Leveling Employer Competition

One of the most important contributions of the anti-sweatshop movement of the past two decades was getting jobbers and retailers in the apparel industry to acknowledge responsibility for working conditions in supplier firms. In California in 1999, anti-sweatshop groups were able to pass AB 633, a state law that provides for apparel jobbers to pay back wages (in an expedited manner) to workers in its contracting shops when the contractor does not pay (Sweatshop Watch, 2000). However, even though most apparel corporations adopted codes of conduct for their suppliers and vendors, and many of them have programs to monitor compliance with these codes of conduct, most apparel corporations viewed their responsibility as policing contractors to adhere to codes and few, if any, intended to actually pass on a greater share of profits through their contractors to workers.

Recently the United Students Against Sweatshops[6] and the Workers Rights Consortium[7] created the Designated Suppliers Program (DSP), a project whereby university licensees would be required to source a significant portion of their products from a list of designated suppliers that have met labor rights requirements. These licensees range in size from big, well-known firms such as Nike that have large contracts with universities to small firms that make souvenirs. By requiring licensees to pay designated suppliers a price high enough to meet labor standards, the DSP will create a 'pass through' of higher wages to workers (Worker Rights Consortium, 2007). This is the first project in many decades to address the distribution of value in supply chains. Although it would only apply to university-licensed products, if it is successful, then it could be replicated in other sub-sectors of the apparel industry.

In the past, leveling the playing field with regard to labor costs was accomplished through employer associations that negotiated with the union for the same terms of the union contract. As the triangular bargaining system declined, however, this leveling of the playing field has been attempted through public and trade policies. For example, in response to advocacy by anti-sweatshop groups, several US cities, including Los Angeles, San Francisco, New York and a number of smaller communities have enacted procurement ordinances that require uniforms and other products purchased by these cities to be manufactured consistent with established labor standards. This sets minimum standards for those who wish to compete for business with these cities (Global Exchange, 2007).

American unions have been keen to insert labor-standards requirements in trade policy, requiring investors to meet established labor standards along with other regulations. Though sometimes seen by the governments and citizens in the receiving countries as being 'protectionist' because unions were trying to protect the jobs of their American members, the effect was nevertheless to set a (labor-standards) floor for those investors who wished to do business in the receiving country. This was clearly the case in Cambodia, where a 1998 bilateral trade agreement with the United States conditioned increased trade opportunities for garment industry contractors to compliance with labor rights as defined by the International Labour Organisation (ILO).[8]

Another way that minimum labor standards are set is through wage and benefits policies. In fact, in the United States where unions have been unsuccessful in increasing wages and benefits for garment workers, passage of increases in local and state minimum wages, paid family leave policies, and mandatory sick leave policies have replaced collective bargaining as the most important tool for improving working conditions. Current efforts by unions and other civil society advocates to pass universal health care policies would also create social benefits that unions have not been able to accomplish through collective bargaining. On a global basis, Jobs with Justice's Asian Wage Floor campaign aims to organize Asian garment worker groups to establish an international minimum wage that would take wage competition out of business competition (Jobs with Justice, 2006).

Consideration could also be given to other ways of stabilizing labor costs, such as by using modern production technologies to help control overtime and by eliminating the piece-rate system (an antiquated system of compensation that leads to sweatshop problems such as unpaid overtime, lack of a minimum wage guarantee, and employee health problems).

Worker Representation

Unions and collective bargaining are effective when they bring employers to the table, yield constructive negotiations, and secure a contract that defines the employer–employee relationship for a stipulated period of time and provides a chance to renegotiate provisions every few years. However, in response to globalization and a decline in market share, garment-worker unions in the United States, Japan, and other developed countries have merged with other unions and shifted their focus away from the apparel sector toward other sectors.

Faced with unbearable sweatshop conditions and intolerable employer abuse, workers in many developing countries have undertaken aggressive organizing campaigns. Examples include the Kenyan unions that organized 30 000 garment workers from 1998 to 2003 (Forbes, 2003); the Mexican union SITEMEX at Kukdong/Mexmode that raised worker wages by 10 percent, 38 percent and 20 percent in successive years (Hermanson, 2004: 17–18); and the Salvadoran union STIT that waged an international campaign for two years against an employer that shuttered its plant because of union activity and won the opening of another plant to re-employ the workers (Quan, 2007). These and hundreds of other courageous efforts like them are now in the forefront of garment worker organizing, and it is likely that any new paradigm for garment worker organizing will be led by workers from these kinds of struggles.

In the absence of union strength, civil society organizations dedicated to labor rights have arisen. Such organizations are located in the United States, China, India, Thailand, Mexico, South Africa, and indeed in almost every country. Unlike unions, which derive power from contracts with employers, these workers' groups often rely on pressure against employers through media exposure, consumer boycotts, and legislative advocacy. The largest of these groups, the Self-Employed Women's Association of India (SEWA), has more than 700 000 members (many of whom are former garment workers) and organizes women workers in contingent sectors into economic cooperatives. It also sponsors literacy and economic self-sufficiency programs, and lobbies local and national governments on behalf of its members.[9] Another example is the Garment Workers Center in Los Angeles, an independent non-profit organization that has been active in organizing non-union workers to obtain back pay and is a member of the Multi-ethnic Immigrant Workers Organizing Network (MIWON), a network of workers centers in the Los Angeles area.[10]

The greatest challenge for unions and worker organizations will be in conceptualizing and carrying out labor-relations strategies internationally. In the 1970s and then again in the 1990s, some unions established 'company councils' of workers from different countries who worked for the same multi-national employer, but those efforts were not sustained (Russo and Banks, 1999; Borgers, 1999). In the 1990s, some general union federations began to advocate for international framework agreements that called for international labor rights to be applied to contractors, however these agreements rarely have effective enforcement mechanisms and do not carry out global collective bargaining.[11] From 1995 through 2005, the Association of Flight Attendants had a contract with United Airlines that covered all 40 000 of its flight attendants with a single collective bargaining agreement, regardless of the citizenship or country where the attendants worked (Quan, 2000).

One of the biggest obstacles to international labor strategies is the resistance of the AFL-CIO and some other international unions to establishment of formal relations with unions in China. This resistance is due partly to long-held beliefs in the AFL-CIO leadership that unions in communist countries do not truly represent workers and because of the Chinese government's harassment and incarceration of union and other human rights activists (Shailor, 2005). However, this hard line has neither improved conditions for Chinese garment workers nor helped the organizing of garment workers worldwide. Conditions in China's garment export sector continue to be horrific, with workers often clocking in at 7 a.m. and clocking out at 11 p.m., having only 1–2 days off per month, and wages so low that they do not even meet the Chinese government's low minimum-wage standards. Because China's apparel exports account for 30 percent of the world's market, and China is not just the largest exporter but also larger than its next five competitors combined (International Textiles and Clothing Bureau, 2007), and because there are more garment workers in China than anywhere else, low labor conditions in China drive down labor standards everywhere. Clearly an alternative to the hard-line labor diplomacy approach must be found because current policies have not worked, and without unity with Chinese garment workers there can be no power for any of the world's garment workers.

In the apparel industry there have been some examples of grassroots workers organizing across borders. One is the campaign of Sara Lee workers in Mexico allying with anti-sweatshop groups in over a dozen countries to pressure their employer to allow them to organize a union of their choice. Another is the case of Tainan Enterprises workers in El Salvador, who worked through the AFL-CIO Solidarity Center to link with Cambodian workers in another Tainan plant to put economic pressure on the company, and with a Taiwanese labor-rights group that shamed Tainan in Taiwan (Quan, 2007). Many garment-worker groups also came together before the expiration of the Multi-Fibre Arrangement to discuss possible strategies in anticipation of a worldwide shift in apparel production that did not happen.[12] However, while all of these efforts were positive developments and the organizing strategies were increasingly sophisticated, they have not yet resulted in a new labor relations system that will structure labor markets in a way that provides workers with growing power.

One new development is the SEIU's Global Cities initiative, a plan that ambitiously attempts to build on the union's Justice for Janitors model. This initiative works through the union international federation, UNI, to organize workers horizontally across 40 important global cities and to leverage vertically up the supply chain from building owners to real estate investors (Lerner, 2007). It aims to build union density in global janitorial markets, a critical element in union power, however it remains to be seen whether any new forms of collective bargaining or other labor-market institutions will be formed as a result of this global organizing.

Finally, while reinventing labor relations systems, consideration should be given to strengthening the leadership of women garment workers themselves. Women garment workers have shown great courage by overcoming company thugs on picket lines in Mexico (Hermanson, 2004), and the very real danger of being shot dead when blocking scab trucks in Thailand (Quan, 2004: 98). They have built accountability systems between rank and file and leadership in their unions in Cambodia, and led the fight against the International Monetary Fund's anti-labor policies in Sri Lanka (AFL-CIO Solidarity Center, 2007). Today as in the past, men still dominate leadership positions in most unions and worker groups, leading Mexican women workers to form a separate group (known as SEDEPAC) so that women would have opportunities to develop as leaders (Quan, 2007), and causing Honduran banana workers to establish a quota for women at all levels of leadership in their unions (Frank, 2005). Much more has to be done to bring women's wisdom and spirit to the higher ranks of leadership in unions and worker organizations.

THE ROLE OF LABOR RELATIONS SPECIALISTS

If the challenge for organizers of garment workers is to construct a strategy that will parlay current achievements into more powerful and sustained labor relations systems, then the challenge for labor relations experts is to find ways of assisting organizers in doing this. Over the last two decades, much work has been done to document sweatshop conditions in the women's apparel industry, and some work has been done to understand the apparel business and identify innovative organizing practices. However, beyond this important work, what is urgently needed is a focus on constructing labor relations systems that will bring increased power to workers on the level of triangular bargaining – systems that will address passing through value in the supply chain, leveling employer competition on labor costs, and increasing union density and worker strength.

Given the expertise of labor-relations experts in education, research and facilitation, work could be developed in the following key areas.

Leadership development: Understanding global labor strategies can be daunting, and programs and classes that prepare garment worker leaders to chart their own futures are critical. Using the technique of popular education, labor educators can help worker leaders link their experiences to a broad analysis of the global apparel industry. Then, armed with that additional knowledge, workers can take steps to create and implement plans for a new labor-relations paradigm in the apparel industry.

Applied research: Though there has been much research on sweatshop conditions, worker advocates still know little about each other's best practices or about the apparel business. Much more must be done to bring to light successful organizing strategies and to explain complex global apparel business practices. This will help garment workers to understand their situation better, uncover strengths and weaknesses in the existing power hierarchy, and identify promising new labor-relations structures.

Facilitated dialogue: Although many actors in the anti-sweatshop movement know each other, almost all operate in a reactive mode, responding to crises that arise. An exception was the recent convening of many groups to address the end of the Multi-Fibre Arrangement (on January 1 2005) and to consider the implications this worldwide trade agreement might have for workers in various countries. However, since 2005 there have not been many international attempts to chart common agendas. Labor experts are in a unique position to convene key practitioners and facilitate discussions regarding common goals, implementation strategies, and the establishment and maintenance of communications networks.

CONCLUSION: BUILDING STRENGTH THROUGH UNITY

Labor relations are about power relationships, and unions establish collective bargaining and organizing strategies with the objective of gaining greater power. The advances in power for garment workers in the first 50 years of the twentieth century were almost eliminated in the next 50 years, and these losses were further intensified by the inability of stakeholders to keep pace with changing power relationships in the global industry. Nevertheless, garment workers in many countries currently carry on the tradition of organizing unions because they know that they are stronger when they build unity among themselves and with others. Moreover, the anti-sweatshop movement has helped spread the word about their issues, and has won so much sympathy from the general public that most apparel corporations have been forced to acknowledge responsibility for sweatshop conditions.

The challenge for garment workers today is to construct new forms of labor relations that raise their standard of living and give them the tools to gain ongoing strength in the face of globalized capital. Labor relations experts can play an important complementary role by providing education that develops stronger worker leaders, carrying out research that is useful to worker organizers, and bringing together key stakeholders to chart strategic goals and paths.

NOTES

1. For further information, see http://www.nlrb.gov/nlrb/shared_files/brochures/basic guide.pdf, p. 25.
2. To see a typical contractor's agreement, go to http://www.bls.gov/cba/reports/ cbrp0241.pdf.
3. For example, for a copy of the Gap's admission of little improvement in labor conditions in its supplier factories, go to http://www.gapinc.com/public/SocialResponsibility/sr_ fac_wwf_id.shtml (accessed 16 August 2007).
4. See http://www.yueyuen.com/hk/annual/2006/E_Yue%20Yuen%20AR-1754.pdf.
5. For information on SACTWU membership eligibility, see http://www.sactwu.org.za/ memunionapply.asp.
6. See www.usasnet.org.
7. See www.workersrights.org.
8. For a report on the ILO's findings in Cambodia, go to http://www.ilo.org/wcmsp5/ groups/public/---dgreports/---dcomm/documents/publication/kd00125.pdf.
9. For more information about SEWA, go to http://www.sewa.org/aboutus/index.asp.
10. See http://www.garmentworkercenter.org/campaigns.php?itemid=27.
11. For an example of the rationale for international framework agreements, go to http://www.union-network.org/UNIsite/In_Depth/Multinationals/GFAs.html.
12. For examples of these kinds of meetings, go to http://www.mfa-forum.net/bangladesh/ docs/eti_post_conf.pdf and www.amrc.org.hk/5205.htm. According to this author's

analysis, a worldwide shift in apparel production did not happen after the Multi-Fibre Arrangement expired for a number of reasons, including: quotas were re-established between China and the European Union and China and the United States; China's apparel development policy changed in 2005 in ways that discouraged garment assembly in mature economic zones; and suppliers in some Latin American and South Asian countries became competitive with China through taking on additional manufacturing responsibilities as "full package" producers.

REFERENCES

Asia Monitor Resource Centre (2005), *Asian Transnational Corporation Outlook 2004: Asian TNCs, Workers, and the Movement of Capital*, Hong Kong: Asia Monitor Resource Centre.

AFL-CIO Solidarity Center and UC Berkeley Center for Labor Research and Education (2007), 'Toolkit for organizers in export processing zones and industries,' published on the Internet at http://www.solidaritycenter.org/content.asp?contentid=689 and http://laborcenter.berkeley.edu/curricula/. Last accessed 12 August 2007.

Bonacich, Edna (2003), 'Pulling the plug: labor and global supply chain,' *New Labor Forum*, **12**(2), 41–8.

Bonacich, Edna, Cheng, Lucie, Chinchilla, Norma, Hamilton, Nora and Ong, Paul (1994), *Global Production: The Apparel Industry in the Pacific Rim*, Philadelphia, PA: Temple University Press.

Borgers, Frank (1999), 'Global unionism – beyond the rhetoric: the CWA North Atlantic Alliance,' *Labor Studies Journal*, 24(1), 107–22.

Dickerson, Kitty (1991), *Textile and Apparel in the International Economy*, New York: Macmillan Publishing Company.

Forbes, Mary Ann of AFL-CIO Solidarity Center (2003), Interview with the author on 8 October in Bangkok, Thailand.

Frank, Dana (2005), *Bananeras: Women Transforming the Banana Unions of Latin America*, Boston, MA: South End Press.

Gereffi, Gary (1994), 'The organization of buyer-driven commodity chains,' in Gary Gereffi and Miguel Korzeniewicz (eds), *Commodity Chains and Global Capitalism*, Wesport, CN: Greenwood Press.

Global Exchange (2007), 'Sweatfree campaigns', published on the Internet at http://www.globalexchange.org/campaigns/sweatshops/, last accessed 8 August 2007.

Hermanson, Jeff (2004), 'Global corporations, global campaigns – the struggle for justice at Kukdong International in Mexico,' draft paper published on the Internet at http://falcon.arts.cornell.edu/sgt2/PSCP/documents/Jeff%20Hermanson.pdf, last accessed 12 August 2007.

International Textiles and Clothing Bureau (2007), published on the Internet at http://www.itcb.org/Documents/ITCB-TD1-07.pdf, last accessed 11 August 2007.

Jobs with Justice (2006), 'India update,' published on the Internet at http://www.jwj.org/news/updates/2006/02.html#in, last accessed 8 August 2007.

Klein, Naomi (1999), *No Logo: Taking Aim at the Brand Name Bullies*, New York: Picador.

Lerner, Stephen (2007), 'Global unions: a solution to labor's decline', *New Labor Forum*, **16**(1), 23–37.

Levine, Louis (1924), *The Women Garment Workers: A History of the International Ladies' Garment Workers' Union*, New York: B.W. Huebsch, Inc.

Quan, Katie (2000), *A Global Labour Contract: The Case of the Collective Agreement Between the Association of Flight Attendants (AFL-CIO) and United Airlines*, Transfer, Brussels: The European Trade Union Institute, 6.

Quan, Katie (2004), 'Global strategies for workers: how class analysis clarifies us and them and what we need to do,' in Michael Zweig (ed.), *What's Class Got to Do With It?* Ithaca, NY and London: Cornell University ILR Press.

Quan, Katie (2007), 'Women crossing borders to organize,' in Dorothy Sue Cobble (ed.), *The Sex of Class*, Ithaca, NY and London: Cornell University ILR Press.

Russo, John and Banks, Andy (1999), 'How the teamster took the UPS strike overseas,' *Working USA*, **2**(5),74–87.

Shaffer, Jono of Service Employees International Union (2005), Telephone interview with the author on 24 February.

Shailor, Barbara (2005), 'Skirting the facts on China,' *New Labor Forum*, **14**(1) Spring.

Sweatshop Watch Newsletter (2000), 'Action Alert,' **6**(4) p. 3.

Tyler, Gus (1995), *Look for the Union Label: A History of the International Ladies' Garment Workers' Union*, New York: M.E. Sharpe.

Worker Rights Consortium (2006), 'DSP program description,' published on the Internet at http://www.workersrights.org/dsp.asp#DSP, last accessed on 8 August 2007.

Yue Yuen Industrial (Holdings) Limited (2006), *Annual Report*, published on the Internet at http://www.yueyuen.com/hk/annual/2006/E_Yue%20Yuen%20AR-1754.pdf, last accessed 7 August 2007.

Zimny, Max and Garren, Brent (1994), 'Protecting the contingent work force: lessons from the women's garment industry,' published on the Internet at http://www.nelp.org/docUploads/zimny.pdf, last accessed 7 August 2007.

12. Immigrant workers and the new American labor movement

Kent Wong and Janna Shadduck-Hernández

INTRODUCTION

Immigrant workers are playing an increasingly important role in the revitalization of the US labor movement. As a truly global immigrant city, Los Angeles (LA) is recognized as a vital site for the renewal of the labor movement, precisely because of its immigrant labor force (Milkman, 2006). In recent years, immigrants have been on the forefront of many of the most successful labor organizing campaigns in LA and in other US communities.

The growing influence of immigrants within the US labor movement has led to stronger alliances between unions and immigrant worker organizations. The partnerships between organized labor, community allies and immigrant worker organizations offer new opportunities to expand immigrant worker power while reinvigorating union membership nationally. As immigrant workers build coalitions across community, labor and ethnic fronts, immigrant workers in unions are beginning to experience better working conditions and increased salaries. Moreover, these alliances have generated new and creative forms of organizing that engage immigrant workers on broader issues of democratization, social justice and economic equality. This process of civic engagement has created new spaces for immigrant workers to become leaders in both the immigrant rights and labor movements.

University programs that focus on supporting and repositioning immigrant workers as central players in society and within contemporary social movements hold the potential of redefining labor and industrial relations programs nationally. The linkages and prospects of coalition building among immigrant workers (both union and nonunion), their communities and labor organizations create important opportunities for labor educators, students and universities. This chapter explores the role of a public university's labor center in revitalizing the labor movement through its redefinition of education as building relationships among immigrant worker communities, organized labor and university students and faculty. Through seminars, workshops, leadership training, university courses and research, the UCLA Center for Labor Research and Education (Labor Center) offers a distinct perspective to higher education's mission to support, advocate for and incorporate the interests and knowledge of diverse and marginalized community constituents, in particular immigrant workers.

IMMIGRANT WORKERS AND THE LABOR MOVEMENT

The largest May Day demonstrations in US history took place on May 1 2006. Millions took to the streets in LA, San Francisco, Seattle, Denver, Chicago, New York, Miami and Houston, to name but a few. In LA alone there were two separate demonstrations on May Day, each mobilizing half a million workers, the largest demonstrations in the city's history.

Ironically these May Day demonstrations were not led by the American labor movement, but by immigrant workers themselves (Wong *et al.*, 2007). The demonstrations were a powerful response to draconian proposals introduced by the Republican-dominated Congress in the form of the Sensenbrenner Bill. Sensenbrenner would have criminalized the estimated 12 million undocumented immigrants living in the United States and also enacted criminal penalties against labor, community and religious organizations that provide assistance to undocumented immigrants.

The US labor movement historically has opposed immigrant rights. Unions were at the forefront of advocating for 'employer sanctions' in the 1980s that imposed civil and criminal penalties against employers for knowingly hiring undocumented immigrants. Employer sanctions unfortunately have rarely been used to penalize employers, but instead have caused further exploitation and hardship to undocumented immigrant workers and exacerbated the abuse within the underground economy.

During the 1999 AFL-CIO convention in LA, a debate erupted on the floor of the convention to change the anti-immigrant position of the labor movement. In 2000, the AFL-CIO Executive Council took a historic step to pass a resolution calling for unconditional legalization for undocumented immigrants, an end to employer sanctions, and an increase in workplace protections for immigrants.

In 2003, UNITE HERE initiated the Immigrant Workers Freedom Ride, inspired by the freedom rides of the Civil Rights Movement. More than 900 immigrants and their allies boarded buses to Washington DC and New

York to demand full rights for immigrant workers. Along the way, 100 separate events in cities and towns throughout the country mobilized support for immigrant rights and brought together labor and community coalitions for immigrant rights. Many of these coalitions formed the nucleus of the spring 2006 mobilization planning committees (Wong and Muñoz, 2004).

ORGANIZING IMMIGRANT WORKERS

For generations, the American labor movement was resistant to aggressively organizing undocumented immigrant workers. Unions viewed immigrants with suspicion and hostility and thought they could be used by employers to undermine wages and working conditions or to break strikes. Unions feared that the threat of deportation would squelch unionization efforts among undocumented workers.

These views proved to be unfounded in the 1990s, which witnessed a new upsurge in immigrant worker organizing. LA led the nation in aggressive organizing campaigns that have reached out and successfully organized immigrant workers.

One of the first national breakthroughs involved the Justice for Janitors campaign in LA. In June 1990, at the height of the organizing campaign, the LA police brutally beat a group of protesting janitors and their supporters. The event received national media attention and intensified pressure on the mayor and city council to intervene. The eventual settlement with the building service contractors resulted in thousands of mainly Latino, immigrant janitors joining the Service Employees International Union (Waldinger *et al.*, 1998).

Also in the early 1990s, the residential home construction industry was paralyzed when thousands of Latino immigrant workers waged a strike that extended hundreds of miles over a five-county area in Southern California. At the height of the strike, workers were chased onto the Hollywood Freeway, one of the busiest freeways in LA, where they staged a civil disobedience action. This marked the first time a major freeway had been shut down by a political protest since the anti-Vietnam War movement. The eventual settlement with the building contractors brought thousands of newly organized immigrants into the Carpenters Union (Milkman, 2006).

The largest factory organizing victory in LA in decades was also won in the 1990s at the American Racing Equipment Company. Twelve hundred predominantly Latino, immigrant workers staged a wildcat strike to protest substandard wages and working conditions. After an intense campaign, the workers prevailed against an anti-union consultant and won union recognition and a contract with the Machinists Union (Zabin, 2000).

In the late 1990s, the largest unionization victory in the country in 50 years was won in LA when 74 000 homecare workers voted ten to one to join the Service Employees International Union. The campaign took over ten years but resulted in substantial pay increases and improved benefits for the low-wage workers, the majority of whom were immigrant women. Through new organizing and mergers with other locals, this union has since grown to become the largest in California with 200 000 workers (Delp and Quan, 2002).

Currently there are major organizing campaigns involving tens of thousands of truck drivers in the Port of Los Angeles and tens of thousands of California hotel workers. Again the majority of these workers are immigrants.

THE UCLA DOWNTOWN LABOR CENTER

On Labor Day 2002, in front of a thousand union and community members, California Governor Gray Davis participated in a ribbon-cutting ceremony that opened the doors to the new UCLA Downtown Labor Center. The Downtown Labor Center is located a few blocks from the LA County Federation of Labor, dozens of union offices and many immigrant rights organizations. It is also in the heart of a large and growing Latino immigrant community and borders Historic Filipino Town to the north and Koreatown to the west.

The Downtown Labor Center has provided unprecedented opportunities to promote greater partnerships between the university and the labor movement and among unions, community groups, worker centers and immigrant workers. It has emerged as a hub of activity that is an important educational resource for faculty and students, labor unions, workers, and community organizations. The 4000-square-foot facility is used for union leadership schools, educational seminars and workshops, conferences (that often bring together faculty, students, labor and the community), and cultural events (including musical performances and art and photography exhibits).

The UCLA Labor Center has an established track record in running successful leadership schools that have been well received by the labor movement, including the first Spanish-language union leadership school in the country, the first Asian American union leadership school in the country, the first African American union leadership school in California, and the first LGBT (lesbian, gay, bisexual and transgender) union leadership school in the country.

THE IMMIGRANT WORKER RESOURCE CENTER

In response to the recent changes in the labor movement, the UCLA Downtown Labor Center has launched the Immigrant Worker Resource Center (IWRC) to address the changing educational needs of the growing number of immigrant workers engaged in organizing.

One central premise of this project is that it redefines the field of labor relations to include both union and nonunion workers. Frequently the field of labor relations has only included unionized workers. The misconception has been that immigrant workers who were not in unions lacked organization. What we have witnessed with the mass mobilizations in the spring of 2006, however, is that immigrant workers have diverse and varied organizational structures, including religious affiliations, worker centers, immigrant rights groups, hometown associations and community-based organizations.

The challenge, then, is to provide new opportunities for immigrant workers to join with the formal labor movement. Unfortunately, the current structures of the American labor movement function as an exclusive club that limits the participation of workers to those who are fortunate enough to work in one of the few workplaces targeted for organizing. Many immigrant workers, particularly those in the underground economy and the contract labor system, will never have the opportunity to join the labor movement unless there is a change in the orientation and organizational structure of labor unions.

There are four basic components of the Immigrant Worker Resource Center. First, the center strengthens ongoing education and outreach to existing unions to educate them about immigrant rights, immigrant workers and the ways that they can successfully organize immigrant workers into unions. Second, the center provides leadership development opportunities for immigrant workers (in unions and other organizations) who share an interest in promoting worker rights and labor and community coalitions. Third, the center promotes partnerships between unions and worker centers to explore new opportunities for collaboration and joint work. Fourth, the center provides service-learning and internship opportunities that enable students to engage in support for immigrant worker rights.

The IWRC offers a series of workshops and seminars for union organizers, representatives and worker-leaders on issues impacting immigrant workers. Workshop topics include immigration reform and immigration policy, social security no-match letters and other employment verification issues, creating effective union contract language to protect immigrant workers, understanding the legislative/electoral system, health and safety in the workplace, building cross-border solidarity, protecting worker rights, and using the media to promote labor and immigration issues.

The IWRC also provides leadership schools for the new generation of immigrant workers in unions and worker centers who are either new to the labor movement or involved in workplace organizing. This includes both workers and activists from unions as well as those who are not yet unionized from immigrant worker centers. The IWRC utilizes a curriculum that is grounded in popular education. The exercises are creative, participatory and respect and draw upon the knowledge of the immigrant workers themselves. Facilitators use a variety of popular education techniques, including popular economics, role-playing, storytelling, forum theater, body mapping and small-group discussions. All of the modules require participants to practice, discuss and reflect on what they are learning.

BUILDING BRIDGES BETWEEN THE LABOR MOVEMENT AND ITS ALLIES

During the past decade, California has experienced the emergence of many new immigrant worker centers. These have become intermediary organizations that represent new immigrants and low-wage workers, advocate for worker rights and engage workers in a process of collective action. In October 2004, the UCLA Labor Center hosted a statewide convention of California worker centers. The worker centers discussed their challenges, engaged in a process of critical reflection and developed a strategic road map for the future.

One major area of concern was to forge deeper relationships between unions and worker centers. Since that convention, the Labor Center has actively promoted strategic relationships between unions and worker centers. For example, the Labor Center has facilitated ongoing meetings between the AFL-CIO and the National Day Laborer Organizing Network (NDLON) to discuss how to develop relations at the national and local levels. The Labor Center has also assisted in negotiations between NDLON and the Laborers Union (LIUNA) to create a partnership to organize day laborers throughout the country (Narro, 2006).

Through the UCLA Downtown Labor Center, the IWRC has built important bridges and strategic relationships between worker centers and the LA labor movement. The IWRC also provides space for nonunion workers from many low-wage industries to learn about the labor movement and to meet union leaders and organizers.

The UCLA Labor Center also connects students with immigrant workers. It conducts student internship programs that allow undergraduates and graduate students, including those studying the law, to assist with labor union initiatives, research projects and other programs that serve the needs of immigrant workers. For the past five years the Labor Center has hosted a Labor Summer Internship Program. This program has been responsible for placing dozens of graduates in full-time positions at unions and community-based worker centers throughout Southern California.

Through their internship experiences, students have worked on a wide variety of research projects and organizing campaigns. From worker outreach to corporate research, these students have gained invaluable skills that prepare them for careers with labor and community organizations. Many former interns from the Labor Summer Internship Program are working in leadership positions in unions and community organizations throughout LA.

Today we find ourselves in a historic moment in LA as stronger relationships are forged between the immigrant rights movement and the labor movement. The recent mass mobilizations of millions of immigrants throughout the country have revealed the potential for this strategic partnership. Many labor and immigrant rights groups have recognized the value of developing immigrant workers as the future leadership of both of these movements. With the mobilization of one million immigrants in May of 2006, and with the active support of a vibrant labor movement, LA has become a central focal point for this new wave of immigrant organizing and worker empowerment. The UCLA Labor Center is developing its programming strategically in order to play a role in facilitating this synergy and building sustainable bridges between immigrants and the labor movement.

THE ROLE OF A UNIVERSITY LABOR PROGRAM IN THE IMMIGRANT RIGHTS MOVEMENT

Associations between universities and communities have had a long history in the United States. John Dewey (1916) encouraged relationships between the two as a path to reestablish communities and universities as co-participants in political, social and educational decision-making. Policy makers, politicians, community members, university administrators and scholars have recently taken a renewed interest in community and university relations as a necessary component in twenty-first-century learning (Boyer, 1990; Kellogg Commission,1999). Today, nearly 1000 campus presidents are part of Campus Compact, a national organization created in 1985 to expand the opportunities of community engagement on campuses.

Most universities promote centers supporting civic engagement or community outreach and development. In many instances, universities have rewritten their mission statements to highlight the call to integrate academic learning and relevant community engagement and to develop relationships of reciprocity and mutual learning across communities and campuses. Yet establishing an integrated educational approach where community engagement, learning and research are respected within university culture remains one of the greatest challenges of higher education (Maurasse, 2001). Many campuses face the additional problem of not being able to attract diverse community members and students, especially working-class immigrant constituents, to participate in their community programs. The reasons cited by scholars range from lack of relationships with diverse communities, time constraints of community members and divergent expectations and interests, to name a few (Shadduck-Hernández, 2006).

As university demographics follow national population trends, minority students, including immigrants and refugee students, are increasingly becoming part of higher education bodies (Vernez and Abrahamse, 1996; NCES, 2003). US immigration over the past 30 years has become progressively diverse. Of the 33.3 million foreign-born residents living in the US, 53 percent originate from Latin America, 25 percent from Asia, 8 percent from other regions such as Africa and 14 percent from Europe. Despite these demographic changes, US educational institutions continue to support Eurocentric models that largely ignore the culture, knowledge and experiences of non-European communities on campus and off (Zúñiga *et al.*, 2000). To address this problem, educators like those within the UCLA Labor Center have called for curricula, research and training in higher education to focus on social relations between students, their communities and the educational institutions that serve them (Chang *et al.*, 2003).

The commitment and mission of the UCLA Labor Center is to facilitate relationships between university students, often from working-class and immigrant backgrounds, and immigrant workers, the industries they work in and the institutions that support them. A recent article in the *UCLA Magazine* (April, 2007) claims that one out of every four UCLA undergraduates was born outside the United States and that 60 percent of the parents of UCLA students are foreign-born. In a sense, UCLA is a microcosm of the city where it is housed; a place where immigrant youth are seeking mobility through educational opportunities, and their families are working in LA's service, manufacturing and construction economies to improve their children's educational prospects. In providing a bridge between a diverse student population and the city's immigrant workforce, the UCLA Labor Center is often bringing the students into contact with their own parents' employment realities.

The Center's labor and workplace studies minor offers undergraduate and graduate courses that explore both theoretical and historical aspects of labor and the labor movement as well as contemporary labor issues related to LA and its vibrant immigrant rights movement. Students are encouraged to participate in internships and community service with unions and community organizations to complement their coursework by working directly with immigrant workers and their allies across the city.

The model of education and research employed at the UCLA Labor Center values educational opportunities through which students acquire relational and participatory experiences based on the students and workers' knowledge, direct involvement, and community research geared to engaged learning, action and social change. At the same time, the Labor Center connects students to immigrant worker leadership opportunities promoted through the IWRC and affiliated worker associations and institutions.

CHALLENGES AND OPPORTUNITIES CONFRONTING LABOR STUDIES

Although it may seem ironic, few academic labor programs are well equipped to contribute to – or even connect with – the revitalization of the American labor movement. The traditional framework of labor-relations (or industrial-relations) programs involves a study of the rules that shape the relations among management, government and labor. In recognition of that framework's limitations, centers of 'labor studies' were established in the 1960s and 1970s at institutions including Rutgers University, the University of Massachusetts and the Pennsylvania State University (Denker, 1981). While these programs have succeeded in educating students about the complexities of labor and workplace relations, most of their focus has been on the relationship between unions and workers who are already union members. Moreover, educational support to worker organizations and examinations of the problems that confront working people on a daily basis usually take place only through extension programs or workshops, not through the academic track of university programs.

The challenge for labor studies programs in a changing postindustrial society is to create dynamic and relevant curricula that engage students and faculty around the multiple facets of the labor movement while continuing to be relevant to workers and labor. Today the immigration question has become a central component in the debate about how to build a strong and renewed labor movement. A growing number of immigrant workers are entering diverse industries and sectors of the US economy.

According to US census data, the 1990s witnessed the largest influx of immigrants during any period in American history, and the immigration continues. From 2000 to 2006, immigration accounted for approximately

45 percent of the change in the US population and nearly half of the net increase in the US labor force. Immigrants represent over 12 percent of all US residents, about 15 percent of the civilian labor force (about 22 millions workers), and 20 percent of low-wage employees (US Census Bureau, 2005).

Below are just a few more figures that shed light on the immigrant worker labor market and union participation nationally (drawn from Capps *et al.*, 2007; Fan and Bartalova, 2007; Migration Policy Institute, 2004):

- Ninety percent of new immigrants work in the private sector for wages and salaries.
- Of the nation's 17.7 million foreign-born wage and salary workers, one in ten are members of unions.
- Of the nation's 15.36 million union members in 2006, 12 percent were born outside the United States.
- Since 1996, the number of foreign-born union members has increased while the number of native-born union members has declined.

The UCLA Labor Center views the political, economic and social phenomena associated with the immigrant rights and labor movements in LA as an important opportunity on which to hinge its educational programming and research efforts. This model can also offer lessons to other centers as we collectively evaluate the changing field of labor and industrial relations. The UCLA Labor Center is committed not only to teaching students about broader labor and workplace issues, but also to building relations with low-wage and immigrant workers, unions, worker associations and organizations outside of the workplace, such as churches, clubs, cooperatives, ethnic organizations and hometown associations.

The UCLA Labor Center provides what labor educator Michael Yates (1998) has called for: a revival of worker-centered, pro-labor education in the United States – labor studies programs that educate and support workers from all types of communities, backgrounds and associations. Yates claims that for labor education programs to effectively impact a broader and more diverse student and worker population, they must collaborate with academic programs that have similarly struggled for recognition and legitimacy, such as African American, Asian American, Chicano and women's studies programs. The UCLA Labor Center is affiliated with a range of faculty and departments such as urban planning, sociology, Chicano studies, Asian American studies, African American studies, history, economics, management and women's studies as a way to broaden our engagement on labor issues with diverse teaching and student bodies.

Some critical observers of US labor studies and labor education programs maintain that such programs do not have a conceptual framework that defines the relationship between academic labor studies and the objectives of the American labor movement. While most academic programs focus on full-time students, today's unions often rely on in-house educational programs to address their immediate needs regarding organizational and technical skills (such as organizing, grievance handling, collective bargaining, arbitration and union administration). Given the crisis in the US labor movement, Barrow (1999) asserts that the time is right for university labor educators and the labor movement to revitalize their relationships in ways that not only clearly frame a collective, 'labor' point of view, but also include a focus on vital social issues like immigration, gender relations and power dynamics.

Faculties within the UCLA Labor Center have recently taken up this challenge and developed a course that focuses on the immigrant rights movement, with particular attention to labor and higher education. The course provides students with an overview of the history of the immigrant rights movement and examines the development of coalition efforts between the labor movement and the immigrant rights movement in LA and nationally. In addition, the course explores the issue of immigrant students in higher education, the particular challenges facing undocumented immigrant students, and the legislative and policy issues that have emerged in relation to this student body. In a complementary course, the mostly first-generation (and some undocumented) students are developing a student publication based on their family histories, interviews and research about UCLA's undocumented student population and the organizations that advocate around this issue.

In 2001, the California state legislature passed Assembly Bill 540, which allows undocumented students to pay in-state tuition at the University of California schools, the California State University schools, and California community colleges. However, these students do not have access to financial aid and many other fellowships or grants, making it very difficult to finish their degrees. The student publication now being developed will highlight the experiences and struggles of talented, undocumented students who are organizing to change state and federal legislation to adjust their immigration status. The publication will include stories, poetry, photography and essays about this particular immigrant experience.

We must remember, however, that educational programs that approach learning from a critical pedagogical and social justice perspective are often met with resistance by conservative forces within higher education. This has certainly been the case of the UCLA Labor Center, which has experienced yearly attempts by the California governor to defund our statewide labor studies programs for the past four years. Politicians, elected officials, unions, students and community organizations have rallied their support for the continued work of the Labor Center as a recognized collective space for skills-development workshops, interactive dialogue, education and research that impacts labor and workplace issues. The Labor Center has an established track record in offering comprehensive labor education courses and coordinating leadership schools that have been well received by the labor and immigrant rights movements.

CONCLUSION: FACILITATING DEVELOPMENT OF A STRONGER LABOR MOVEMENT

The UCLA Labor Center has become a major facilitator of leadership development and relationship building between unions, worker centers, community groups and students. Its goal is to build stronger labor and economic movements throughout LA. At the downtown site, most LA unions and community partners, including ethnic and student organizations, immigrant rights groups and immigrant worker associations are using this space for their meetings, educational programs and community and labor events. For the past five years, the site's availability to multiple partners in the LA labor and immigrant rights movements has greatly increased the university's visibility and has changed the perception of the university within the city's working-class and immigrant communities.

Immigrant workers from unions and worker centers from across LA County met recently at the UCLA Labor Center to engage in open discussions about their perceptions of one another, how they can begin to forge relationships across common worker issues, and how these institutions can support each other. Conversations such as these are commonplace at the Labor Center and are creating a new vision for immigrant worker leadership at the local, state and national levels. Such dialogue captures the spirit of the Labor Center and underscores its role in facilitating partnerships that can defend workplace rights and build leadership in advancing low-wage worker and immigrant rights.

The UCLA Labor Center has chosen to respond to the question of how academic institutions can revitalize labor and industrial relations by focusing our educational programs on the growing constituency of immigrant and working-class students on our campus, the immigrant workers in LA's union halls, and LA's large and diverse labor force. By providing a critical space for dialogue and learning across industries, immigrant workers and diverse students, we envision our role as educators in building a framework that redefines the relationship between academic labor studies and the objectives of the American labor movement. We call on university administrators, fellow labor educators, union leaders, community members, students and immigrant workers to join us in this effort.

REFERENCES

Barrow, Clyde W. (1989), 'Pedagogy, politics, and social reform: philosophy of the workers' education movement', *Journal of Theory, Culture and Politics*, **2**, 46–66.

Boyer, Ernest L. (1990), *Scholarship Reconsidered: Priorities of the Professoriate*, Princeton, NJ: Carnegie Foundation for the Advancement of Teaching.

Breese, Kristine (2007), 'Upward bound', *UCLA Magazine*, April, 22–8.

Capps, Rand, Fortuny, Karina and Fix, Michael (2007), *Trends in the Low-Wage Immigrant Workforce*, Washington, DC: Urban Institute, March.

Chang, Mitchell J., Witt, Daria, Jones, James and Hakuta, Kenji (2003), *Compelling Interest: Examining the Evidence on Racial Dynamics in Colleges and Universities*, Palo Alto, CA: Stanford University Press.

Delp, Linda and Quan, Katie (2002), 'Homecare worker organizing in California: an analysis of a success strategy', *Labor Studies Journal*, **27** (1), 481–96.

Denker, Joel (1981), *Unions and Universities: The Rise of the New Labor Leader*, Montclair, NJ: Allanheld, Osmun and Co.

Dewey, John (1916), *Democracy and Education*, New York: Macmillan.

Fan, Chuncui Velma and Batalova, Jeanne (2007), 'Foreign-born wage and salary workers in the US labor force and unions', Washington, DC: Migration Policy Institute.

Kellogg Commission on the Future of State and Land Grant Universities (1999), *Returning to our Roots: The Engaged Institution*, Washington, DC: National Association of State Universities and Land Grand Colleges.

Maurasse, David J. (2001), *Beyond the Campus: How Colleges and Universities Form Partnerships with their Communities*, New York: Routledge.

Milkman, Ruth (2006), *LA Story: Immigrant Workers and the Future of the US Labor Movement*, New York: Russell Sage.

Migration Policy Institute (2004), *Immigrant Union Members and Trends*, Washington, DC, MPI Report, No. 7, May.

Narro, Victor (2006), 'Impacting next wave organizing: creative campaign strategies of the Los Angeles worker centers', *New York Law School Law Review*, **50**, 465–513.

National Center for Education Statistics (NCES) (2003), *The Condition of Education 2003*, US Department of Education, Institute of Education Sciences, http://nces.ed.gov/pubs 2003/2003067.pdf.

Shadduck-Hernández, Janna (2006), 'Here I am now! Critical ethnography and community service-learning with immigrant and refugee undergraduate students and youth', *Ethnography and Education*, **1** (1), 67–85.

US Census Bureau (2005), *American Community Survey and Census Data on the Foreign Born by State*, Washington, DC.

Vernez, George and Abrahamse, Allan (1996), *How Immigrants Fare in US Education*, Santa Monica, CA: Rand.

Waldinger, Roger, Erickson, Chris, Milkman, Ruth, Mitchell, Daniel J.B., Valenzuela, Abel, Wong, Kent and Zeitlin, Maurice (1998), 'Helots no more: a case study of the Justice for Janitors campaign in Los Angeles', in Kate Bronfenbrenner, Sheldon Friedman, Richard W. Hurd, Rudoph A. Oswald and Ronald L. Seeber (eds), *Organizing to Win: New Research on Union Strategies*, Ithaca, NY: Cornell University Press Press, pp. 102–20.

Wong, Kent and Muñoz, Carolina Bank (2004), 'Don't miss the bus; the immigrant workers freedom ride', *New Labor Forum*, **13** (2), 61–6.

Wong, Kent, Narro, Victor and Shadduck-Hernández, Janna (2007), 'The 2006 immigrant uprising: origins and future', *New Labor Forum*, **16** (1), 50–56.

Yates, Michael D. (1998), 'An essay on radical labor education', *Cultural Logic*, **2** (1), 1–17.

Zabin, Carol (2000), 'Organizing Latino workers in the Los Angeles manufacturing sector: the case of American racing equipment', in Ruth Milkman (ed.), *Organizing Immigrants: The Challenge of Unions in Contemporary California*, Ithaca, NY: Cornell University Press, 150–68.

Zúñiga, Víctor, Hernández-León, Rubén, Shadduck-Hernández, Janna L. and Villarreal, María Olivia (2002), 'The new paths to Mexican immigrants in the United States: challenges for education and the role of Mexican universities', in Stanton Worthham, Enrique G. Murillo, Jr. and Edmund T. Hamann (eds), *Education in the New Latino Diaspora: Policy and the Politics of Identity*, Westport, CT: Ablex, pp. 99–116.

Conclusion: the future of industrial relations, a.k.a. work and employment relations

Thomas A. Kochan

INTRODUCTION

It is the perfect time to celebrate the achievements of the first century of industrial relations (IR) and make the transition to the study of work and employment relations in the forms they exist today. Why? This field of study and practice is now well into an era that parallels the conditions that led to the emergence of IR over a century ago.

The Webbs and John R. Commons and their colleagues and students created this field as Britain and the United States were transitioning from an agrarian to an industrial economy with all the attendant changes in the nature of work, the workforce and family life. The fundamental problem identified by these founding scholars was that the institutions and laws governing work had not changed or developed fast enough to keep up with the changes in the economy. The results: Workers experienced income declines, employment disruptions and uncertainties, and harsh working conditions; societies experienced increased conflict and sporadic violence; and the variance in employer behavior increased. Some employers chose to take advantage of excess labor supply and wage competition by 'sweating labor' and suppressing worker efforts to form unions, while others tried to follow newly emerging 'scientific' principles in managing their workforce.

As Joel Cutcher-Gershenfeld notes in his chapter, the United States, Britain, and most other developed nations are now in the midst of another transition – from an industrial economy to a service and knowledge-based economy. Once again, the economy, workforce and work–family relationships have changed while institutional and policy adaptation has lagged far behind. Again, as a result, worker wages have stagnated, employment has become more volatile, inequality has increased, and employers have adapted in varied ways. As the old institutional order no longer suffices to take wages out of competition, some employers have chosen to participate in a 'race to the bottom' by seeking to put work where it can find the greatest labor cost advantage and other employers have engaged in workplace and human resource innovations to attract and retain the most productive and innovative talent available.

Bruce Kaufman notes in his chapter that IR succeeded in taking off and growing for at least three quarters of a century in the United States because the work of its founders laid the intellectual foundation for the New Deal policies and associated institutions that supported the nation's industrial economy. For the new or renewed field of work and employment relations to experience the same success, it must prove to be equally intellectually sound and useful, both in laying a foundation for a new set of public policies and in establishing a new set of employment practices better fitted to the economy, nature of work, and workforce of our time.

The authors of the preceding chapters lay out many of what I believe are the building blocks of a modern approach to the study of work and employment relations and do a good job of stating why a multidisciplinary approach to the field is still needed. I will draw on their ideas and add a few of my own here in an effort to look forward in a positive and optimistic way and close the door on laments about the declining fortunes of the field we are retiring. As with most transitions, however, not all of what has come before should be abandoned. In this specific case, several core principles of the field are as relevant and needed today as when first developed.[1]

CORE PRINCIPLES

John Budd reminds us that values, normative assumptions, and ethical considerations lie at the heart of any social science discipline. IR has well articulated values. These start, as Kaufman notes, with the recognition that labor is more than a commodity. Labor is done by humans who have free will, the capacity to learn, and can be motivated to use more or less of their capacities. Moreover, because labor (work) is done by humans it has a moral dimension as outlined in Catholic encyclicals from 1891 to 1991 and equivalent writings of many other religions.

These are the starting points for arguing, as Budd does, that the objectives of this field of study need to include but not be limited to efficiency (which, in contrast, is the case in classical and neo-classical economics). Equally valued objectives are equity (fairness) and the ability to exercise free will through voice or other actions at work.

Labor does not operate in atomistic spot markets governed by the invisible hand of perfect competition, but in relationships with employers (we will come to the issue of independent contractors and the self-employed a bit later). As Cutcher-Gershenfeld notes, the label 'industrial' does not fit as many of these employers as when the field was born. So that term may need to be retired and replaced with something more descriptive of the different types of employment alternatives present in today's labor markets. Nevertheless, labor or work is still embodied in relationships between and/or among two or more interested parties. That leads to another normative premise. These relationships embody a mix of conflicting and shared or common interests that need to be resolved and improved or enhanced to the extent possible. The insight of Commons and other institutionalists who embodied what Budd labels the pluralist model of employment relations is that these conflicting and shared interests are natural and enduring features of employment relations, not ones that can be totally eliminated by market forces or managed away by good practices.

This does not mean that practices cannot be invented or adapted to improve the inherent tradeoffs among the core objectives of efficiency, equity and voice. On the contrary, this is what a good deal of research and innovation in this field seeks to do. Organization development, interest-based bargaining, knowledge-based or high-performance work systems, labor–management partnerships, lateral alignment, *et cetera*, are just some modern counterparts to innovations of an earlier era, such as scientific management, human relations, job-control unionism and collective bargaining, and personnel management. The search for ways to improve the tradeoffs and/or expand the pie needs to continue. Indeed, the performance of an employment relations system should be judged, as Budd suggests, by its ability to generate an acceptable balance among efficiency, equity and voice. I would add as another performance indicator the ability to improve any one of these objectives without reducing the others.

The founders of IR helped invent and develop institutional economics in recognition that the atomistic and timeless (ahistorical) assumptions of classical and neo-classical economics did not capture the dynamic and social/collectivist nature of labor market activity. This too has proved to be an enduring feature of work that has now been embraced with new vigor not only by many economists, but also – as John Godard, David Lipsky and Ronald Seeber, and Michael Piore each point out – by sociologists and organization theorists. The early institutionalists and their second and third generation students who created the study of internal labor markets recognized what has become a founding tenet of contemporary economic sociology, namely that work is embedded in a set of social structures and networks (some of which are internal and some of which are external to any given employment relationship). The richness and quality of these networks affect the performance of an employment relations system.

WHAT IS NEW?

If the preceding are the enduring features of the study of work and employment relations that deserve to be carried over from IR, what changes are needed? Again, many of the key points were made in preceding chapters and need only be summarized here.

Work

The nature of work has changed dramatically. The physical aspects of work have not been eliminated. Otherwise, why would we all be so tired at the end of the day? But the knowledge, analytical, and learning dimensions of work – previously the province of managers, scientists, and entrepreneurs – now extend to more, arguably all, of those who work. The assumption of scientific management that conception and execution of work should be separated by a division of labor between management and workers no longer holds, especially in a world where the physical aspects of labor cannot be taken out of competition.

Only by designing work systems that draw out workers' knowledge, for the purposes that include generating innovation and increasing productivity, can workers compete in markets that are not limited by space, time or national boundaries. Moreover, in service-based economies more workers are in direct contact with customers, clients, patients, and students – that is, with other humans who react to and influence the quality of employment relationships. This adds more interpersonal or emotional content to work than was the case with much of industrial work. It also adds a lateral dimension to work relations that the traditional IR paradigm left under-developed. It is not just the quality of relationships between workers and managers that matter, but also the quality of relationships across complex lateral relations (in supply chains, with co-workers, and with final customers) that must be factored in as both a cause and an effect of the quality of an employment system.

Significant research on knowledge-based work systems and related employment practices has been underway for over two decades. Consistent with the methodological traditions introduced by the early institutionalists, most of this work has been carried out using both quantitative and qualitative methods in specific industries. The cumulative evidence from this body of work is that knowledge-based work systems can be linked to production or service methods in ways that enhance productivity, product and/or service quality, and employment outcomes – wages, job satisfaction and learning.

Yet there is no market or technologically driven path to the diffusion of such systems. This, therefore, calls for policies and institutions capable of supporting diffusion. Thus, on this issue IR/work and employment researchers are doing a good job of laying the intellectual and analytical foundations for one feature of a twenty-first-century employment policy, namely an active initiative for diffusing knowledge-based work systems and supporting organizational practices.

There are, of course, more changes in the nature of work than the development of knowledge-based work systems. Work now takes place in a wider array of alternative employment configurations. Some of the labels used to describe these variations include standard and non-standard, formal and informal, and contingent and permanent work. Workers fall under numerous labels such as contractors and consultants, and work can be temporary, permanent, part-time, full-time, virtual, home-based, self-employed, and so on.

Yet much of employment policy continues to assume work is done in a fixed location with a single, easily identifiable employer and with employees attached on a full-time, long-term basis. Adapting employment policies and institutions to meet the needs of this increased variety of work settings is a vital intellectual challenge. Researchers have done a good job of documenting the size and trends in these different types of employment relationships, and we are learning more about the effects of different employment arrangements on efficiency, equity and voice. The task ahead is to figure out how to translate the evidence from this research into an updated set of employment policies and enforcement strategies that accurately reflect this variety of work settings.

Workforce

Diversity is the catchall word for capturing the need to shift thinking from a workforce composed mostly of male breadwinners to one with a rich mixture of men and women and native and foreign-born people of multiple races and ethnic backgrounds. This increased diversity poses at least three significant policy and institutional challenges.

First, while the shift from an agrarian to an industrial economy increased the separation of work and family, cultural, technological and economic changes have now combined to reduce the separation in roles and increase the interdependence between work and family life. Nearly all advanced economies have recognized this and have work–family policies in place that go beyond the minimalist policies of the United States. This provides an international laboratory for research and learning when US policy makers are ready to address this changed reality.

Second, issues of discrimination on the basis of race, religion, nationality, and other grounds have been the subject of policy intervention since the

1960s, but access to enforcement remains problematic for a large number of workers. Alternative dispute resolution and other enforcement models have been proposed by researchers and are likely to feature more prominently in the future. Because these alternatives are controversial and their effectiveness relative to standard enforcement remains open, there is a significant opportunity for research and evaluation.

Third, managing immigration flows and protecting and enforcing the rights of workers who cross national boundaries (on a temporary or long-term basis, either legally or illegally) looms as one of the biggest unresolved intellectual, policy and institutional challenges of our time.

Once again, the three issues noted here do not exhaust the changes in the workforce that merit attention by contemporary work and employment-relations researchers or policy makers. The key is to recognize the work-force shifts that challenge the unstated assumption that policies and institutions should be designed with some ideal worker – male breadwinner with a wife at home – in mind.

THE KEY 'ACTORS'

In his classic *Industrial Relations Systems* John Dunlop used the term 'actors' to describe the organizations and groups that interact and – subject to the constraints posed by markets, technology, and the distribution of power in society – shape the processes and outcomes of an employment relations system (Dunlop, 1958). He focused on three key actors: government, employers, and unions. These remain sensible starting points, but today they need to be supplemented by other groups: non-governmental organizations (NGOs), labor market intermediaries, and international bodies such as the International Labor Organization, World Bank, World Trade Organization and the International Monetary Fund. This is not an exhaustive list of the 'actors' that shape modern employment relationships. The point is that today there are multiple actors that need to be considered. But let us start with an updated view of Dunlop's chosen three.

Unions

IR scholars have privileged unions as institutions for providing workers with a collective voice at work and in society. Indeed, most of the authors of the chapters in this book (present company included) have both participated in research on unions and criticized each other (and themselves) for privileging unions too much. Because of this emphasis, there is close to a general consensus (but see the chapter by Daphne Taras for a counterpoint) that the decline of unions has contributed to the decline in the field.

This does not mean that the study of worker organizations, including traditional unions, should be abandoned. Indeed unions and other groups and organizations that aggregate worker interests are as critical today as ever before. Yet the field should neither be solely identified with the study of unions or be so uncritical of their strategies and performance so as to be blinded to the need for more varied forms of worker voice and representation.

The proliferation in the variety of groups and organizations advocating for workers is due to increased diversity in at least three areas: the workforce, the variety of employment settings, and management strategies. As the chapters by Katie Quan and by Kent Wong and Janna Shadduck-Hernandez show, the range of worker advocacy and support organizations operating in today's labor markets includes NGOs that use advances in information technology to publicize violations of labor standards, professional associations that lobby policy makers and educate members (but do not bargain directly with employers), and worker centers and ethnic associations. The definition of labor organizations or unions needs to be expanded to take into account these varied forms and perhaps others yet to be invented.

The decline in worker voice and the rise of alternative forms of voice pose challenges and opportunities for labor policy makers. As William Gould points out, the case for updating and reforming America's tired and ineffective labor law has been made over and over again in scholarly articles, commission reports, and legislative debates. Yet the quarter-century political gridlock between business and labor and their political allies continues. This cannot, and likely will not, go on forever. If and when the political forces align in ways that allow for passage of a new or updated labor law, the key question will be whether the changes seek to just reinforce and strengthen workers' rights to gain a voice at work in the same fashion as was embodied in the 1935 National Labor Relations Act or whether new options will also be opened to reflect changes in the labor force, the nature of work and work systems, and the economy.

There is no shortage of research from which policy makers can draw ideas for labor law reform. Gould makes reference to legal reforms embodied in a bill favored by many in the labor movement, The Employee Free Choice Act. My own reading of the research on this issue is that the passage of this bill in its present form or in some marginally modified form would constitute a necessary first – but far from sufficient – step in updating labor law to fit the needs of the contemporary workforce and economy. This will remain a fertile area for research and policy debate in our field for a long time to come.

Despite the growth of new worker advocacy organizations, the majority of workers in the United States and most other countries have no formal organization representing them directly at their places of work. Yet the same basic assumptions or values guiding our field apply in these relationships. Conflicting and shared interests are still at play and the objectives of efficiency, equity, and voice (or freedom to act) are just as central. The admonitions of the authors of this volume might simply be summarized as it is time to bring these different, seemingly unrepresented or underrepresented, employment relationship forms back in to our field of study.

Employers

Considerable progress has been made in research spanning the last quarter century in unpacking the black box of management. While many scholars have acknowledged differential interests within management organizations for a long time, recent research has examined different managerial strategies and the internal relationships and workings of employment-relations specialists, line managers, and senior executives. Growing attention has also focused on the comparative analysis of corporate governance regimes and their effects on employment relationships. This increased interest reflects a proposition that management is now in a more powerful position to influence and shape employment relations than labor organizations or government. While this may always have been the case, much of IR research over the first three-fourths of the twentieth century implicitly viewed unions and/or government as the driving forces of change. Which 'actor(s)' dominate in the future is an empirical question worthy of continued attention. The key is to remain open to the heterogeneity of 'management' as an actor.

As several of the authors in this book have noted, the study of employers, managers, human resource management practices, and the like, has historically been an important part of our field and needs to remain so. Studying management should not be equated with abandoning a pluralist view of employment relationships. The key is to continue to conceptualize management or employer organizations as actors most directly interested in promoting efficiency, while holding their organizations accountable for also meeting equity and voice objectives in employment relationships. Increasingly, as Quan points out in her chapter on the garment industry, responsibility for meeting these objectives is shared across the boundaries of employer organizations in complex supply chains or other networks of contractors. Rethinking human resource management models and practices to address this reality will be one of the key intellectual and institution-building challenges of our time.

Government(s)

Globalization has made it harder for national governments to regulate employment relations. However, it has not rendered national policies impotent; therefore, the substance of national policy options and the study of how national policy is enacted and administered remain central to our field. Indeed as Taras points out, it is this public or national perspective that sets this field of study apart from typical approaches of organizational behavior and/or human resource management scholars in most business schools.

Budd makes a compelling case for assessing the full range of government policies against their effectiveness in meeting efficiency, equity, and voice objectives. This would be ideal, but may not be politically realistic given the incremental nature of policy making. Current political reality should not, however, keep work and employment relations researchers from approaching the task of evaluating any specific policy action with this more comprehensive, system-wide perspective in mind. It was the scholars' broader view and the politicians' step-by-step legislative and administrative actions that produced what we now look back on as a coherent package of New Deal policies.

Globalization has restored interest in transnational comparison and typologies, something with a long tradition in our field dating back at least as half century to the controversial typology of 'industrial systems' and 'elites' presented in *Industrialism and Industrial Man* by Clark Kerr, John Dunlop, Frederick Harbison and Charles Myers (1960). Nick Wailes, Russell Lansbury and Jim Kitay apply a recent and equally controversial 'varieties of capitalism' typology to analyze employment relations in the auto sector of different countries and demonstrate the value and also the limits of its broad categories. They show not all countries fit into the proposed typologies and that considerable variation across organizations within countries remains to be explained. Their findings parallel the critiques of a large body of work that followed publication of the categories offered by Kerr and his colleagues.

The chapter by Wailes, Lansbury and Kitay underscores why comparative IR research has increasingly tended to take into account variations across and within national boundaries that involve nuanced analytical distinctions and concepts. The style of comparative research that dominated IR in the past century – which focused on broad comparisons of national systems – is slowly but surely being replaced by the work of research teams composed of scholars from different countries who bring knowledge of their culture and institutions to the study of specific industries, occupations, or issues (such as global sourcing of work, migration, trade, inequality, and so on). This is a welcome development and one that should continue to feature prominently in research in our field in the years ahead.

OUR NICHE

IR found its place in twentieth-century social science by drawing and building on the concepts and methods of multiple disciplines to address the critical work and employment problems of the day. I agree with Piore that this will continue to be the way we can add value and create our social science niche in the future. Indeed, the biggest breakthroughs in theory and research in our field have come when individuals and groups from multiple disciplines have worked together on a shared set of problems.

The early institutionalists mostly drew on economics as their basic discipline. Today, other disciplines including sociology, history, law, political science and psychology are making equivalent contributions to various work and employment issues. Indeed, each of these disciplines has experienced an upsurge of interest in these topics in recent years. Yet leaving the study of work and employment relations solely to scholars from the basic disciplines risks losing the holistic perspective needed to shape effective policies, institutions, and practices. That is why the range of academic programs, professional associations, and publication outlets reviewed by Immanuel Ness, Bruce Nissan, and Charles Whalen need to continue to be part of the research, teaching and communication landscape of our field.

CONTEMPORARY CHALLENGES AND OPPORTUNITIES

Problem centered, holistic or multi–disciplinary research thrives best in an environment where researchers can rally around a big, widely recognized problem or challenge. The Manhattan Project, the Marshall Plan, the War on Poverty, are all examples of challenges that have rallied scientists from multiple disciplines to engage in informed discourse and build on each others' findings. If I had to pick a candidate for this purpose today, I would say it is the need to build a new social contract at work that fits the interests and expectations of the parties to modern employment relationships.

The social contract that governed employment relations in post-World War II America evolved out of the New Deal legislation, the work of the War Labor Board, and the interactions of labor and management in collective bargaining in the immediate post-war years. That social contract evolved not out of the invisible hand of market forces or technological changes, but out of the combined effects of a change in public policies, the growth of new institutions, and the actions of the key 'actors' that were fitted to the market and technological environment of the era. The implied compact was that wages and living standards would advance in rough tandem with growth in productivity.

This compact broke down in the 1980s. Between 1980 and 2005, productivity grew by 70 percent while average workers' wages remained essentially flat. IR scholars played key roles in helping develop and nurture the post war social contract through research, policy activism, and in some cases hands-on administration and assistance. Our generation will be celebrated for its achievements if we do the same in the years ahead.

I believe we are well positioned to meet this challenge if we now stop lamenting and debating how or why the field of IR from which we have come has declined and focus on the growth opportunities and challenges open to us in the modern world of work and employment relations.

NOTE

1. I have avoided duplicating citations that can be found in preceding chapters of this book.

REFERENCES

Dunlop, John T. (1958), *Industrial Relations Systems*, New York: Henry Holt.
Kerr, Clark, Dunlop, John T., Harbison, Frederick and Myers, Charles (1960), *Industrialism and Industrial Man*, Cambridge, MA: Harvard University Press.

NA →

Index

academic programs
  in history of industrial relations
    18–26, 143–8
  problems of interdisciplinary
    industrial relations 170–71
  science-building 34–5, 42–3, 147–8,
    156, 165
  social capital and labor movement
    decline in United States 94, 95,
    104–5, 107
  see also business schools; business
    schools and marginalization of
    industrial relations in Canada;
    degrees; extension programs;
    Immigrant Worker Resource
    Center (IWRC); MBAs; PhDs;
    UCLA Labor Center;
    universities
Academy of Management (AOM) 19,
  129, 131, 146, 147
accreditation, business schools in
  Canada 125, 126
actors 70, 71, 230–34
  see also employers; government;
    organizations; unions
administrative law in the United States
  78, 79–80
adversarial employment relationships
  71, 75, 79
AFL-CIO 20, 149, 151, 205, 206, 212,
  216
Age Discrimination and Employment
  Act (1967) 118
agency 180–181
  see also control; power relations
alternative work practices (AWPs) 76
American Arbitration Association
  (AAA) 95, 98–100, 106
American Economic Association
  (AEA) 9, 144
American Manufacturing Association
  (AMA) 95, 103

American Racing Equipment
  Company 213–14
Americans for Democratic Action
  (ADA) 95, 102
Andrews, John B. 16
anti-discrimination policies and laws
  118, 119, 229–30
anti-sweatshop movement 199–200,
  202–3, 204–6, 207, 208
apparel industry, women's *see* labor
  relations in the women's apparel
  industry
arbitration 98–100, 117–19, 120
Asia 127, 128, 184, 187, 198, 199, 203,
  204, 218
  see also Asian market economies
    (AMEs); Cambodia; China;
    India; Japan; South Korea;
    Taiwan
Asian market economies (AMEs)
  182–3, 189
Assembly Bill (540) 221
Association for Labor Relations
  Agencies (ALRA) 95, 101
Association for Union Democracy
  (AUD) 95, 102–3
association journals 149–50, 156
associations 94, 95, 98–101, 106, 107
  see also association journals;
    employer associations;
    organizations; individual
    associations
Australia 175, 179, 182, 186, 187, 188,
  189
automotive industry *see* globalization
  and employment relations in the
  automotive industry

Bachrach, P. 73
Baratz, M. 73
Barrow, Clyde W. 221
Befort, Stephen F. 51, 55, 56–7

behavior, in institutional environments
    approach 70
behavioral research methods 68–9, 81,
    167–8
benchmarking, in business schools in
    Canada 125–9, 130, 134, 138–41
benefits 196–7, 203
Bhave, Devasheesh 49, 52, 53
Bonacich, Edna 201
books 129, 132, 133, 134
brand power 202
Britain *see* England; United Kingdom
Brown, J. Douglas 34
Budd, John W. 44, 48, 49, 51, 52, 53,
    55, 56–7, 58, 60, 61
business journals 126, 127–9, 130, 147
Business Roundtable 95, 103
business schools 145–6, 147
business schools and marginalization
    of industrial relations in Canada
    abandonment or infiltration? 133–5
    and business strategy of business
        schools 124–8
    and CIRA membership 123–4
    Fordism and production of next
        generation of scholars 132
    and research publication 128–32
    training students 133
    and union membership 123
business unionism 166
Byrd, Barbara 145

California 204–5, 212, 213–17, 218–19,
    220–23
    see also University of California
Cambodia 203, 206
Canada 23–5, 71, 75–7, 120, 123, 175
    see also business schools and
        marginalization of industrial
        relations in Canada
Canadian Industrial Relations
    Association (CIRA) 123–4, 131–2
capital allocation, and varieties of
    capitalism 176–7
capitalism 35, 43, 44, 78–9, 165
Chamber of Commerce (US) 95, 103
change 74, 177, 179–81, 188–90
Cheffins, B. 179
China 182, 183, 185, 186, 187, 188,
    189, 199, 201, 205

Chrysler 184
citations 128–9, 131, 132, 134, 138–41,
    154
civic virtue 91–2, 93
Civil Rights Act (1964) 119
class 180, 218
Coase, Ronald H. 41, 49
codes of conduct 199, 202
cohesive social groups 164
collective bargaining
    in the automotive industry 186
    and employment relationships 27
    and explicit objectives of industrial
        relations in Europe 59
    and history of industrial relations
        144
    and institutional environment of
        Canada compared to England
        75–6
    and labor and employment law in
        United States 117, 118, 119,
        120, 203, 205
    and National Labor Relations
        Bureau (NLRB) 111, 112,
        116
    and new institutionalism 168
    research in United States 68
    and social capital and labor
        movement decline in United
        States 97–8, 99, 100, 106
    in teaching industrial relations
        60–61, 144, 147
    in the women's apparel industry
        196–7, 205
Colvin, Alexander J.S. 57, 58
commercial relations 42
commodity theory of labor 39–41,
    42–4, 53
Commons, John R. 8–9, 16, 17, 22, 33,
    35, 168, 227
community–university relations
    217–19, 222–3
comparative research 233–4
competition 124–8, 134, 195–6, 198,
    200, 203, 207
competitive demand/supply labor
    market model 37–8, 39–41, 42–4,
    45
competitive markets 51, 52–3, 55
complete labor contracts 41, 42

conditions of employment *see* terms and conditions of employment; working conditions

conferences 20, 22, 26, 129, 131, 132

conflict 54
see also interest disputes; labor–management disputes; strikes

Congress 112–13, 119, 166, 212

consolidation, journal publishing 152–3, 156

construction workers 213

consumers 36, 44, 202

continuity 177, 188–9

contract workers 186–7, 190

contractors 195–6, 197, 199, 200, 201

contracts 41, 42, 68
see also terms and conditions of employment

control 54
see also agency; power relations

cooperative employment relationships 72, 75–7

coordinated market economies (CMEs) 70–71, 175, 176, 177, 179, 182, 183, 189

coordination problems, and varieties of capitalism 174–6

Cornell University 145, 153, 163

corporate governance, and varieties of capitalism 175–8, 179

corporate journal publishing 151–6

corporate social responsibility 199, 202–3

corporatism 72, 73

corporatization, universities in the United States 155

critical model of employment relationships 54, 55, 56

cross-disciplinary approaches *see* multi-disciplinary approaches

Crouch, C. 174, 177, 178, 180, 181

Cutcher-Gershenfeld, Joel 17, 18, 27

Darbishire, Owen 59, 60

degrees 94, 104–5, 126–7, 216–17

Delp, Linda 214

democracy 52, 55, 91-2, 93, 102–3

democratic rights 37

deregulation 20

Designated Suppliers Program (DSP) 202–3

developing countries 22, 198–200, 204

development studies 170

Dewey, John 217

Dickerson, Kitty 198

differentiation 176, 177

disciplinary fragmentation, in labor and employment journal publishing in United States 143–8, 155, 156

dispute resolution 57–8, 112, 117–19, 120
see also arbitration; collective bargaining; mediation; negotiation

distribution, in the women's apparel industry 201

diversity 218, 222–3, 229–30

division of labor 17

Dunlop, John T. 26, 56, 163, 166, 168, 169, 230

economic sociology 168–9, 227

economic welfare 55–6

economics 143–4, 168, 169
see also economic sociology; economics journals; institutional economics; labor economics; neoclassical labor economics; new institutional economics; varieties of capitalism

economics journals 143, 146, 147

education 207, 208
see also academic programs; business schools; degrees; Immigrant Worker Resource Center (IWRC); MBAs; PhDs; students; teaching industrial relations; UCLA Labor Center; universities

efficiency
and commodity theory of labor 39, 44
and competitive demand/supply labor market model 43, 44
as explicit objective of industrial relations 51, 52–3, 55, 56, 57–9, 61, 226, 227

egoist model of employment
relationship 53, 54, 55, 56, 57
El Salvador 204, 206
elections, secret-ballot 111, 112, 113,
120
electronic journal publishing 149, 150,
152–3, 154, 156, 157
Employee Free Choice Act (2007) 80,
113, 120, 231
employer associations 197, 203
employers 44, 78–80, 112, 113–14, 115,
116, 232
employment relationships
competitive demand/supply labor
market model, rejection of
37–8, 39–41, 42
explicit theories 53–4
globalization and employment
relations in the automotive
industry 186–8, 189–90
in history of industrial relations 33
and institutional economics 45–6,
227
and institutional environment 71,
75–7, 79
quality and quantity 228
and revitalizing industrial relations
48–9
and science-building in 'three faces'
of industrial relations 34, 42
and stakeholder relations 26–8, 227
England 32–3, 75–7
enterprise governance 187, 188
enterprise unionism 58–9
*Ephemera: Theory and Politics in
Organization* 157
Equal Employment Opportunity
Commission (EEOC) 119
equity 37, 44, 51–3, 55, 56, 57–8, 59,
61, 226, 227
ethical values 36–7, 39, 44, 226
see also morality
ethnic groups 54, 55
see also foreign students; immigrant
rights; immigrant workers and
the American labor movement
Europe 16, 59, 70, 178, 184–5, 198–9,
218
see also England; Germany; Ireland;
Sweden; United Kingdom

extension programs 145, 215,
219

facilitated dialogue 207, 216, 222–3
factory workers 213–14
fairness *see* equity
family–work policies 229
federal agencies 20, 94, 95, 96–8, 106,
107
Federal Arbitration Act (1925) 118–19
Federal Mediation and Conciliation
Service (FMCS) 20, 95, 96–7, 106
feminism 54
fields of study, defining 33–4, 49–51
see also multi-disciplinary
approaches; individual fields of
study
Financial Times 126, 127–9, 130, 147
firms, and varieties of capitalism 175–8
First Amendment 116
Ford 184, 185
foreign students 127–8
'free' contracts 78, 79, 80, 114, 120
free market capitalism 35, 43, 44, 78–9
funding 134–5, 145, 153–4, 156

Gap 199
garment industry, women's *see* labor
relations in the women's apparel
industry
Garment Workers Center 204–5
General Motors 184, 188
Gereffi, Gary 200–201
Germany
cooperation in employment
relationships 72
coordinated market economy 70–71,
175, 177, 179
corporatism and social democracy
as nation state paradigms 72, 73
globalization and employment
relations in the automotive
industry 182, 185, 186, 187, 189
works councils 57, 115–16
Gershenfeld, Gladys 27
Gifford, Kathie Lee 199
Gingerich, D. 176
Global Cities initiative 206
global collective bargaining 205
globalization 177, 198–200, 233

globalization and employment
  relations in the automotive
  industry
  automotive assembly industry 184–8
  broadening the varieties of
    capitalism approach 182–4
  conclusions: change, continuity and
    hybridization 188–90
Godard, John 68, 69, 74, 75, 76, 77, 79,
  80
good faith bargaining 113, 115, 117
government 9, 34, 37, 44, 233–4
  see also federal agencies; nation state
    paradigms; state

Hall, Peter A. 70–71, 174–6, 177, 178
Hermanson, Jeff 204, 206
high-commitment human resource
  management (HRM) 76
higher education *see* academic
  programs; business schools;
  degrees; MBAs; PhDs; students;
  teaching industrial relations;
  UCLA Labor Center; universities
history journals 143, 146
history of industrial relations
  choices and principles, post World
    War II 18–21
  disciplinary fragmentation, effect on
    labor journal publishing in
    United States 143–8
  and human resource management
    (HRM) 9–10, 19, 232
  immigrant workers and the
    American labor movement
    212–13
  importance for the future 7–10
  'industrial' to 'industry,' terminology
    22–6, 227
  labor relations in the women's
    apparel industry 195–200
  origins of industrial relations 15–17,
    32–3
  'three faces' of original industrial
    relations 34–7
  unions 20, 22, 31, 144, 147, 164–6
homecare workers 214
Howell, C. 174, 179, 180
human beings 10, 36–7, 38–9, 44, 53,
  92, 226

human capital 91, 176–7
human resource management
  (HRM)
  and equity 52
  field of study in the United States
    68–9
  high-commitment 76
  and history of industrial relations
    9–10, 19, 232
  and labor relations publishing in the
    United States 146, 155
  single theory 49
  terminology 22, 23–5, 167
  and unitarist model of employment
    relationships 53
  university departments in the United
    States 146, 147
  and voice 52
Human Resources Division, Academy
  of Management 19, 131, 146
human rights 36–7, 39, 44, 199, 205
hybrid systems 185–6, 189

ideology 36–7, 44
immigrant rights 212–13, 215, 216,
  217, 220, 221, 230
Immigrant Worker Resource Center
  (IWRC) 215–16, 219
immigrant workers and the American
  labor movement
  challenges and opportunities
    confronting labor studies
    219–22
  conclusion: facilitating development
    of a stronger labor movement
    222–3
  historical perspective on immigrant
    rights 212–13
  Immigrant Worker Resource Center
    (IWRC) 215–16, 219
  labor relations in the women's
    apparel industry 204–5
  organizing immigrant workers
    213–14
  partnerships 216–17
  UCLA Labor Center 214, 215,
    216–17, 218–19, 220–23
Immigrant Workers Freedom Ride
  212–13
immigration, United States 219–20

imperfect markets 55
incomplete labor contracts 41
independent contractors 41, 42
independent journal publishing
150–51, 152
India 204
individualism 35, 78, 79
individuals *see* human beings
Industrial and Labor Relations Review
144, 146, 153
industrial peace 164, 165, 188
industrial relations
contemporary challenges and
opportunities 234–5
core principle 37–41, 45, 226–7
crisis in field of study 1–2, 31, 45,
48, 68–9, 123, 146–7, 154–5,
163–6
(*see also* business schools and
marginalization of industrial
relations in Canada)
history (*see* history of industrial
relations)
institutional environments approach
(*see* institutional environments
approach to industrial
relations)
meta-paradigm (*see* meta-paradigm
of industrial relations)
our niche 234
redefining the field 167–71
research methods 21, 28, 38–9, 68–9
single theory 48, 49, 50–51
terminology 8, 17, 22–8, 33, 34, 167,
227
'three faces' 34–7, 41–4
*Industrial Relations: A Journal of
Economy and Society* (*IR:JES*)
144, 153, 156
Industrial Relations Research
Association (IRRA) 7–8, 9, 19,
22, 144, 150, 166, 167
see also Labor and Employment
Relations Association (LERA)
Industrial Revolution 15–16
'industrial' to 'industry,' terminology
22–6, 227
industrialization 15–16, 22
industry councils 20
'industry studies' 22, 26

information 41, 42
see also books; conferences;
journals; publication of
research
innovation 26, 176–7
insider corporate governance 175, 176
institutional change 74
institutional complementarity 175–6,
181
institutional economics 8, 45–6, 68,
227
institutional environments approach to
industrial relations
illustrations 74–80
prospects 80–82
tenets 69–73
institutional norms 72–3, 74, 77, 78–80
institutional rules 70, 72–3, 74, 77
institutions 37, 39, 48–9, 70
interdisciplinary approaches *see* multi-
disciplinary approaches
interest disputes 117, 120
international benchmarking, in
business schools in Canada 125–7
International Labor Organization 33,
44, 62, 203
international labor rights 205
International Ladies' Garment
Workers' Union (ILGWU) 194,
196, 198, 201
international trade agreements 198,
203, 206, 207
international unions 194, 196, 198,
201, 205–6, 213, 214
international worker organizations
205–6
Internet journal publishing 149, 150,
152, 153, 154, 156, 157
internship programs 215, 216–17, 219
investors 201–2
Ireland 175

Jackson, G. 176, 179
Jacoby, Sanford 78, 79, 178
janitors 206, 213
Japan
Asian market economy (AME) 182,
183
coordinated market economy 70,
175, 177, 179

employment relations in the
automotive industry 182, 183,
184–5, 186, 187, 188, 189–90
employment relations in the women's
apparel industry 204
enterprise unionism and explicit
objectives of industrial relations
58–9
unions, decline 204
voluntarism and explicit objectives
of industrial relations 59–60
job security 186–7
jobbers 195–7, 199, 200, 201, 202
Jobs with Justice 203
joint employers 196
journals 128–31, 132, 134, 135,
138–41
see also labor and employment
journal publishing in the United
States
Judge, Timothy A. 125, 128
Jurgens, U. 176
Justice for Janitors 206, 213

Katz, Harry C. 59, 60, 98, 189
Kaufman, Bruce E. 1, 17, 20, 31, 32,
37, 38, 39, 41, 44, 45, 48, 49, 52,
54, 61–2, 68, 69, 79, 146, 147, 148,
156
Keller, Berndt 31
Kerr, Clark 144, 233
knowledge-driven economy 17, 22, 26,
28–9, 225–6, 228–9
Kochan, Thomas A. 19, 22, 54, 61, 68,
98, 184, 185
Kuhn, Thomas S. 50

labor, in competitive demand/supply
labor market model 38, 39–41, 42
*Labor: Studies in Working-Class
History of the Americas* 157
labor and employment journal
publishing in the United States
historical perspective on disciplinary
fragmentation 143–8
looking ahead 155–7
recent trends 148–55
association journals and
independent publications
149–51

financial stability and academic
excellence 153–4
risks of corporate publishing
154–5
from small publishers to large
corporate publishing 151–3
labor and employment law 39, 44, 55,
75, 77, 78, 115–16, 120, 186, 187,
196
see also labor and employment law
in the United States
labor and employment law in the
United States
anti-discrimination law 118, 119
collective bargaining under NLRA
114–16
dispute resolution procedures
117–19, 120
and explicit industrial relations 56–7
and free market economy 78
future of 119–20, 231
immigrant rights 212
labor and employment organizations
96–7, 102
National Labor Relations Board
(NLRB) 80, 111–14, 115, 116,
117
and New Deal 81, 111, 226, 234
and origins of industrial relations
16, 17, 20
and public sector 116–17
reform 80, 112–13, 120, 231
union protection 166
Labor and Employment Relations
Association (LERA) 19, 20, 21,
22, 81, 95, 100–101, 107, 131, 146,
147, 150, 153–4, 165–6, 167
see also Industrial Relations
Research Association (IRRA)
labor–community relations 26, 27
labor contracts 41, 42
see also terms and conditions of
employment
labor costs 195, 196, 197, 198–9, 200,
203, 204, 207
labor demand curve 38, 39–40
labor economics 46, 147, 169, 227
labor–family relations 26
Labor History 146, 156
labor–labor relations 26

labor–management disputes 42, 57–8, 117, 144, 147, 164, 188
  see also dispute resolution; strikes
labor–management relations 18, 19–20, 21, 26, 27, 40, 150, 152–3, 188
labor markets 61, 62
  see also labor demand curve; labor supply curve
labor movement
  decline in United States 56, 77–80, 81, 112
    (*see also* social capital and labor movement decline in United States)
  and history of industrial relations 19, 166
  and labor journal publishing 149, 150, 151, 152
  in the women's apparel industry 196
  see also immigrant workers and the American labor movement; unions
labor problems 35–6, 43–4, 143–4, 164–5, 167
labor relations experts 206–7, 208
labor relations in the women's apparel industry
  conclusions – building strength through unity 208
  industry globalization and new anti-sweatshop movement 198–200
  role of labor relations specialists 206–7
  towards a new paradigm 200–206
  triangular bargaining 195–8, 199, 203
Labor Research Review (*LRR*) 151
labor rights 113, 116–17, 119, 199, 202–3, 205
  see also immigrant rights
labor standards 44, 199, 203–4, 205
  see also minimum standards
labor studies 144–5, 146, 147, 155, 219
Labor Studies Journal (*LSJ*) 145, 149
labor supply curve 38, 40–41
Lansbury, R.D. 181, 184, 185, 189
Latin America 198, 199, 204, 218
  see also El Salvador; Mexico

law *see* administrative law in the United States; anti-discrimination policies and laws; labor and employment law; labor and employment law in the United States; public law; state laws
lay-offs 187
leadership development 206, 207, 208, 214, 215, 216, 217, 222
lean production 185, 186, 189
Lerner, Stephen 206
Leung, Kwok 124, 134
liberal market economies (LMEs) 70, 71, 73, 175, 176–7, 179, 182, 183, 189
liberalism 72, 73
libraries 149, 152, 153, 154, 156, 157
litigation 117, 118–19
locked labor-market actors 197–8, 200
lockouts 113–14, 120
logistics, in the women's apparel industry 201
Los Angeles 204–5, 212, 213–17, 218–19, 220–23

Madison, James 92
management 68–9, 81, 146, 169, 232
  see also labor–management relations
management–labor relations 18, 19–20, 21, 26, 27, 40, 150, 152–3, 188
management–management relations 27
management prerogatives, and National Labor Relations Act (1935) 113–14, 115
management–union relations 144, 147
Manning, Alan 40
marginal products, in competitive demand/supply labor market model 39, 40
market-based theories 143–4
Marxism 54, 164, 165
Maslow's hierarchy of needs 37
mass production 185–6, 195
Masterman, Margaret 48, 50
MBAs 125, 126, 127, 128
McKersie, Robert B. 26, 27, 54, 168
mediation 96–7, 99, 106
Mediterranean variety of capitalism 178

membership
  of organizations 93, 123–4, 131, 146,
      149, 150, 198
    and social capital and labor
        movement decline in United
        States 94, 100–101, 102,
        103–4, 105–6
  of unions 116–17, 123, 198
meta-paradigm of industrial relations
  cross-disciplinary and multiple
      theoretical perspectives 48, 49,
      50–51
  explicit comparative studies 58–60
  explicit industrial relations 54–8
  explicit objectives 51–3, 54–62
  explicit theories 53–4, 55–7
  implications for teaching 60–61
  toward a common intellectual vision
      61–2
meta-paradigms, defined 48, 50
Mexico 199, 204, 205–6
Middle East 127, 128
Midwest Center for Labor Research
    151
Milkman, Ruth 213
minimum standards 52, 53, 55, 57, 59,
    203, 205
MIT 21, 163, 167, 170–71
mobilization biases 73, 74, 80
monopsony labor markets 40
moral hazard 42
moral philosophy 52, 143
morale 40–41
morality 36, 39, 164–5, 170, 226
  see also ethical values; moral
      philosophy
multi-disciplinary approaches
  and fields of study 50
  in history of industrial relations 8,
      18–19, 21, 33, 34, 35, 144–5
  importance 227, 234
  and labor journal publishing in the
      United States 152, 156, 157
  and meta-paradigm of industrial
      relations 48, 50, 51, 52, 53, 54
  redefining industrial relations
      167–71
UCLA Labor Center 220
Multi-Fibre Agreement (1974) 198,
    206, 207

multiple theoretical perspectives 48, 49,
    50, 51
Muñoz, Carolina Bank 213
mutuality 75–7

nation state paradigms 72–3, 74
National Academy of Arbitrators
    (NAA) 95, 100, 107
National Association of
    Manufacturers 95, 103–4
National Coordinating Committee for
    Multiemployer Plans (NCCMP)
    95, 102
National Industrial Conference Board
    33
National Labor Relations Act (Wagner
    Act) (1935) 75, 79, 110, 111, 112,
    113, 114–16, 117, 231
National Labor Relations Act's
    Garment Provo 196
National Labor Relations Board
    (NLRB) 80, 95, 98, 106, 111–14,
    115, 116, 117, 166
National Policy Association (NPA) 94,
    95, 101
National Right to Work Committee
    (NRTWC) 95, 103
negotiation 168, 196–7
neoclassical labor economics 46, 147,
    227
  see also commodity theory of labor;
      competitive demand/supply
      labor market model; egoist
      model of employment
      relationship
New Deal 81, 111, 226, 234
new institutional economics 41, 167–8
  see also institutional environments
      approach to industrial relations;
      varieties of capitalism
New Labor Forum (*NLF*) 151, 152
New Zealand 59, 175
Nike 199, 203
Nissen, Bruce 145
nonunion contractors 197
nonunion jobbers 197, 199
nonunion rights disputes 57–8
nonunion workers 216
norms 37, 39, 72–3, 74, 77, 78–80, 226,
    227

North America 184–5
　see also Canada; United States

occupational psychology journals 146
occupational sociology journals 146
optimal allocation of resources 43, 44
organizational behavior 146
organizations 94, 95, 97–8, 102–4,
　105–6
　see also associations; voluntary
　　organizations; worker
　　organizations; individual
　　organizations
outcomes of work 36–7
outsider corporate governance 175–6
overseas sourcing 198–9

paradigms 48, 50, 72–3, 74
　see also meta-paradigms, defined;
　　meta-paradigm of industrial
　　relations
partnerships 215, 216–17, 222
path dependency, and varieties of
　capitalism 180
Patterson, S. Howard 16
peer-reviewed journals 131, 132, 150,
　151–2, 153–4, 157
perfect information 41, 42
performance-related pay 186
Perspectives on Work (*POW*) 150,
　153–4
PhDs 127, 132
physical capital 91
pluralism 53–4, 55–6, 57, 91–2
policy 18, 19, 21, 26, 55, 56, 169
　see also anti-discrimination policies
　　and laws; family-work policies
political economy 168
politics 52, 154, 164, 165, 179, 180,
　231
politics journals 143
Pontusson, J. 179, 180, 181
positive statement, in core principle of
　industrial relations 38–9
power relations 54, 55, 56, 200–202,
　206, 207, 208
　see also agency
practice 18, 19, 21, 144–5, 165, 169,
　207
　see also problem-solving

problem-solving
　business schools in Canada 129, 134
　in history of industrial relations 8
　labor journal publishing in the
　　United States 156
　versus science-building 147–8
　and social sciences 21, 28, 234
　in 'three faces' of original industrial
　　relations 35–6, 43–4
　and unions in industrial relations
　　research 165
　see also practice
procedural justice 52
process-based teaching of industrial
　relations 60–61
production chains 201, 202
professional associations 94, 95,
　98–101, 106, 107
professional journals 143, 149–50, 156
profits 195–6, 197, 200–201
property rights 36, 37, 78, 79
psychology 52, 53, 146, 168
public law 118
public policy 55, 56, 169
public sector 22, 34, 116–17, 123
publication of research 128–32,
　138–41
　see also books; conferences; journals
Putnam, Robert D. 89–90, 91–3, 101,
　106, 107

quality 176, 177, 228
Quan, Katie 204, 205, 206, 214

ranking 125–9, 130, 134, 138–41, 147,
　154
relations 26–8, 91–2, 227
　see also community–university
　　relations; employment
　　relationships; labor–family
　　relations; labor–labor relations;
　　labor–management relations;
　　management–management
　　relations; partnerships; power
　　relations; production chains;
　　stakeholder relations; supply
　　chains; triangular bargaining;
　　union–management relations
representation 37, 111, 112, 117, 204–6,
　232

research methods 21, 28, 38–9, 68–9, 169
retailers 199, 200–201, 202
retaliation, employer 113, 116
revenue 94, 97–8, 99–100, 102, 103, 105–6
'revolution' 16
Rezler, Julius 22, 25
rights *see* democratic rights; human rights; immigrant rights; labor rights; property rights; rights disputes
rights disputes 57–8, 117
Rockerfeller, John D., Jr. 33
rules 70, 72–3, 74, 77

SAGE 149
salaries 126
    see also wages
Samuels, Warren J. 9
Scholarly Publishing and Academic Resources Coalition (SPARC) 157
science-building 34–5, 42–3, 147–8, 156, 165
sciences 50, 167–9, 170
scientific management 16, 228
scientific method 38–9
secret-ballot elections 111, 112, 113, 120
sectoral bargaining 58, 59
self-actualization and self-development 37
Self-Employed Women's Association of India 204
Sensenbrenner Bill 212
Service Employees International Union (SEIU) 201, 206, 213, 214
sessional instructors, business schools in Canada 133
Shaffer, Jono 201
Shailor, Barbara 205
Sharpe (M. E., Inc.) 151–2
single discipline-defining theories 48, 49, 50–51
skill development 186
Slichter, Sumner 36–7
Sloan Foundation 20, 22, 134–5
small journal publishing 151–2
social action 70, 164, 180–81

social capital 89, 91–3, 167
social capital and labor movement decline in United States
    conclusions 105–7
    findings 96–105
        college and university programs 104–5
        federal agencies 96–8
        neutral and professional associations 98–101
        organizations allied with business 103–4
        organizations allied with unions 102–3
    methodology 94–6
    theory of social capital 91–3
social contract 234–5
social democracy 72
social groups 164
social justice 37, 44, 221–2
social movements 144–5, 169
social problems 8, 167, 171, 221
Social Science Research Council (US) 33, 35
social sciences 21, 28, 50, 143, 167–71, 226, 234
Social Sciences and Humanities Research Council of Canada (SSHRC) 132, 133
social welfare function 37, 44
society, and employment relationships 27
Society for Human Resource Management (SHRM) 19
sociology 54, 146, 168–9, 227
Solow, Robert 40
Soskice, David 70–71, 174–6, 178
South Korea 175, 182, 183, 184, 185, 186, 187, 188, 189
stakeholder relations 26–8, 227
standards 44, 199, 203–4, 205
    see also minimum standards
state 9, 179, 180
    see also government; nation state paradigms; state laws
state laws 120, 221
Stiglitz, Joseph 44, 62
Streeck, W. 176, 179, 180, 181
strikes 42, 60, 98, 113, 116, 118, 196, 197, 213–14

students 126–8, 132–3, 135, 202–3, 218, 219, 220, 221, 222–3
supply chains 27, 200–203, 228, 232
Supreme Court (US) 113–15, 117–19
sweatshop conditions 196, 197, 198–9, 200, 204, 205, 207
  see also anti-sweatshop movement
Sweden 182, 185, 186, 187, 189
Swenson, P. 177, 181
Synergy system 152, 153

Taft-Hartley Act (1947) 96–7, 102, 115, 117
Taiwan 201, 206
Taras, Daphne 78, 80
Taylor, Frederick W. 16
Taylor & Francis 152, 156
teaching industrial relations 60–61, 133, 134, 144–5, 147, 170–71, 215–16
  see also academic programs; business schools and marginalization of industrial relations in Canada; universities
terminology 8, 16, 17, 22–8, 33, 34, 167, 227
terms and conditions of employment 36–7, 39, 42, 44, 57, 113–14, 186–7, 189–90
textbooks 133
Thelen, K. 180
theology 52, 62
theory 18, 19, 21, 48, 49, 50-51, 53–4, 55–7
  see also multiple theoretical perspectives
'three faces' of industrial relations 34–7, 41–4
Tocqueville, Alexis de 92
town-gown divide 129, 134
Toyota 184, 185, 188, 189
trade unions *see* unions
transaction cost theory 176
triangular bargaining 196–8, 199, 203
truckers 201
tuition fees 127, 221

UCLA Labor Center 214, 215, 216–17, 218–19, 220–23
unemployment 10, 187

unfair labor practices 111
union contractors 197, 199
union jobbers 197
union–management relations 144, 147
unions
  capitalism as moral problem 164–5
  decline in Japan 204
  decline in United States 56, 77–80, 81, 112, 120, 146, 147, 155, 165, 188, 199, 204
    (*see also* social capital and labor movement decline in United States)
  and explicit industrial relations 55–6, 57, 58–61
  globalization and employment relations in the automotive industry 186, 187–8
  in history of industrial relations 20, 22, 31, 144, 147, 164–6
  and immigrant workers 213, 214, 215–16
  institutional environment Canada compared to England 75–7
  as key actors 230–32
  and labor journal publishing 149, 150, 151
  and labor law in the United States 166
  membership 116–17, 123, 198
  and models of employment relationships 54
  and politics 164
  public sector 116–17, 123
  in revitalized industrial relations 48–9
  rights disputes 57–8
  in teaching industrial relations 60, 144–5, 147
  in the women's apparel industry 196, 197–8, 199, 200, 201, 202, 203, 204, 205–6, 207, 208
unions–human resources' professionals relations 26
unitarist model of employment relationship 53, 54, 55, 56, 57
United Association for Labor Education (UALE) 146, 149
United Kingdom 58, 59–60, 71, 75–6, 175, 179

see also England
United Nations 62
United States
  adversarial employment
    relationships 71, 79
  community–university relations
    217–19, 222–3
  explicit industrial relations and
    employment and labor
    legislation 56–7
  explicit industrial relations and
    public policy 56, 57
  globalization and employment
    relations in the automotive
    industry 182, 184, 185–6, 187,
    188, 189
  history of industrial relations 15–16,
    17, 18–21, 22–6, 33
  labor movement and union decline
    56, 77–80, 81, 112, 146, 147,
    155, 165, 188, 199, 204
    (*see also* social capital and labor
      movement decline in United
      States)
  labor relations in the women's
    apparel industry 195–200, 201,
    202–3, 204–5, 206
  liberal market economy 71, 73, 175,
    177, 179
  liberalism as nation state paradigms
    72, 73
  New Deal era 81, 111, 226, 234
  PhDs in business schools 132
  pluralist model of employment
    relationships 53–4, 92
  public sector unions 116–17, 123
  research methods in industrial
    relations 68–9, 81–2
  social capital 89, 91–3
    (*see also* social capital and labor
      movement decline in United
      States)
  teaching industrial relations 60, 133
  union membership 116–17, 123,
    198
  university corporatization 155
  see also immigrant workers and the
    American labor movement;
    labor and employment journal
    publishing in the United States;
    labor and employment law in
    the United States
United Students Against Sweatshops
  202–3
universities
  and community relations in the
    United States 217–19
  corporatization 155
  historical perspective on disciplinary
    fragmentation in the United
    States 143–6
  labor journal publishing in the
    United States 149, 151, 152,
    153, 156, 157
  and labor relations in the women's
    apparel industry 202–3
  and problems of multi-disciplinary
    investigation 170–71
  see also Cornell University;
    Immigrant Worker Resource
    Center (IWRC); MIT; UCLA
    Labor Center; University of
    California; University of
    Wisconsin
University and College Labor
  Education Association (UCLEA)
  149
University of California 144, 145, 153,
  156, 167, 221
  see also Immigrant Worker Resource
    Center (IWRC); UCLA Labor
    Center
University of Wisconsin 144, 145, 163
  see also 'Wisconsin School'

varieties of capitalism 70–71, 73, 74,
  174–81
  see also globalization and
    employment relations in the
    automotive industry
voice
  and ethical/ideological approach in
    original industrial relations 37
  as explicit objective of industrial
    relations 51, 52–3, 55, 56, 57–8,
    59, 61, 226, 227
  and human resource management
    (HRM) 52
  and labor and employment law
    reform in the United States 231

Volkswagen 187
voluntarism 58, 59–60, 75–6
voluntary organizations 92–3, 95–6,
    100–101, 107

wages
    in competitive demand/supply labor
        market model 38, 39–41, 42
    and equity as explicit objective of
        industrial relations 52
    globalization and employment
        relations in the automotive
        industry 186, 189–90
    immigrant workers and the
        American labor movement
        213–14
    and institutional isomorphism 168
    and labor relations in the women's
        apparel industry 195–7, 199,
        202, 203, 204, 205
    see also salaries
Wagner Act (National Labor Relations
    Act) (1935) 75, 79, 110, 111
Wailes, N. 177, 180
Waldinger, Roger 213
Walton, Richard E. 26, 27, 54, 168
Webb, Beatrice 32–3
Webb, Sidney 32–3
Weber, Max 17
Whitley, R. 182–3
Wiley-Blackwell 149, 152, 153, 156
'Wisconsin School' 33, 168
Witte, Edwin E. 8–9
Womack, James P. 26, 185
women's apparel industry *see* labor
    relations in the women's apparel
    industry
Wong, Kent 212, 213
work, nature of 228–9
work–family policies 229
Work in America Institute (WAI) 94,
    95, 101

work slowdown 114–15
worker centers 216, 219
    see also Immigrant Worker Resource
        Center (IWRC); UCLA Labor
        Center
worker organizations 204–5
workers
    diversity 229–30
    labor relations in the women's
        apparel industry 195–7, 199,
        200, 201, 204–6, 207, 208
    see also immigrant workers and
        the American labor
        movement
Workers Rights Consortium 202–3
working-class students 218
working conditions
    and equity as explicit objective of
        industrial relations 52
    of immigrant workers, and the
        American labor movement
        213–14
    in women's apparel industry 196,
        197, 198–9, 200, 201, 202, 204,
        205, 207, 208
    see also anti-sweatshop movement;
        terms and conditions of
        employment
Working USA (*WUSA*) 145, 148,
    151–2
works councils 57, 115–16
World Bank 89

Yamamura, K. 179, 181
Yates, Michael D. 220
Yeung, H. 182–3, 189
Yoder, Dale 35

Zabin, Carol 214
Zagelmeyer, Stefan 51, 55
zero transaction costs 41, 42